Our Raci

Few people today would admit to being a racist, or to making assumptions about individuals based on their skin colour, or on their gender or social class. In this book, leading psychologist Geoffrey Beattie asks if prejudice, more subtle than before, is still a major part of our everyday lives.

Beattie suggests that implicit biases based around race are not just found in small sections of our society, but that they also exist in the psyches of even the most liberal, educated and fair-minded of us. More importantly, the book outlines how these 'hidden' attitudes and prejudices can be revealed and measured, and how they in turn predict behaviours in a number of important social situations.

Our Racist Heart? takes a fresh look at our racial attitudes, using new technology and fresh experimental approaches to show how unconscious biases influence our everyday actions and thinking. These groundbreaking results are brought to life using the author's own experiences of class and religious prejudice in Northern Ireland, and are also discussed in relation to the history of race, racism and social psychological theory.

The book will be of great interest to students of psychology, sociology, and cultural studies, as well as those who work in human resources and to all those who have experienced prejudice in their daily lives.

Geoffrey Beattie was Head of Psychology at the University of Manchester from 2000 to 2011 and is currently Visiting Professor at the University of California, Santa Barbara.

His previous work has either won or been shortlisted for a number of major awards. He has also presented several television series on BBC1 and Channel 4.

Our Racist Heart?

An exploration of unconscious prejudice in everyday life

Geoffrey Beattie

Routledge
Taylor & Francis Group

LONDON AND NEW YORK

First published 2013
by Routledge
27 Church Road, Hove, East Sussex, BN3 2FA

Simultaneously published in the USA and Canada
by Routledge
711 Third Avenue, New York, NY 10017

Routledge is an imprint of the Taylor & Francis Group, an informa business

British Library Cataloguing in Publication Data
A catalogue record for this book is available from the British Library

Library of Congress Cataloging in Publication Data
Beattie, Geoffrey.
Our racist heart? : an exploration of unconscious prejudice in everyday life /
authored by Geoffrey Beattie.
     p. cm.
Includes bibliographical references and index.
ISBN 978-0-415-61296-8 (hb : alk. paper) —
ISBN 978-0-415-61299-9 (pb : alk. paper)
1. Prejudices.   2. Racism—Psychological aspects.   I. Title.
BF575.P9B34 2012
303.3'85—dc23

                                                                2012007195

ISBN: 978-0-415-61296-8 (hbk)
ISBN: 978-0-415-61299-9 (pbk)
ISBN: 978-0-203-10091-2 (ebk)

Typeset in Century Schoolbook
by RefineCatch Limited, Bungay, Suffolk

Printed and bound in Great Britain by the MPG Books Group

This book is dedicated to the memory of Alan Gilbert, Vice Chancellor and President of the University of Manchester from 2004 to 2010.

Alan was an inspirational leader who made sure that equality and diversity were cornerstones of our new institution.

This book explores why things might not have changed as quickly as he would have liked them to, before his untimely death.

Contents

Figures

Tables

Acknowledgements

I am very grateful to Patrick Johnson, from the Equality and Diversity Unit at the University of Manchester who urged me to explore the issues raised in this book, and to the Equality Challenge Unit for further encouragement and support. My initial interest in measuring implicit attitudes and analysing their effects on behaviour was carried out through the Sustainable Consumption Institute at the University of Manchester, funded by Tesco, and I am very grateful to them for their support for another aspect of my research.

My main research assistant for this work was Laura McGuire who was invaluable (and a joy) from start to finish.

I have written about my background in Belfast previously in *Protestant Boy* (Granta, 2004) and a novel *The Corner Boys* (Victor Gollancz, 1998) and I thank both publishers for permission to reproduce the relevant sections here. Some sections about implicit attitudes to the environment appeared first in *Why Aren't We Saving the Planet? A Psychologist's Perspective* (2010) and I thank Routledge for permission to reproduce these sections here, in a slightly different form. Graham Richards made some very useful comments on an earlier draft of the manuscript and I thank him for his helpful suggestions. Mick Billig and David McNeill reviewed the book in manuscript form and the words of encouragement from these two (inspirational) academics helped me greatly.

PART I

Challenged by history

Introduction: approaches and avoidances

This is a book which explores an important and I would say timely topic, namely what kinds of prejudices and biases might be operating in everyday life in contemporary British society, revolving around race and ethnicity, especially in the broad area of employment. I say 'timely', but equally I could have said 'timeless' because this issue has been debated and argued about for decades. It is a highly charged debate and the emotions associated with accusations of racial prejudice and the counter-accusations that often greet them are intense. On the one hand we have claims of 'prejudice at work', 'racial discrimination' and 'ethnic bias', sometimes based on 'hard facts' like employment statistics, which seem to indicate significant inequalities attributable to race or ethnicity. On the other side, and often equally loud and passionate, we have statements like 'forget it, prejudice is a thing of the past', 'We are fair and transparent in all of our dealings, especially when it comes to issues to do with employment', and 'Don't you see that some people are trying to get some extra advantage by crying "prejudice" whenever, and wherever, they can?' These latter opinions are often expressed by fair-minded but exasperated individuals, and the opinions are based directly on their years of experience in the world of work; they have conducted numerous interviews, they have advertised posts and shortlisted in the most fair and transparent ways they can manage. What more can they do? The emotions on both sides show no signs of diminishing and the gulf, if anything, is widening. There is a chasm of misunderstanding and almost certainly mistrust.

In this book I take a novel approach to this problem. What if both sides are right? What if we are all, at a conscious level, no longer prone to the prejudices of the past based around race or ethnicity? What if we are all scrupulously fair in all of our dealings, especially when it comes to employment because, after all, we know how serious accusations of racial bias might be in this context? But what if at some deeper level, there is some system that is quite capable of operating independently of this conscious system; another system which is more susceptible to biases based on differences in race or ethnic background? And what if this system is allowed to operate in particular social contexts without challenge and without any top-down editorial control? And what if this alternative system of thought and decision-making throws up results that sometimes surprise us all, fair and rational creatures that we are? And even when these biased outcomes are pointed out to us, we think to ourselves that there must be some other rational explanation for all of this. This is the idea that I will be exploring in this book. I say that it is novel, but, of course, nothing is really that new in psychology. Some of the early researchers had great and enduring insights. This book has its intellectual origins in the classic work of Leon Festinger (1957) on cognitive dissonance, but more particularly and more directly in the work of Gordon Allport (1954) on prejudice and it also has strong and direct links with the work of Anthony Greenwald, who pioneered new techniques and methodologies for revealing the working of this hidden, deeper, 'implicit' system. I try to take this work into slightly new territory, that's all, right into that most liberal of institutions, the modern British university, and I ask what biases might operate there, as candidates apply for jobs and are shortlisted or not. I will also tell a story along the way about some of the prejudices that I have seen in my own life, and describe how prejudice sometimes operates in loud, vociferous and unambiguous forms, but sometimes in more subtle and quieter ways.

Why do I do this? Why don't I leave myself out of the story? One reviewer of this book suggested that I do so in order to establish my 'credibility as someone who, despite being a white male, has considerable first-hand experience of prejudice in action (from his childhood and adolescence in an impoverished Protestant enclave in Belfast before and during the "Troubles", fortuitously attending a privileged school to boot by passing his Eleven-Plus)'. He may be right, credibility has always been quite important to me as an author and as a psychologist (how could it be any other way?), but I would probably turn this the other way around. It was my experiences in growing up in Belfast that got me interested in prejudice in the first place, prejudices to do with religion (obviously), prejudices to do with social class, prejudices to do with neighbourhood and belonging and identity, prejudices to do with weight and body shape, prejudices to do with hope and aspiration, prejudices to do with knowing your place or not knowing your place. I saw these prejudices all around me and I sometimes felt their effects personally, although some of the effects, no matter how deeply felt they were, are quite hard to pin down when it comes down to it, and even harder to quantify. But perhaps it is easier to be specific and concrete about that most obvious of all prejudices, racial/ethnic prejudice. Here, at least, we have things like employment statistics to guide us, and the apparent inequalities in employment opportunity based on the self-categorisations of individuals as White or Black and Minority Ethnic (BME), statistics that, to my mind, do really require some explanation. These apparent inequalities in the rates and conditions of employment between BME groups and the majority White population are a major issue in the UK today, and elsewhere (Bassanini and Saint-Martin 2008). After controlling for age, socio-economic status and number of years in education, research shows that BME groups, in a range of countries, seem to continue to face a significant 'net' disadvantage in terms of gaining access to, and remaining in, the labour market (see Bassanini and Saint-Martin 2008). Evidence of labour market discrimination on the grounds of ethnicity has been reported in Australia (Booth, Leigh and Vaganova 2009), Canada (Pendakur and Pendakur 1998), France (Lefranc 2010), Germany (Kogan 2011), Greece (Drydakis and Vlassis 2010), North America (Bertrand and Mullainathan 2004), New

Zealand (Tobias, Bhattacharya and White 2008), Sweden (Nordin and Rooth 2009), and the United Kingdom (Wood, Hales, Purdon, *et al.* 2009).

One technique that has been frequently used to identify possible bias in the labour market is what is termed 'correspondence testing' (see Jowell and Prescott-Clarke 1970). In a typical correspondence test for racial bias, written job applications are randomly assigned either a traditional Anglo-Saxon sounding name or an ethnic minority name and are then submitted for advertised vacancies. Bias can be identified if there is a difference in the proportion of applicants who are short-listed as a function of their perceived ethnicity (typically White versus non-White). Bertrand and Mullainathan (2004), for instance, randomly assigned either Anglo-Saxon (e.g. Emily) or African American (e.g. Lakisha) names to over 5,000 fictitious CVs, which were then sent in response to a range of job advertisements in Boston and Chicago. They found that White candidates were 50 per cent more likely than non-White candidates to be offered an interview. Similarly, the results of a Swedish field study (see Carlsson and Rooth 2007) demonstrated that second generation Swedes were, on average, ten percentage points less likely to be invited for interview if the applicant had a Middle Eastern rather than a traditionally Swedish sounding name. In the UK research shows that ethnic minorities not only have to send, on average, 74 per cent more applications than non-Whites to secure an interview (Wood *et al.* 2009) but, once in employment, they face lower hourly earnings and lower levels of occupational attainment, compared to equally qualified Whites (Heath and Li 2007).

It is hardly surprising that I, as a social psychologist, am interested in racial or ethnic prejudice as an incredibly important social (and indeed moral) phenomenon but I am also interested in it as an example of something much broader, namely prejudice based on perceived difference. From this point of view I am introducing my own experiences not to bolster my credibility in this one domain (racial prejudice) that I will never directly experience but rather to map out a broader range of relevant phenomena, some of which will, one day, maybe get the same sort of treatment and analysis which we can now carry out on prejudices connected with race. The reader can ultimately judge for him or herself because the narrative of the book explains my decision to engage in the research in the first place. This narrative beginning in Chapter 2 also explains why I am not that naïve to the likely emotional effects of suggesting that many people may be unconsciously subject to racial or ethnic bias.

Coincidentally, I was interested to read Mick Billig's recent 'landmark article' in the *British Journal of Social Psychology*, where he offers an anniversary critique (50th anniversary) on how to write social psychology. He argues that:

> social psychologists tend to produce unpopulated texts, writing about 'fictional things' rather than people. Social psychologists assume that their technical terms are more precise than ordinary language terms. The author contests this assumption. (Billig 2011: 50)

This new book of mine is heavily populated not just in terms of its style of language (in places at least) but also in terms of its subject matter. Ordinary lives, including my own, are dissected alongside new (sometimes quite technical) psychological experiments, which are used to produce original data. To my mind, real psychological understanding requires both a description of lived experience and the systematic testing of ideas, no matter how controversial, with whatever techniques are available.

So this is a book about prejudice, especially racial or ethnic prejudice, but in the context of other types of prejudice. Both race and ethnicity are, of course, difficult and often emotionally charged terms with complex semiotic and cultural histories. According to Goldberg (1993: 62):

> The concept of race seeped into European consciousness more or less coterminous with the exploratory voyages of discovery, expansion, and domination in the latter part of the fifteenth century. The French term race and the

German *Rasse* derive from the Italian *razza* and the Spanish *raza*, general terms that came to reflect the discovery and experience of groups of beings very different from, indeed strange to the European eye and self. From its inception, then, race has referred to those perceived, indeed, constituted as other.

Again according to Goldberg (ibid.):

The earliest recorded English use of the term 'race' occurs in 1508, in a poem by William Dunbar. It seems possible that the term's significance was a derivative of an earlier sense of race as 'root', applicable to vegetables or herbs (1450). Races were taken, loosely speaking, as population groups of different roots, suggestively rooted in the geographical soils of different regions.

Coincidentally, Dunbar in his poem seems to be taking a liberal view on race; he is effectively saying that back-biters ('bakbyttaris') are to be found in all races (see Banton 1998: 17–43 for the original; and Arber 2007 for the translation).

The Oxford English Dictionary records the different meanings of the term 'race', first as a 'breed or stock of animals' (1580) and roughly at the same time, as a 'limited group of persons descended from a common ancestor' (1581) and later, but only slightly later, as a 'tribe, nation or people considered of common stock' (1600). As Goldberg points out, since its inception, concepts of biological origin ('common ancestor') and social origin ('tribe, nation or people considered of common stock') have been conflated and intertwined in the definition and understanding of race. This continues to the present day. Thus, *The Oxford English Dictionary* defines race as 'a group of people descended from a common ancestor', as in 'a prince of the race of Solomon', as well as 'a group of people sharing the same culture, history, language, etc.; an ethnic group', as in 'we Scots were a blood thirsty race then.' This does, of course, make the concept of race inherently ambiguous, and indeed somewhat problematic. Some critics say that it is worthless, at least in terms of some of its particular meanings. Thus, Richards (1997: x) writes: 'Races as objectively existing biological entities do not exist. The traditional concept of "race" cannot be reconciled with current understanding of the genetic nature of human diversity.' More practical definitions of race, in the meantime, have tended to move away from identifiable patterns of lineage (based on primarily biological criteria). For example, the concept of 'Black' in the US once meant having a 'trace of black ancestry' (or colloquially a 'drop of black blood'), but now it is more about self-concept and self-identity, resulting from a process of self-definition and self-ascription to the category itself. However, as Goldberg points out, there is something interesting and revealing in this process of self-ascription. In discussing the process, he writes:

> You are what you take yourself to be (at least within the parameters of State-defined categories). That people generally continue to classify themselves as they traditionally have been, that they are even asked to classify themselves on this criterion, suggests that behind the principle lies the expectation that they will take themselves racially to be what they 'naturally' are. (Goldberg 1993: 87)

Sollors (1986) and others have discussed how many of the social groups talked about in racial terms in the past are now often discussed in primarily ethnic terms. Goldberg (1993: 75) writes:

> Why and when the terms are interchangeable in this way may have much to do with the referential history of the groups in question, though not necessarily. So Jews, Blacks, Hispanics, and Japanese in the United States may now be referred to as either race or ethnic group.

But he adds an interesting footnote to this: 'Because of their connotative histories, the latter seems more benign. This may be changing, however, as the phenomenon of "ethnic cleansing" in Bosnia suggests' (ibid.: 75). There seems to be some general process at work in all of this, where people recognise the limitations of using terms that have biological lineage at their core while at the same time needing terms that allow them to categorise and differentiate.

> That races may emerge, submerge, or evaporate in the referential lexicon of social groups has in part and relatedly to do with the sorts of processes by which ethnicities form and emerge, with the (self-)explanation stressed for their formation, and with the politics of general group reference at the time in question. The general processes of ethnic group formation, or what is generally called 'ethnogenesis', turn primarily on boundary construction and on the internalization and naturalization of identity by social subjects. (ibid.)

Again, in contemporary society, self-definition and self-ascription are important aspects of ethnicity (and will be key to this book) although, as in much of life, ethnicity may be contested and much more problematic in certain cases.

The approach that I take is very much rooted in the psychology of the individual mind, and ultimately at some ill-defined point in the future (perhaps) on the organisation of the human brain in terms of basic neuroscientific principles. This reflects my own particular theoretical bias, that of a social psychologist with a particular interest in social action and social cognition, attempting to understand the world of everyday affairs by focusing on the decisions and actions, many of them social, which individuals perform as a function of their beliefs and values. Some would see this as problematic. Richards (1997: xii) writes that: 'Psychology's earlier tendency to view racism as an individual-level quasi-psychopathology was, however well meant, inadequate. Indeed, such a position may well avert attention from more pertinent social and economic factors.' But, of course, one can examine biases and prejudices to do with race and ethnicity at the individual level to see how they might feed into 'pertinent social and economic factors', like employment. This is one core aspect of the operation of ethnic bias which, to my mind, requires more detailed and careful scrutiny. And, of course, one should not begin by assuming that any such biases are 'quasi-pathological' in nature. It remains to be seen what exactly their essence is: pathological, quasi-pathological or entirely functional at some psychological level.

Another bias that underpins the book is the assumption that many of the decisions that we make in everyday life do not appear to be a result of great reflection, the weighing up of the pros and cons of any particular choice. They seem to be faster than this, sometimes very fast and non-reflective, almost automatic in their speed; they seem to come from nowhere but they have enormous social consequences for people, for societies and for cultures. Stanovich and West (2000) identified these kinds of decisions as resulting from one of the two great systems of the human mind, the so-called (and very bland-sounding but somewhat Orwellian) 'System 1'. This is the system which, for example, analyses the emotion in a picture of a human face and anticipates what the person in the picture might do next as a result of their emotional state. Here is how the psychologist Daniel Kahneman (2011: 20) describes our reaction to the picture of an angry woman:

> You did not intend to assess her mood or to anticipate what she might do, and your reaction to the picture did not have the feel of something you did. It just happened to you. It was an instance of fast thinking. System 1 operates automatically and quickly with no sense of conscious control or influence. System 2 is the conscious system, which allocates attention to mental activities that require some thought.

In Kahneman's words 'The operations of System 2 are often associated with the subjective experience of agency, choice and concentration' (ibid.: 21). We may think of ourselves as rational, logical creatures, with a firm foundation in the operations and processes of System 2, but we will see that in many domains, including decisions to do with race and perceived differences in ethnic background, that System 1 will often take over and guide us to particular outcomes.

So where does this particular academic bias of mine come from in terms of my own experiences? It comes from many years of work analysing the social actions of individuals, considering their language and their non-verbal actions, and my discovery that, time and time again, these two sorts of social action, one considerably more reflective than the other, can be discrepant, not congruent and sometimes downright contradictory, even when people appear to be in a generally reflective mode. We have known about these apparent contradictions for some time, since Gregory Bateson and colleagues formulated the concept of the 'double bind' in 1956. One aspect of which was the sometimes inconsistent nature of human communication (there were other additional social and relational factors necessary to capture fully the double bind concept), often with verbal and non-verbal channels that seemed to contradict each other. In one classic example, described by Bateson, the mother of a schizophrenic patient visited her son in hospital, and when he put his arm around her, she automatically stiffened (a System 1 response in modern terminology), he removed his arm as a consequence and she said 'Don't you love me anymore?' (a System 2 response which is conscious and controlled). Bateson pointed out that this behaviour, of course, puts the recipient (the son) in an impossible situation. What should he do next? Should he hug her again and pretend that he hadn't noticed her bodily response (or indeed any bodily responses)? Should he laugh off all of these types of non-verbal action and live in a world where they have no meaning and no consequence? Should he stand there, doing nothing, immobile? Herein, Bateson argued, lie the very origins of a form of maladaptive behaviour that we call schizophrenia.

But this is a very specific, somewhat anecdotal example of something much more general and now much more systematically studied. My view is that talk in human interaction is a complex multi-channel activity, which necessarily involves the expression of thoughts and ideas through both language and certain expressive movements (particularly the expressive movements of the hands and arms; see McNeill 1992, McNeill and Duncan 2000; Beattie 2003), as well as involving social communication (about emotions and relationships) and the structuring of the interaction (see Beattie 1980, 1983) using other forms of non-verbal behaviour (facial expression, eye gaze, posture, interpersonal distance, head movements, etc.) as well. The expressive movements of the hands and arms are often imagistic, and indeed iconic, in form and closely temporally integrated with the speech itself. Ideas are jointly expressed through the speech and these movements although we often need experiments to demonstrate this conclusively (Beattie and Shovelton 1999a, 1999b, 2000, 2001, 2002a, 2002b, 2005, 2006, 2011). But all of this has led David McNeill (2000: 139) to the startling conclusion (in some quarters) that 'To exclude the gesture side, as has been traditional, is tantamount to ignoring half of the message out of the brain'.

There are different conceptual models of how this whole process of talk and action, in the form of speech and gesture, cooperate together to communicate meaning. McNeill proposed a model based on the concept of the 'growth point' – the minimal unit of an imagery–language dialectic.

A growth point is a package that has both linguistic categorical and imagistic components, and it has these components irreducibly. It is a minimal unit in the Vygotskian [1986] sense, the smallest package that retains the property of being a whole; in this case the imagery–language whole that we see in synchronized combinations of co-expressive speech and gestures. (McNeill 2005: 105)

In McNeill's model, the construction of meaning and talk is 'a dynamic, continuously updated process in which new fields of oppositions [his terminology for a particular understanding of context] are formed and new GPs [growth points] or psychological predicates are differentiated in ongoing cycles of thinking and speaking' (ibid.: 107). McNeill argues that this model can explain the form and timing of the gestural movements that accompany speech. In an example where a participant retells a story, the concept of the growth point is illustrated when someone says verbally 'drops it [a bowling ball] down the drainpipe'. The accompanying gesture has a distinctive shape and is not the gesture shown in the original story. McNeill's conclusion is that 'The gesture and sentence . . . reflected the speaker's conceptualizing of the cartoon as much as the objective cartoon content' (ibid.: 121). McNeill's model in which he makes speech and gesture absolutely integral to the process of meaning generation gives us a new way of analysing talk to glimpse the conceptualisation process of utterances in real time.

Another influential, but very different, model was the Information Packaging Hypothesis (IPH) developed by Kita (2000). The IPH considers speech and gesture to be independent cognitive streams in speech, running simultaneously. The IPH is a modular conception of speech and gesture with the two modules conceived as 'separate' intertwining streams. McNeill says that the imagery in the gesture is categorised linguistically whereas in the IPH gesture is viewed as visual thinking. The IPH requires an interface for the imagery and gesture modules for the exchange of relevant information. McNeill's growth point model does not have such an interface because here gesture and language combine dialectically (see McNeill 2005: 132). These are models designed to show how the systems cooperate to express meaning, jointly and coherently; though sometimes the meanings expressed by the two systems do not match (which would seem to imply a degree of independence in functioning), and this can be very revealing when it does occur (Goldin-Meadow 1997). In one study with Doron Cohen and Heather Shovelton, we analysed people who had been actively encouraged to 'lie' about some factual details in a story that they were telling (I put 'lie' in inverted commas because it was not a very big lie with any real social consequences, unlike many of those that we tell in everyday life). But what was interesting was that the gestures became less frequent and shorter in these lies, and sometimes the form of the gesture simply no longer matched the content of the speech. The image in the gesture represented what they had actually seen rather than what they were now describing in the lie itself (Cohen, Beattie and Shovelton 2010).

Thus, there are a number of significantly different theoretical interpretations of the exact relationship between gesture and speech but they all agree on a number of theoretical points; mainly that gesture, a form of non-verbal action, is an essential component of talk and that communication between conversational partners depends critically upon this component (see also Beattie and Shovelton 1999a, 1999b, 2001, 2005, 2011). The other thing they all agree on is that our very conception of the nature of human communication has been changing in the past few years.

But there is one other important feature of gestural communication that is particularly relevant here. Speakers may have considerable awareness of how their speech is unfolding in real time but they seem to be much less aware of the exact form and timing of their gestural movements. Cienki and Müller (2008: 94) wrote that 'Gestures are less monitored than speech and they are to a great extent unconscious. Speakers are often unaware that they are gesturing at all.' Danesi (1999: 35) argued that, 'when people speak they gesture unconsciously, literally "drawing" the concepts they are conveying orally'. Nelson (2007: 96) stated that:

> gesture is a parallel component of human verbal communication, sometimes used unconsciously to accompany the message conveyed by words (Goldin-Meadow 1997) . . . [gestures] are often acquired and used without conscious intent. To the extent this is the case, it verifies the continuing existence of a mode of unconscious meaning unconsciously expressed.

I have on the computer screen in front of me a short video-recording of a young, dark-haired woman with a kind face and a dark fringe swept to one side explaining to an unseen interviewer how she would buy sustainable low carbon footprint products in a supermarket in these environmentally friendly times (see Beattie 2010). She refers to these as the 'good' products. The high carbon footprint products are, in her words, the 'bad' products. She says explicitly and unambiguously: 'if they were next to each other and it was obvious that one was good and one was bad then you would go for the good one'. But her accompanying hand gestures, which are highly meaningful but largely unconscious, seem to contradict this basic statement. In one gesture she uses the left hand opening and closing and raised slightly above (and in front of) the right hand to signify the 'good' products. In her next gesture she uses the right hand with a very similar configuration and hand shape to represent the 'bad' products. The choice between the 'good' and the 'bad' is being physically enacted in the space in front of her body. But the critical third gesture when she talks about the actual moment of choice itself, and accompanying the words 'then you'd go for the good one', is executed in that part of the space in front of the body used to represent the 'bad' high carbon footprint products. In other words, she says that she would choose the 'good' products, but her nonverbal action seems to be suggesting that she would choose the 'bad' ones.

What is also interesting about this young woman is that although she says explicitly and consciously that she is very pro-low carbon (and very 'green' in terms of her attitudes), other measures of 'implicit' attitude (which we will come to later) suggest that she is not (see Beattie 2010). But she clearly does understand the social desirability of saying that she is 'green'. In other words, her opinions, expressed in her speech, are clearly not congruent with her underlying implicit attitude. And there is something else here as well. She repeatedly makes circular movements of the right hand when she displays her choice, as if there is some discomfort, some dissonance (to borrow Festinger's term), associated with the unconscious signalling of that choice, and her intonation is also a little unusual: it sounds incomplete, as if she does not want to fully commit herself. One might even speculate that by making the gestural movement in the first place, towards that point in the gestural space where the high carbon products are symbolically located, she allows herself to reduce her state of 'dissonance' by being true to herself. Festinger (1957: 97), after all, wrote that 'If public (i.e., forced) compliance is elicited, then the private opinions are dissonant with the cognitive elements corresponding to the overt behavior'. However, despite the compliance forced by social desirability, some overt behaviour here (the iconic gestural action depicting choice between 'good' and bad' products) remains consonant with the private opinion. Thus, given that people generally act to reduce dissonance, for example by changing their underlying attitude to make it consonant with overt behaviour (and we usually only think of what people say as the 'overt behaviour' here), you could argue that the production of this particular gesture alongside the speech allows the implicit attitude to be held without this particular psychological challenge.

This is just a couple of seconds of social action, but to me it raises many important issues about how we might approach analysing human behaviour.

The first issue it raises is that it reminds us that there are different components of social action, and not just what people say in their words and sentences. I take the point that we give meaning to the world through language and that the language we use in our everyday life does not just reflect the world out there in any simple or straightforward way, rather it actively constructs it (Potter and Wetherell 1987). The world we live in is effectively made through our use of language. After all, the categories of high and low carbon products have to be constructed as such; they are not straightforwardly available (and the categories seem to vary considerably from one individual to another, where individuals have to borrow and shape concepts like 'air miles', 'seasonality', 'local', 'organic', 'the nature of their shipping conditions', etc. to arrive at some flexible and often vague category). Labelling one category as 'good' and one as 'bad' is another active constructive process, which depends on broader cultural views on sustainability as well as certain value judgements. Representing consumer choice as an actual decision point between adjacent 'good' and 'bad' items is a highly metaphoric and schematic construction of the nature of such choice. And there are those who have argued, persuasively in my view, that this constructive process can, and should, become a major focus of scholarly activity in psychology; just as it is elsewhere in other disciplines (see, for example, the classic Potter and Wetherell

1987), even when it comes to understanding racism (Wetherell and Potter 1992).

But for me this focus of study on language alone is simply not sufficient. I do not want to conclude that everything in the end is just language. I do not agree with the extreme 'relativist' views expressed by the likes of Edwards, Ashmore and Potter (1995). I understand it when they say that even something physical and tangible like thumping a table (which they regard as 'a bedrock of reality that places limits on what can be treated as epistemologically constructed or deconstructible') has to be encoded as such for us to get the point, but then they take it a step too far (way too far) to my mind. They write:

> It is surprisingly easy and even reasonable to question the table's given reality. It does not take long, in looking closer, at wood grain and molecule, before you are no longer looking at a 'table'.

They then continue on a slightly different tack:

> 'When the table is assaulted it is not the whole of it that gets thumped, but only a bit of it under the fist or hand or fingers, or tips of (some of) the fingers. What exactly is warranted by this – just the bits hit? What makes it a bit of a table? And for whom? (Ibid.: 29)

This is starting to veer a bit off target, especially because it is the concept of 'thumped' rather than 'table' that is more problematic and interesting in terms of use of language in this example. Who cares what bit of the table was thumped, the question is was it 'thumped' at all? That's what I want to know. Or was it merely hit?

In the case of that other great 'realist emblem' (in their words) 'death', they are even more off track. They attack the argument by Craib (1986) who railed against the irresponsibility of turning everything into discourse. They are attempting to maintain their essential position (in the face of Craib's onslaught) that there is no such thing as a 'version-less reality'; all that we have, they say, are linguistically coded versions of reality. Craib (ibid.: 484) wrote:

As I write this, an area of Tripoli has been laid waste by
a number of aircraft currently (I hope) sitting on the
ground a few miles down the road from my Ivory Tower.
Some 100 people (not very many by modern standards)
have been killed. They were not killed by words neither
are they dead because the rest of the world decides to
call them dead. Their death was brought about by the
employment of a disproportionately immense amount of
scientific and technical knowledge. If we can only see
this knowledge as just another story, then we too deserve
to fall victim to it.

Edwards and his colleagues' response to this persuasive
and very well-made point is:

Look closer at the commonsense conception of death,
and, like the table, it starts to disappear: resurrection,
the afterlife, survival of the spirit, the non-simultaneous
criteria of brain death, the point when life support might
as well be switched off, cryogenic suspension, the precise
(how precise), moment of death . . . Death is never simple.
We have far too much interest in it for that. (Edwards
et al. 1995: 36)

I find this argument facile and slightly infuriating.
Language is our most important symbolic tool, and language
is clearly both constructed and constructive even when it
comes to death and destruction, for example, in the construction of the nature of the 'victim' in acts of terrorism (see
Beattie and Doherty 1995), or in the construction of more
routine and 'ordinary' acts of violence by the perpetrators of
the violence themselves (Jordan and Beattie 1998). But there
is a harsh reality out there that sometimes words cannot
disguise or negate [he said, thumping the table; which bit of
the table was not even remotely relevant]. There are dead
people, and people dying, regardless of what types of victims
they have become through our constructive use of language.
I believe that nuclear bombs kill large groups of people (and
in my home town of Belfast, Semtex from Libya killed smaller
but still very significant numbers) and I also believe that in

the end sometimes it is the action that matters, regardless of how it is encoded or talked about. Try explaining to the relatives of those killed on Bloody Sunday or Bloody Friday in the Troubles of Northern Ireland that if you look closely enough at the commonsense concept of death, then it starts to disappear.

I want to study and to understand more fully choices and decisions and actions in the area of race and ethnicity, and not just the language we use. I am not alone in this. Read, for example, Frantz Fanon's description of White people's unconscious behavioural responses to the Negro, sometimes at the 'instinctual, biological level' (Fanon 2006: 70), often much more powerful and telling than any language they use (and quite possibly a 'neurotic' behavioural response in many senses). I want to study choices, decisions and actions that are often completely silent (and not, therefore, themselves embodied in language but still dependent on language through cultural understandings) and yet highly meaningful, as I attempt to simulate parts of our everyday life in experiments. Of course, these silent decisions are based on our cultural background which is heavily discourse based, but I will leave that particular nexus to others to unravel. These choices and decisions will subsequently be coded in language on many occasions, they may be commented on, reflected upon, contested, justified, argued about, but sometimes they will not. They are essentially actions (sometimes very simple like a tick on a page) that result in very significant consequences ('smiles all round, you've got the job') and I am deeply interested in the movements and the micro-behaviours that seem to be connected to these choices (even patterns of eye-gaze as our attention locates relevant information on a CV). And the reason for this focus is that I want to understand the behaviours that may contribute to biases in employment. I do not want to focus just on what people say about 'fairness', or 'transparency' or even just analyse their justifications as to why they short listed x but not y. I am not even much interested in the present book in what they say about 'race' or 'ethnicity', how they construct it, how they give it meaning or why (although some will see this as an extraordinary admission). I will treat these as non-problematic for present purposes, and often follow the bureaucratic language of employment statistics, and the processes of self-ascription, like White, non-White, BME or not. I want to see what actually happens when people make decisions, regardless of whether it's formulated in language or not (some of the very detailed analyses of what happens when people make decisions can be found in Appendix 2). And sometimes the decisions, those split second actions, will have to be so quick (a matter of milliseconds) that there will actually be little opportunity to encode any stimuli into words to allow linguistic categorisations to occur and for language to do what it does.

But, there is another important point that I need to make here. I do not believe that we just give meaning to the world through our use of language. I believe that we also give meaning to the world through our actions. These are often as important as what we say, and I do not just mean the actions of the hands as they accompany speech, sometimes redundant, sometimes adding new information, sometimes contradicting it (Beattie 2003). I mean other actions, like offering someone a job or not, like sitting next to someone or not, like smiling in one way rather than another, like shifting uncomfortably in someone's presence, or being at ease. These actions structure our social world and give it much of its essential meaning, with or without language (see also Beattie 1986).

The second issue that this short video-clip raises in my mind is that I have grounds for believing that this gesture–speech mismatch is not accidental or random or just one of those little errors of everyday life, like the typographical error that I have just made and corrected immediately. My grounds for believing this derive from experimental techniques that we will subsequently come to, and that I have used to 'understand' this individual participant (at least, in terms of revealing her underlying implicit attitude). In other words, I am using an essential process of triangulation to focus on the occurrence or non-occurrence of certain micro-behaviours. Discourse analysis, especially now that it is connecting more with the Conversation Analysis of Gail

Jefferson, developing out of the pioneering work of Sacks, Schegloff and Jefferson (1974), can and sometimes does address issues of the accompanying non-verbal behaviour, but my own feeling here is that these behaviours are simply too multifarious, complex and common to be incorporated into transcripts in the same way as the features of the speech stream itself (Jefferson 1985), without the powerful lens of a theoretical perspective to guide the focus and the analysis. Conversation Analysts argue that we have to include everything in our transcripts because we cannot rule anything out on an *a priori* basis. But I do not want to be overwhelmed by data; I do not want to be in a position where I cannot see the wood for the trees. For this reason I will be using experiments, based on simulated situations of some importance, to guide the analysis of particular non-verbal behaviours in particular contexts.

The third issue that this short clip raises is that human beings may well be contradictory in some situations, as Allport and Festinger and others have noted, going this way and that at the same time. It raises questions as to whether individuals do even know their own minds. They might well do, of course; the hesitation and the gesture of the young woman with the dark fringe could after all be prompted by this simple desire to look good, to avoid admitting that she doesn't give a damn about carbon footprint. But there is always the possibility that human beings don't know either way, that there is some alternative system chugging away (System 1), guiding us much of the time, and that the gesture reflects this. The gesture might be signifying some choice guided by certain types of process that the speaker herself does not understand or even know about, but nevertheless it is a choice, symbolically enacted, with real psychological consequences for the young woman herself. But this, of course, is just a hypothesis. But if it were to be the case, what else might be being directed by this alternative and hidden system? What else lurks beneath? And how do issues to do with race and ethnicity fit into all of this? Could some unconscious and implicit system lead to biases and prejudice in employment around race? And that really is the subject of this book.

- Employment statistics suggest that there are inequalities which may well be attributable to race or ethnic background.
- Prejudice can often be seen in language use but there is much more to prejudice than that. Prejudice is also found in action.
- Some psychologists believe that mapping the language of racism may be sufficient; I don't.
- Our actions (even when we are in a reflective mode) are often discrepant with our words.
- Some decisions in life are made very quickly and do not seem to be based on much reflection.
- Some decisions in life are made so quickly that the choices are not linguistically encoded.

2

A room steeped in the past

This is a serious room, sturdy and solid, with a slightly musty smell like a certain kind of old Victorian church. You breathe in more deeply and you can tell that it's not a church, it is just a similar smell to it, highly evocative in the way that some smells are. It almost controls your emotions, in a way that Marcel Proust would surely recognise. You find yourself lowering the tone of your voice as you go through the door, quite unconsciously; as if you know that you are entering a solemn place, perhaps more a court rather than a church. This is Victorian splendour, in that modern Gothic style, presumably designed to remind you of order and position and hierarchy. The smell alone sees to that.

I take my seat on what look like pews at the back opposite the large rectangular oak table. The President of the university, Alan Gilbert, sits in the middle of the table on the far side, directly in my eye line, but I can move behind the pillar to my left when I want to avoid what feels like eye contact. The Deputy President, Nancy Rothwell, sits to his left, the Registrar to his right. The Vice Presidents for Teaching and Learning, Research and External Affairs sit side by side in a line then an arc from the Vice President, stretching then arcing around the side of the great table. The Heads of Schools, like me, sit wherever they like, in principle that is, but there is always a certain regularity and order in where they choose to sit. There must be something comforting about a familiar position. The Head of School of Mathematics always sits in the same place near the entrance, the Head of School of Physics on the main table down towards the left, the Head of School of Dentistry on my far right, where he rotates his upper body a great deal as he listens, you can see the side of his head more than most. And I sit towards the back like some naughty schoolboy, but I sit here for my own good reasons, in a position to watch everything that goes on in this great, almost pompous, room. I am a psychologist after all. Where else would I sit, right in the middle of the action, where I can see nothing?

There is a regularity and an order in the meetings, in the positioning, in the opening remarks, in how the questions to the President are phrased, in how the President looks to the Registrar (sometimes for reassurance, sometimes not), in how the President makes his points and how we nod attentively. And here we conduct the great business of the provincial university. It is a star in the firmament of provincial universities, but it is a provincial university nonetheless, founded in Victorian times by one of the great merchants of the city of Manchester, John Owens. Owens made his money by shipping calico and coarse woollens to China and India and North America and then invested in the new great railway system, eventually leaving £96,654 to establish the college that bore his name. This later became the University of Manchester. Alfred Waterhouse was the architect of these Oxford Road buildings that opened in 1886, and much of the other great Victorian splendour of Manchester. And this is the council chamber with its gothic arches and serious wood. A painting by Willem Wissing hangs above the President's head; it is a painting of Mary II when she was Princess of Orange. In the painting she looks down, her right arm folded across her chest just below her bosom; her left hand is positioned on some kingly looking purple robes. She looks a little wistful, maybe even a little sorrowful. The extraordinary point about the painting is that her eyes seem to follow you no matter where you sit on that back pew. I noticed that from the beginning, from my first moment in that room some ten years ago. At first I thought that it was me. Occasionally in meetings, when I was feeling a little bored, I would move my head from side to side to check if she was still looking at me, but she always was, like some great psychological ploy in the positioning of this seventeenth century painting in this serious Victorian chamber. The painting was there to remind you about public display and watchfulness, about standards, academic and personal, about decorum, about reputation.

The President outlines our considerable research achievements in the last Research Assessment Exercise and the Heads around the table nod with a certain amount of self-satisfaction and pride. There is a white marble sculpture to my right, carved by Harry Bates in 1886. It is 'Socrates Teaching the People in the Agora'. Here Socrates sits in dialogue with his pupils. Socrates has a long stick, the pupils look engrossed in what he is saying. He points towards them with his right hand, as if making a fine point, and the pupil behind him listens in on the conversation, his head in his hands, engrossed, picking up on every word. I catch myself looking towards this white sculpture. It is that pointing gesture, it never looks right to me, and the President notices this slow, almost thoughtful turn of my head, and I catch the movement in his eyes as if he wants to see what I am looking at. But his eyes draw me back to the main business, the approaching Senate vote and the proposed changes to the Teaching and Learning Curriculum to enhance 'the student experience', modern terms that jangle uncomfortably at times in this old-fashioned room. The President gestures forcefully when he talks about the importance of this review and I watch the shape and the trajectory of his gesture to see where it lands and to see how serious he is. Then I think of this gesture of Socrates and I am momentarily distracted again.

These meetings are terribly benign and terribly civilised. The 23 Heads of Schools at this biggest university in the UK in consultation with the senior management team, in many ways setting the future landscape of British higher education in terms of everyday, practical action. But today there is an additional item on the agenda set by the Vice President for Equality and Diversity, to be presented by the Head of Equality and Diversity at the university, Patrick Johnson. Since the formation of the University of Manchester in 2004 which combined the much older Victoria University of Manchester (which grew out of Owens College) with the

University of Manchester Institute of Science and Technology, there has been a Vice President for Equality and Diversity to drive forward the equality agenda. But despite all their best efforts and all of their implementation of new policies and procedures ensuring the broadest possible range of applicants for posts, many of the top positions are still held by male academics from an extremely narrow ethnic background. The Vice President for Equality and Diversity makes this point almost immediately, 'Just look around you, what do you see?', he says in his fine RP accent, almost cut glass, and sure enough in this room there are very few who display much by way of ethnic diversity, apart from the Vice President for Equality and Diversity himself and the person he has invited along to speak.

The heads glance around uncomfortably, like school-boys who have been caught out, or fear that they are going to be accused of something that they have not actually done. From the back pew I can detect a noticeable change in terms of bodily communication: their upper bodies tighten a little, hands knitting together, arms folding as if they know they are in for a telling off, a mixture of defence and indignation, when they know deep inside that it is not their fault. It's the body language of false accusation and injustice. They have worked hard to get here to this great Victorian room; they have forged significant academic careers. They have made personal sacrifices in their family life to build their curricula vitae to get ahead in the academic game; they have forged personal and political connections to allow them to progress through School Boards and Executive Committees. Now they are in this great serious room with colleagues who have been on the same or parallel journeys to themselves. They are among friends. They enjoy each other's company and enjoy the implicit references and shared humour; there are many shared values, and yet now they are being told off. It is being suggested that they at the university have failed because there are not more brown, black and yellow faces in this great Victorian room.

Patrick begins his presentation and you can see them bristling. He presents a series of hypothetical situations in which unwitting prejudice and discrimination could be operating in the advertising, shortlisting and interviewing of candidates for university posts. He points out that academics often like to recruit candidates explicitly from 'a good stable', a good university and a good research group from within that university. 'How many times have you heard that concept mentioned when advertising and short-listing for posts?' 'Many times,' I whisper to the Head to my left, expecting to hear a unity of affirmation, but there is just silence, not just from him but from around the room. 'The problem with the concept of a good stable,' continues the speaker, 'is that we recruit candidates from research groups that we already know and we appoint people who are familiar to us, and similar to those that we have already got. We need to think outside the box, to think differently, to be divergent.' I can hear the sharp expulsion of air from a grey-haired man in a grey suit sitting in front of me. I cannot see his face but I can imagine his facial expression. It would be one of mild anger, perhaps more than mild anger, a justifi-able response, in his mind, to a gross accusation of unfair-ness. 'But can I remind you of how Manchester did in the last Research Assessment Exercise?', he says indignantly.

We came fourth after Oxford, Cambridge and London. We have been climbing a mountain to get here. Are we to give up these lofty ambitions just because of political correctness? Should we start ringing up the University of Bolton or the University of East London now for them to suggest possible candidates rather than Oxford or Cambridge? We always recruit the best regardless of colour; we do not discriminate either negatively or positively on the basis of colour, creed or ethnic background. Let me remind you that Manchester was founded by a Nonconformist so that students would not have 'to submit to any test whatsoever of their religious opinions'. Manchester has always been a nonconformist and radical city and this is reflected in the university. Manchester in my view is completely colour blind.

The anger has made the speaker lift out of his seat ever so slightly; he slumps back down and glances from left to right for support. I glance around the room too, but for a different reason, to see what colour blindness has bought us: an all-White cast that is bristling with indignation at the hint that something might not be quite right.

But the invited speaker does not stop there; he has reserved his *coup de grâce* for the final part of his talk. He says that he knows that we are all, rationally at least, completely non-prejudiced and non-racist; he knows we have read the diversity literature and agreed with every word of what we should and should not do. He doesn't believe that any of us actively discriminates in any sort of conscious way against women or people from different ethnic backgrounds. 'But,' he says, 'what happens if we do this unconsciously and implicitly without conscious awareness or knowledge? Research from the United States by a psychologist called Anthony Greenwald suggests that this may well be the case.'

The already muffling silence of the room just increases, as a long silent pause opens up in front of us all like some gaping chasm. 'What happens,' he was effectively saying, 'if this great Victorian room, full of the great and good of Manchester academia is full of unconscious racists who have no knowledge of their cognitions and judgements when it comes to matters of race, and whose behaviour has been influenced in subtle and unconscious ways by these beliefs and attitudes? What happens if we all have racist hearts no matter what we say?' He then dares to fill the silence himself, by briefly outlining the research on racism mainly carried out in the United States which suggests that the explicit attitudes that people openly hold and espouse may not be that closely related to measures of implicit attitudes when it comes to questions about race. He even mentions the empirical finding that in the United States White people explicitly have a slight preference for White people, on traditional self-report attitude scales, but implicitly, on the basis of these new psychological measures, they have a much stronger preference for White people. But more extraordinarily, Black people may say that they have a preference for Black people in attitudinal surveys, but implicitly many seem to have a preference for Whites. So the research from the United States suggests that we are all biased against Black people; even some Black people themselves, even they are racist, but against their own race. I can see why the speaker has mentioned these results; it would suggest that we are all in this together. He might be as guilty, if that's the right word here, as the next man in terms of implicit and unconscious bias against Black people. The theoretical point is that none of us know how we feel inside, we need special complicated tests devised by psychologists to tell us, and the truth may be very disturbing indeed and this may explain the absence of people from different ethnic backgrounds in this serious room, full of serious academics, engaged in the serious business of improving a British university.

The speaker may have mentioned these results in a conciliatory manner, but this is not how it is perceived. The point about serious academics, and this room is full of serious academics, is that they want good empirical facts, rigorous designs, conceptual critiques. Patrick's case studies ('anecdotes', says the Head to my left, 'and sometimes they are not even plausible anecdotes') and non-specialist review of the psychological literature seem to provoke them further. You can almost sense the palpable hardening of attitudes in that room. The mood seems to be that we do what we do and the Research Assessment Exercise proves that we do it well. Why should we let the PC brigade interfere with any of this?

Even I could feel myself bristle to some extent, for more personal reasons. I may be a White male who may not stand out in this room full of White males in grey suits, but I come from what universities these days would probably describe as a non-traditional background. But my diversity, such as it is, is not visible, or may not be visible from the outside, in the way that skin colour or ethnic background is, but nevertheless it often leaves me feeling a little bit different from the majority of my academic colleagues. This is felt difference, remembered difference, difference on the inside. It has been like that for a long time, indeed ever since I was a child because, when I was 11, my world changed in an instant. When I was 11, I passed the Eleven-Plus. This was a test that had been designed to measure a child's intelligence, and on the basis of the outcome of this one test you were directed to one type of school rather than another. Now this might not seem that significant a life event in the grand scheme of things, but trust me it was, for me and for countless others. It took me away from my working class neighbourhood and allowed me to go to a grammar school that offered me tremendous possibilities. It offered me a future, and for that I am, of course, extremely grateful. But it also exposed me to certain prejudices based around social class and social background, many of which seemed to be implicit, but some of which were, on occasion, quite explicit. This school taught me many lessons about life, some of them were very personal and very, very painful.

- People do not like to be accused of being racist, and people definitely do not like to be accused of being unconscious racists.
- Many people are sceptical of the idea of implicit racism, perhaps to protect themselves; perhaps they are sceptical for good reasons.
- You need to be careful how you introduce the topic of implicit racism; you never know who might be in the audience.

3

Early lessons in prejudice: spoken and unspoken

It was a Saturday morning; I will never forget that, the excitement of the weekend, music on the radio, augmented by this anxious wait for the results to come. 'You have to be patient,' my mother would say. 'It'll take them a long while to mark all those wee tests.' I was up already that morning, early for me. We liked to lie to lunchtime on a Saturday, the way that working class families often do. I was jittery with expectation, and the brown envelope came, eventually, clattering through our letter box, as thick and as heavy as a slab of Irish soda bread.

'Is it thick or thin?' my older brother shouted down the stairs, from bed. He hadn't bothered to get up, but I knew he wasn't asleep. He was nervous as well. 'Thick,' I shouted back, fumbling to open it. 'Oh shite, he's passed.' My brother, you see, hadn't passed the Eleven-Plus but he did know enough to appreciate the significance of the thickness of the envelope. We were no longer in the same boat – I had been pushed out and I now had to swim away to strange and foreign shores. He eventually went to university but he had to take a much more circuitous route.

I had chosen the poshest-sounding school on the list the Local Education Authority had sent out – Belfast Royal Academy. There were a few other schools with 'Royal' in the name as well but this one sounded the poshest of the lot. It was to me at that time just a name, not a real institution, nor even a real building as seen from the outside. I had never actually seen it. It was just a typed line on an A4 sheet of paper, but it had a great-sounding name like the Taj Mahal or the Empire

State Building, and it could have been as distant. I didn't know where any of the schools were. None of them were anywhere near my particular part of Belfast, a little loyalist 'ghetto' in north Belfast. I put 'ghetto' in inverted commas because that was how it came to be referred throughout the history of the Troubles, and quite a famous ghetto at that for all the wrong reasons. At the time it was just the 'turn of the road' to us, as vague and yet as specific as that to anyone who knew Belfast. After I passed the exam, and not before, the school asked to see me, probably quite sensibly because nobody had passed the Eleven-Plus from St Mark's Primary School in Ligoniel for maybe thirteen or fourteen years. The Eleven-Plus, by the way, turned me into a kind of local celebrity; people would stop me in the street and press sixpences into my hand. Despite my shyness, this felt good. It wasn't that Ligoniel necessarily produced children of below average intelligence, incapable of passing this particular examination; it's just that there was no special preparation for the Eleven-Plus at St. Mark's. Whilst other schools were running special courses on how to perform in the 'culture-fair' tests that made up the Eleven-Plus, St. Mark's just didn't bother; nobody ever explained why, it was just the way things were. The attitude seemed to be 'why bother?', but I am sure that the thinking was much more sophisticated than that. My mother had even threatened to move me to a different school to prepare for the test, but I had resisted fiercely, I wanted to be with my mates, I wanted to stay in the gang, and it was convenient as she could pick me up on the way past from the mill at lunchtime for our banana sandwiches and tea for lunch.

I was being given my big chance – a chance of an education, but first I had to get through the interview. My mother took the day off work from Ewart's mill, in Ligoniel, to go with me. She worked in the carding room, where the flax dust tends to give you a very pronounced and very distinctive cough. My father gave us directions to what he always insisted on calling the Royal Academy School. I wasn't sure whether it was the same place as Belfast Royal Academy or a completely different institution. I had this notion that we might arrive at the wrong school and wait for hours to see a headmaster who wasn't expecting us. 'Don't let me down,' my mother whispered as we got off the bus. The bus driver wished me well. He could see that I was apprehensive, as well I might be. He knew my father, who worked as a mechanic on the buses at the Falls Road depot. It was us versus them – 'Show them what you're made of, sonny', he said as I got off. I thought this was the last thing I wanted to show them. This day, more than any other, I knew I could not afford to be myself.

The headmaster himself interviewed me; apparently this was quite significant as he normally didn't do the interview. I'm not sure that he knew exactly where Ligoniel was, he had probably never made it to that particular ghetto, even though he did look very learned. He wore a black gown that flapped as he came into the room, with chalk rising from the gown into the air; the flapping sound was like the sound of some great and slightly frightening bat. I found him intimidating in many ways, and not just because he reminded me of a great, blind bat unsettling dust into the air as he moved. He asked a few simple and friendly questions and I provided a few simple and truthful answers, sometimes directed to the floor, sometimes to the chalk rising from his shoulder as he talked and gestured, to avoid eye contact, and very occasionally directly into his watery, sad eyes. I was a very shy boy with strangers, and here I was trying to be accurate and truthful in my answers, and not 'too cheeky', as my mother would have put it. 'Don't stare at your elders and betters,' she would say, 'it's very rude; it's very cheeky.' So I would stare sometimes at the shoulders and hope that my interlocutor couldn't tell the difference between that and something more forward, a gaze at the eyes themselves, looking into the gateway to their soul, and affording them with a gateway into mine. I was truthful all the way through the interview, until that is, he asked me about the last novel I'd read. Now let me get one thing clear – mine was not a deprived home, it was a condemned mill house, granted, damp and squat, almost shaky on its foundations, with no bath and a dark, black toilet in the yard. You had to leave the light on in the backroom when you went to the toilet, so that you could find the latch on the toilet door. And once you were inside you had to pull the door shut behind you if you wanted any sort of privacy and sit there in the total darkness. Indeed, I can remember the electric light installed into the

*outside toilet by my brother who was a spark, and the differ-
ence that made when you had to go to the toilet after dark. And
this was Belfast in the 'swinging' sixties and decadent seven-
ties and power-suited eighties, not Victorian England or the
England of the twenties or thirties. The house was not exactly
comfortable but it was not a deprived home.*

*There were books in the house, lots of them, invariably
obtained as prizes from St. Mark's church or Sunday school,
usually for 'excellent attendance', but sometimes merely for
'good attendance' (and what a disappointment that was; my
mother felt that we had let ourselves down with merely 'good'
attendance). But they were just that – prizes. Nobody really
read books in my house, although we did read a lot of comics
and magazines. I did, however, take encyclopaedias to bed
with me every night – encyclopaedias of science, encyclopaedias of art, encyclopaedias of sport, encyclopaedias of pets,
encyclopaedias of fish, encyclopaedias of famous men,*
The Everyday Encyclopaedia, The Encyclopaedia for the
Younger Generation, The Living World of Science,
The Wonder World of Nature. *As long as it was an encyclopaedia, I'd read it, but I wasn't really interested in novels at
the time. My knowledge of literature was very restricted but I
did have an encyclopaedia of famous authors. So when he
asked me about the last novel I'd read, my heart sank abruptly,
like a float pulled under water on a high river in the streams
around Crumlin. But luckily I'd been to the King George V
Memorial Hall the previous Sunday to see the film* Gulliver's
Travels. *From my* Encyclopaedia of Famous Authors *I knew
it had been written by Swift, J. (1667–1745). The only problem
was that my mates and I had been chucked out shortly after
the interval for throwing marbles, first at each other and then
down into the stalls. We always took bags of marbles to the
cinema, by the way, it was a big part of going to the cinema.
(The only exception was when we went to see the X-certificate
midnight movies, the horror movies that is, at the Park
Cinema, on the Oldpark Road, where we'd take old rags to
first soak in the toilet, then hurl down from the upper circle
during the Hammer House of Horror movies.) It was really
funny sitting there in the dark, in the front row of the upper
circle, watching somebody get the first marble out, showing it*

*round to all the suppressed giggles and then there would be
the little underhand throw, and then the silence as we waited
and listened to where it would land. Maybe one or two would
go astray but soon they would hit their target and you would
hear the yell, with everyone else around the unfortunate victim
going 'shooooooosh', on the assumption that somebody was just
making a racket to spoil the film for all the rest of us. 'Keep it
quiet down there,' my friends would shout out, muffling their
hysterical laughter, 'we're trying to watch the film up here.
Not like you clowns down there in the cheap seats, down there
in the basement where you belong.'*

But that day in the interview, it was Gulliver's Travels *or
nothing: I was short on plot – I had missed a lot of it after all
because of all the excitement with the marbles (the lights had
been switched on after the interval because someone had
caught sight of one of the marbles coming from our direction
in the glow of the projector) but I was very good on visual
description. I got to the point where we'd been chucked out
and said, 'would you like me to continue?' The headmaster
said that he'd heard enough. He was already impressed by my
visual imagination – by my ability to conjure up complex
visual images and detailed scenes full of description and
action from the written word. I was in.*

*I went to the official school outfitter to be kitted out –
official school blazer, tie, white shirt, grey flannels, cap, rugby
shirt, cricket flannels, athletics vest, shorts. A cap! My brother
pored over the details of the school uniform when they were
sent out, as if they were for him one kit for winter and one kit
for summer sports; he was transfixed, some garments I had
never heard of, like flannels. 'What the fuck are flannels?' I
asked in that excited way of mine. 'Trousers', explained my
brother, 'they're just grey trousers with a crease in them.
They're nothing to get too excited about.'*

*It was a brave new world that I was entering and it scared
the life out of me. It took two buses to get to my new school, or
one bus and a long walk; all my friends from my street could
dander together down to theirs in their little clump of a gang.
I have always said that there is a lot to be said for school
uniform. On the surface at BRA, or great BRA, as we all sang
in the school song, we all looked very much the same. Below*

the surface everything was different. I could never understand how anyone could be so unworldly as to write a school song praising a great bra. I used to snigger at the words, my fellow pupils told me not to be such a 'pleb'. I didn't really know what a 'pleb' was. 'Plebeian, Beattie,' they would explain, 'you're just a plebeian.' I, fortunately, was none the wiser, but my brother loved the way that we referred to each other by our surnames, like some great English public school.

> *'That's how they do it at Eton and Harrow, you know. It's all "Smith, put your flannels in your cricket bag" and "Jones, help him pack the wickets", all Smith this and Jones that. You're not allowed to use Christian names. Nobody will even know that you're called Geoffrey down there. You'll just be Beattie to them."*

But great BRA did broaden my horizons. I met children who had been to America for their holidays. I met a girl who had been to Saudi Arabia! I'd never even been across the water, as they say in Ireland. And when I opened my mouth, I stuck out a mile. My accent was as thick as buttermilk. But it wasn't just my accent; it was my whole style of speaking. I was surprised to hear eleven-year-olds say, 'He's such a sarcastic and ostentatious person.' I used to look the words up at night in my Little Oxford Dictionary, *and practise them the next day. 'Don't be so sarcastic, Henshaw,' I'd say. 'Why, Beattie?' 'Because I'll stick my toe right up your arse. That's why,' I'd say. The polite 'ass' instead of the much more common Belfast-sounding 'arse' came much later. My mother thought that I was starting to talk awfully proper. 'With our Geoffrey it's always "ass this" and "ass that", these days,' I heard her tell one of her friends. 'He'll be saying "bottom" next if he's not careful.'*

My linguistic habits were deeply ingrained – my accent, my vocabulary and my whole style of speaking – even at eleven. Now one marked feature of the Belfast dialect is the regular occurrence of the expression 'you know'. At times 'you know' almost seems to act as a universal punctuation mark. 'I have to get a couple of buses here in the morning, you know, sir, that's why I'm a bit late, you know. Sorry sir, it won't happen again, you know'. Both pupils and staff tormented me about this, rolling their eyes every time I said 'you know'. One day, during a history lesson and in front of the whole class, the deputy headmaster decided to rid me of this irritating, nasty little working-class linguistic habit once and for all. 'I know that I know, Beattie. Would you kindly stop saying "you know"? It's you who doesn't know what you're talking about.' The more he insisted, the more I kept saying it. My anxiety was going right through the roof. He told me to get a grip on myself, and I tried, you know, I really tried. I learned to hate the sound of my own voice. My speech set me apart – I could never be part of the BRA crowd, one of the BRA boys, as long as I continued to speak like that. It was visible for all to see – fellow pupil, teacher, headmaster – there was no hiding it. It wasn't a passive blemish either, which could be covered up with suitable cosmetics. It was active, moving, and dynamic; it drew attention to itself. I just had to open my mouth and there it would be – out of its cage, circulating the room, with everyone staring up at it. I would be asked to give an oral account of Gladstone's contribution to British politics, and even the stupidest and least imaginative boy in the class could snigger at my attempt, because of how I spoke.

When we had to write essays at school, about what we did on our holidays, and other pupils wrote adventurous, and true, stories about meeting members of the Saudi Royal Family in Saudi Arabia; I wrote about hitch-hiking to a seaside resort called Portrush about sixty miles from Belfast, because that's all I did. The other pupils asked me if trips to Portrush were really the best I could do. So I started using my imagination, and I started making things up, trying to forget who I was and where I was from. One year I went to Egypt for my holidays, or so one of my third form essays says. I was quite good at the description of the place, because after all there were photographs of the Sphinx, and the bazaars of Cairo, in my Boys' World Atlas, *but I wasn't so good at what the 'natives' were like. (The* Boys' World Atlas *was always a bit thin on its description of actual people.) So I had to bluff it again; 'We didn't meet many of the natives,' I said imperiously in my essay, 'so it is not possible for me to surmise what they were actually like.' I was starting to sound like them, at least in essays, at least in the written word, even if I didn't care much for the content of the essays or the sentiments I was expressing. The funny thing was that I could only use words like 'surmise', when I was quite self-consciously playing the part of the boy from BRA. It never generalised to my other world, my real world.*

My essays were second rate, or worse, third rate, because it wasn't at all clear whether the journalists who wrote these magazine articles had been there in the first place. However, one day I decided that enough was enough, and this happened very suddenly; it was right in the middle of one of these essays one long Sunday afternoon. I quite literally stopped writing an essay about my favourite uncle who was a big game hunter, just back from Africa, one and a half pages in, and ripped it up and threw the pages all over the front room. I had suddenly felt very angry but I wasn't sure why. My mother ran into the room, I have no idea what she thought that I was ripping up. 'I can see you've lost the head today. You'll be ripping all your books up next and I'll have to pay for them.' But I was calm, and I started the essay again, on a clean sheet of paper, this time about a real uncle, my Big Uncle Terry, who went down to the bar with my father every Saturday night, and was mauled not by any lion, but by our fox terrier, Spot, when he came home later reeking of drink, the thirteen or fourteen pints of Guinness oozing out of his pores as he and the dog wrestled on the settee in the front room, the dog yelping and snarling as my uncle threw him from the settee to the chair and back. 'That dog only goes for him when he's had a drink,' my mother always said. 'He must be able to smell the Guinness off him. He always tries to give him a wee nip when he's just back from the bar.' She never liked to say that our wee dog had actually bitten him; that would have been a very serious matter. 'If that dog ever bit anybody, I'd have him put down,' she would say, 'is that blood coming from your neck, Terry, what caused that? It couldn't be the wee dog, it never bites; Spot only nips people in a playful way when they've had a drink. That dog is clair-voyant; it can always tell when you've had a wee drink.'

I tried to describe what a fight was like, because on some Saturday nights when I was waiting for my father and my uncle to come out of the bar, I had witnessed the police, the

RUC, black and sinister, their truncheons already out, pulsating in their hands with anticipation, lay into some drunks outside Paddy's, our bar at the bottom of Barginnis Street. I call them 'drunks' but they weren't drunks (which sounds like a full-time pursuit or an occupation), they were just my neighbours out on a Saturday night, it was Robert's da from up the street, and Michael's uncle from down below the baker's, and that man with the thin grey hair who lived up the Hightown on his own in a wee shack of a house, staggering out of Paddy's at closing time, not drunks; just neighbours a little bit past merry. This was the real thing, or a real thing, and I had never seen it written about in terms of how it really presented itself, the shouting without saying much, all slurred and profane, the swearing that went on and on, then quick sudden movements of black sticks in the night, and not even that many, staccato movements. These things were always over very quickly, and more shouting, 'you're beat . . . I'm far from fucking beat', then silence and low moans, a split head or two, seeping blood into the rain on the pavement. And the torrent of accusations and recriminations and more swearing, and deep voices stepping back into the shadows, and my heart pounding in my chest as I stepped back into the doorway. And women with their coats thrown over their shoulders arriving to take their men home after their night out, and these sad, sheepish, sorrowful expressions on the men, who knew they were in trouble now alright. There was no real narrative to it, sometimes it hardly made sense, just a wee spot of bother, a wee scrap, and I found that I was good at describing it, but only because I'd been there, standing in the shop doorway, waiting for my da and my uncle in the rain, just some terrified child, waiting expectantly for those he loved. I didn't even have to use the word 'surmise' once. Writing about my real life, and my real uncle seemed risky in some way, as if I was confessing too much, but my English teacher liked them.

I was, by the way, in the 'A' set for every subject on the curriculum except English, in which I was in the 'D' set, which never really made sense to me in terms of my pattern of exam marks. I had always performed as well in the English exams as in any other subject. I always assumed that it was some-thing to do with my accent, as if they couldn't bear Shakespeare being read with my strong Belfast accent. But after this essay and the one that followed it about this majestic dog I looked after from down the street, called Keeper, things changed. Keeper was half-Alsatian and half-Collie. It was faithful and protective of me, and vicious with all other animals, but usually only when provoked. Keeper was both intelligent and half-wild, because his elderly owner had Parkinson's disease and couldn't look after him properly. So I looked after him and took him for walks up the hills that surround Belfast, never with a lead, and he followed me to the bus stop every day and stood until I got on the bus and then made his lonely way back to our street to wait for me. But on one of these walks one Sunday afternoon he spotted a sheep down below in the next field, and ran after it to kill it. I couldn't get the dog to come back until after. I wrote about this and what might have happened next if anyone had witnessed it. I was suddenly moved mid-term and mid-week into the 'A' set without any real explanation and only with an expressed sense of wonderment by my teacher that I had ever ended up in the D set to begin with.

I suspect that this recognition by my English teacher that there was something in these essays changed my life as much as anything before, and for that I am extremely grateful. I stopped trying to describe or explain my experiences to Solomon, and the like. They went their way, I went mine. Not inferior anymore, just different. But in my seven years at the Academy I didn't once invite any Academy boy or girl to my home and the toilet without a light and the backroom with little wallpaper because the walls were too damp for wallpaper. One friend did, however, come uninvited on one occasion, but he just wanted help with his homework and he didn't stay long. One of my mates set fire to his school blazer by popping a lit cigarette into his pocket before he left. His father returned about half an hour later with the scorched jacket and stood in the middle of my front room, tense and irate ('steaming', my friend said), as my mother categorically denied that it had happened in her house, and that he was wrong to make such accusations. She had genuinely seen nothing and assumed that his accusations were the result of prejudice on his part and little more. I hadn't seen the butt of the cigarette being flicked into the pocket but I had seen the smirk of one of my mates soon after and I knew that this meant something. I just wasn't sure what it meant at the time; not until later, when we were left on our own. This particular mate of mine was murdered during the Troubles.

And to be honest I never really felt part of that great school. Rather than mingle at lunchtimes I went for a run and had a late school dinner on my own. It didn't seem that lonely or that unusual, except perhaps in its frequency and except perhaps looking back. I did this every single day, which with the passage of time seems very significant indeed. One of my mother's best friends was the dinner lady so she would serve me late and give me two apple crumbles. I thought that the teachers always implicitly regarded me as quite different from the rest (but, of course, this could have been my imagination).

In a chemistry class one day, and it was the A class for 'A' level chemistry and therefore full of serious students, I remember once laughing too loudly at a letter that our teacher, an old wizened spinster with bad teeth, was reading from an ex-pupil who had gone to Cambridge. The letter was meant to be an inspiration to us all. Maybe, we could make it to Cambridge one day if we tried hard enough. There was some word in this letter that I found hysterical; I can't remember what the word was now. I think it may even have been the word 'scholar'. It was an unfamiliar word, or unfamiliar in that particular context, that just sounded ludicrously pompous to me. It sounded funny at the time, don't ask me why now. I laughed out loud. It was a sudden, uncontrolled splutter of laughter, a plebian sort of sound; it was only me who saw the joke and the sound seemed to echo in the wood-clad laboratory. Maybe I had expected others to laugh at this word, prompted by my anticipatory guffaw – I had liked to think of myself as a bit of a funny man in class, never taking anything too seriously, or that's how I liked to portray myself, always able to get others to join in – but not this time. The teacher paused almost mid-word and hesitated, as if fighting for control, then exploded in a rage at me. She was so angry that spit was coming out of her mouth, from between her bad teeth, as she shouted; she slammed the letter onto the bench of the lab and stormed off. In my view, she got far too angry given the nature of the offence. I could see something in her eyes, as she glanced back, just the once, which said something about boys like me from that part of town, from the 'turn of the road', from that loyalist ghetto that bred such violence and such resistance. No matter how you try with them, that was what her eyes were saying, no matter how hard you try, and Lord, I have been trying. She asked to speak to me outside, after she had calmed down, just in case I didn't understand the implicit messages, and she said slowly and calmly, 'Beattie, you come from the gutter, and that's where you are going to end up, mark my words. I'm never wrong about these things.' These words have been burned into my memory for decades. I stared back at her with resentment and a fury that I really felt inside, but did not dare express. I could have hit her, that's what I felt like doing, and that's what many from my street would have done, or cried, but luckily I didn't do either. I just nodded my head in aggressive, sharp little movements with every word she said, and stared back at her and kept control.

One other day, the headmaster caught me brazenly displaying a symbol (unintentional or not) of my lower class background. It was my socks. He sent me home for wearing socks that were too gaudy, they had black and white diamonds on them, rather than being plain grey or black, like those provided by the official school outfitter. He told me to go home and change them immediately. I was breaking school rules flagrantly and deliberately right in front of him. Every boy has many pairs of plain black or grey socks, he said, but I was deliberately choosing not to wear them. But, in reality, I had no spare socks to change into, that was all I thought to myself; I wouldn't have worn these particular socks to school if I'd had a choice, the other two pairs of socks that I actually owned were wet and had been left trying to dry in front of a dead fire that gave off no heat. We didn't have a washing machine or a dryer to launder socks, so socks were washed by hand and left about the place, where they stayed damp for days. I knew that I had nothing to change into that day, so I walked to the school gates and went home and took Keeper out instead. We walked up the Hightown and past the quarry and onto the top of Napoleon's Nose at Cavehill, so I could sit looking down onto the Antrim Road and the houses of the boys from the Academy and the playing fields of this great school with their white rugby posts standing out like some optical illusion, and this other world that seemed to be passing me by.

I had my hair cut very short, I wanted to be a skinhead, and he called me the 'shaveling'. I didn't know the word. He knew that I didn't know it. 'Joyce, boy,' he said. 'Joyce.' Or it could have been 'Just, boy, just,' until he said it all again a few days later, enjoying his little joke. My scholarship was sometimes very thin, on a knife edge. He knew that as well. I learnt the course material well; they couldn't fault me on that. We didn't have Joyce at home, or anybody else like Joyce for that matter. Joyce wasn't on the course, so I didn't know anything about him or his fancy language. I looked up 'shaveling', and Joyce when I got home in my books and encyclopaedias. It is strange trying to work out the discourses of everyday life from a dictionary. 'Derogatory; a priest or clergyman with a shaved head. A young fellow, youth.' He might have been insulting me, it was hard to tell. Dictionaries never give you the whole story. It depends on how he meant it. I couldn't be sure exactly which meaning he was implying. It's hard trying to learn language from a dictionary. It's like learning a foreign language. You can only get so good at it in the end.

He told me that if I got a haircut like that again he would send me home until it grew. I should have a proper schoolboy's haircut, and not one like somebody from the criminal classes. As if only certain classes produce criminals. I thought they were to be found in every walk of life myself.

There has to be some convergence somewhere though, and I realised that when it came to A levels, we'd all have to race through the same dark tunnel, perhaps into the light at the end. I was determined that I was going to be prepared, I had to be self-motivated though – my mother told me that if I kept reading all those books that I'd need glasses before I was twenty, and everyone would call me 'speccy four eyes'. I worked on a low card table in our front room, with the television on permanently in the corner, and with my mother's friends dropping in for a chat. I learned to cope with this and many other distractions.

It wasn't so bad for my family, there were only three of us (my father had passed away at this point, as many working class fathers did in their early fifties in this environment). The

Rock family, two doors up in Legmore Street, had eleven in an identical two up and two down house. There was nowhere for them to sleep, let alone do homework. I got grade As at A level in Maths, Physics and Chemistry, which in those days was exceptional even though it is the norm now, and a D in Russian, which I studied in my spare time as an additional subject with minimal formal tuition. I chose Russian as this additional subject not because of any great socialist or communist ideals but because I thought that this Slavonic language suited my own harsh Northern Protestant sound in a way that French didn't. (I regarded reading French aloud in class as one of the worst punishments imaginable and this punishment was often administered; I have never felt comfortable trying to speak French as a consequence.) It must have been an odd sight as my mother's friends popped in to see her, and I sat there declining Russian verbs, partly in my head, partly out loud with this low guttural sound, on this low yellow card table in front of them.

'Is that son of yours talking to himself again?' Minnie used to say, not able to recognise the words coming out.

'That boy should be out on the street corner with his friends, not stuck behind that wee table in the front room with his mother. That's not natural for a boy his age. Not a bit of wonder he talks to himself.'

It must have been an odd sight, in this wee house, with the slimy damp walls (you could run your hand over the walls and they were as wet as if you had put them under a tap), with the wallpaper hanging off, not just at the corners but halfway down, me just sitting there in a school blazer with a crown on the crest, learning a language from a country that I would never visit, reciting Dostoevsky and Gogol, Pushkin and Turgenev. Looking back I am sure that it was a wonderfully strange sight, but I always thought, despite everything, it must have been a wonderfully positive sight for the casual onlooker.

I am reminded of what W.I. Thomas wrote about the psychology of race in *The American Journal of Sociology* in 1912:

Booker Washington [that great foreteller of the Civil Rights Movement in the US], who has been wiser than we in the education of his own race, says one of the saddest sights he saw during a month's travel in the South was 'a young man who had attended some high school, sitting in a one-room cabin, with grease on his clothing, filth all around him, and weeds in the yard and garden, engaging in studying a French grammar'.

Thomas's prefacing comment on Booker Washington's observation is:

Our education for white children in the past was atrocious, and when we transferred this, including English syntax and sometimes even the dead languages, to the lower races we got results logically to be anticipated.

This leads into a quote from Petrie (1895):

The harm is that you manufacture idiots. Some of the peasantry are taught to read and write, and the results of this burden, which their fathers bore not, is that they become fools . . . His intellect and his health have been undermined by the forcing of education.

Here in these short, convoluted sentences the 'lower races' and the 'peasantry' are all rolled together into a neat little bundle, a bundle of despair, who should not have to suffer the 'burden' of education. Perhaps, I too might have been a sad, pathetic little sight for any educated visitor, but what should I have been doing instead – maybe hanging around the corner with my mates, like Minnie suggested, maybe trying to dry out the walls with blotting paper stolen from school, so that the wallpaper might stick to them for a few hours more, maybe contenting myself with my social position in this damp, little mill house?

I was aiming for grade As because my family could readily understand what they meant – top grades. I never did fancy trying to explain the significance of grade Bs in terms of percentiles or whatever to them. But A levels were more importantly my passport to university – away from Legmore

Street, away from a Belfast caught up in the Troubles, away from great BRA, although, of course, my mother would never forgive me for leaving. My brother had moved on from being a spark and he had gone to climb foreign mountains (and died out there in the Himalayas), and I was all she had left. 'You always said that you would come home when you finished your studies, but I knew you were lying. I can see right through you,' she always said accusingly. But I tried to explain that I had never finished my studies, I was still studying now, still an academic with books to read. I always reasoned that I would never find student digs as cold or as damp as my home, and I was right. Things could only get better in many aspects of my life. The university set me free from my roots and my speech over the years started to change slowly and, I assume, unconsciously, because I never consciously and deliberately decided to change how I spoke as I adapted to new circumstances, eventually getting a first from the University of Birmingham and doing my PhD at Cambridge. But there has always been a degree of felt difference, and I know that even today when I speak, despite my many, many hours of interviews on TV and radio, on Radio 4 and the World Service and the BBC News and News at Ten, there is something distinctively lower working class in my particular phraseology and accent and the fact that I still say 'you know' when I get a little flustered or excited (or when I am lying, which my mother always liked to point out). Not everyone can read my class from my speech, but I know that some can, I can see it in their faces, and it's not my imagination, despite all the books that I've now read (and indeed written); that sly fleeting look of condescension and superiority, and I automatically think of Thomas and Petrie and Booker Washington and the 'burden' of my education that brought me into this Victorian room in Waterhouse's great gothic university.

But if Anthony Greenwald is right then at least it gives us some hint as to why leading universities and many of the top public and private firms do not have the right proportion of people from ethnic backgrounds (and maybe from lower working class backgrounds although I have no idea of what the figures are here, but I suspect for all sorts of reasons that those with middle class backgrounds are similarly overrepresented in academia). This is nothing to do with anything that we can control in any conscious and rational way, this is something much deeper, but we know from a hundred years of psychology that even some of the deeper things can ultimately be changed, so it need not necessarily be a disempowering idea.

But was there any truth in what Patrick was saying? I had spent the last two years attempting to measure implicit attitudes in the area of sustainability and attitudes to the environment, which culminated in the book *Why Aren't We Saving the Planet? A Psychologist's Perspective*, so I was starting with a little bit of background in the area, but I had never seriously thought of questions of ethnic diversity before; this was as good a time as any to start. We agreed to meet in the week after his talk, and I decided to begin research in this area, not primarily to win the hearts and minds of those academics in that room (although I thought that that could be a consequence of the work), but to expose hearts and minds, as much as anything else. I suspected that the processes of implicit or unconscious bias are closer to my own heart than Patrick might have imagined when I agreed to the research programme in question. But I didn't have the inclination to explain it properly to him at that moment in time.

- Never assume that men with white skin in grey suits have not themselves been subject to implicit biases.
- Biases to do with social class may be implicit as well as explicit.
- Implicit biases can produce anger in the victim; I know, I have often been angry.

4

Who needs the Negro?

Sometimes a topic is so vast, so overwhelming, that it is a little difficult to know where to start. Those interested in promoting a fairer university wanted me to explore possible implicit or unconscious biases, but I needed to understand the social and historical background for all of this, particularly with regard to race and ethnicity. I had my own experiences to draw upon, so I knew a little about how prejudice can operate, but, of course, religious prejudice in Northern Ireland, with its accompanying neighbourhood segregation, is one small part of something much bigger and I wanted to think more generally about issues to do with racial or ethnic prejudice.

It was difficult knowing how far back to go to understand the possible roots of implicit or unconscious biases to people from different ethnic backgrounds. I spent a long morning in the John Rylands library at Manchester thinking about all of this, with that smell of dust in the air, before even being able to request a book. I flicked through the library catalogue with titles like *Who Needs the Negro?* (see Wilhelm 1970). It reminded me how life had changed in the last 50 or so years, on the surface at least. I picked up *The Negro American*, buried deep in the library store room. The book seemed like a good place to start because it had a foreword by Lyndon B. Johnson who was then still President of the United States. This seemed to me to be a clear indication of how pressing the 'problem' of the Negro American then was. He starts the book by writing:

Nothing is of greater significance to the welfare and vitality of this nation than the movement to secure equal rights for Negro Americans. This Administration is dedicated to that movement. It is also dedicated to helping Negro Americans grasp the opportunities that equal rights make possible. (Johnson in Parsons and Clark 1965: v)

This book is a collection of papers by the American Society of Arts and Sciences that was especially put together for a White House conference, which Johnson specifically called 'to fulfil these rights'. This book documents the centuries of overt bigotry against the Negro. Of course, some people were suggesting that many types of overt bigotry had now gone, but it did not mean that prejudice more generally had been eradicated; rather it may now have been pushed down below the surface, and possibly even further down from the conscious mind into the unconscious mind. Some were saying that it was all now implicit rather than explicit but still exerting its nefarious influence, still influencing every possible choice, even in universities, the most rational and logical of institutions.

The Negro American is a major historical document, detailing the explicit history of bigotry that Black people have faced for centuries in the United States. John Hope Franklin offers a historical view on 'The two worlds of race' (1965: 47), in which he writes:

For a century before the American Revolution the status of Negroes in the English colonies had become fixed at a low point that distinguished them from all other persons who had been held in temporary bondage. By the middle of the eighteenth century, laws governing Negroes denied to them certain basic rights that were conceded to others. They were permitted no independence of thought, no opportunity to improve their minds or their talents or to worship freely, no right to marry and enjoy the conventional family relationships, no right to own or dispose of property, and no protection against miscarriages of justice or cruel and unreasonable

punishments. They were outside the pale of the laws
that protected ordinary humans.

All of this work is perhaps best viewed through the
various laws and regulations, explicitly and carefully formulated, which document how Black people were to be treated.
For example, the South Carolina code of 1712 had special
laws 'as may restrain the disorders, rapines, and inhumanity
to which they [black people] are naturally prone and inclined
. . .' (ibid.). Even when the founders of the United States
commenced their armed revolt against England in an effort
to secure their independence, the basic idea of the inferiority of the Negro in both intellectual and moral terms had
become part of the common understanding of life, explicitly
stated when necessary, but only explicitly stated as a formu-
lation of what everybody already knew. General George
Washington set out one order to recruiting officers detailing
who should be enlisted into the revolutionary army. They
were specifically ordered not to enlist 'any deserter from the
ministerial army, nor any stroller, negro, or vagabond, or
person suspected of being an enemy to the liberty of America
nor any under eighteen years of age'. As Franklin (ibid.: 48)
so sharply puts it: 'In classifying Negroes with the dregs of
society, traitors, and children, Washington made it clear
that Negroes, slave or free, were not to enjoy the high privi-
lege of fighting for political independence.' Negroes were in
the same category as deserters, tramps and traitors, not to
be trusted, not to be relied upon and not to be allowed as
compatriots in battle. It turns out that Washington later
changed his policy, but presumably not necessarily his
underlying opinion, when more than five thousand Negroes
enlisted to fight the English. In modern terms, his policy
may have changed, his explicit attitude may have changed a
little, but his implicit attitude surely would never have been
touched by the sheer necessity of having to increase the size
of his army.

Even Thomas Jefferson, who was strongly opposed to
slavery (and according to Franklin, if he had been able to
do so, he would have condemned it in the Declaration
of Independence), in no way considered the Negro to be

equal to the White race. In Jefferson's own words he did not want to:

> degrade a whole race of men from the work in the scale of beings which their Creator may perhaps have given them . . . I advance it therefore, as a suspicion only, that the blacks, whether originally a distinct race, or made distinct by the time and circumstance, are inferior to the whites in the endowment both of body and mind.

So here we see something that we might call the 'benevolent paternalism' of the time: someone concerned for the rights of others while recognising their essential inferiority.

These were some of the views of the Negro established from the start of American society, prevalent in the War of Independence, prevalent in the development of the American state, and even when it was thought that Negroes should be educated and trained, they should be educated and trained in particular ways. Thus in 1794, the American Convention of Abolition Societies recommended that Negroes be instructed in 'those mechanic arts which keep them most constantly employed and, of course, which will less subject them to idleness and debauchery, and thus prepare them for becoming good citizens of the United States' (Franklin 1965: 50). Of course, contained within this recommendation are clear and explicit stereotypes that the Negro is inherently subject to 'idleness' and 'debauchery' and that education and training has to somehow lead them away from this natural state to which they are inclined.

Now presumably one might think that universities should offer an alternative perspective on all of this, that being the beacons of scholarship that they are, interested in learning, knowledge and truth, then they should perhaps have been telling a slightly different story. But this fundamental understanding of the Negro as somehow intellectually and morally inferior was enshrined not just in political doctrine, not just in judicial doctrine, but also in academic doctrine. Thus again according to Franklin (ibid.: 52):

In 1826, Dr Thomas Cooper said that he had not the slightest doubt that Negroes were an 'inferior variety of the human species; and not capable of the same improvement as the whites'. Dr S. C. Cartwright of the University of Louisiana insisted that the capacities of the Negro adult for learning were equal to those of a white infant; and the Negro could properly perform certain psychological functions only when under the control of white men. Because of the Negro's inferiority, liberty and republican institutions were not only unsuited to his temperament, but actually inimical to his well-being and happiness.

In other words, the great academies of the time were giving support to the view that the Negro capacity for learning was similar to that of a white infant, and that control over the Negro was not only not a negative thing, but was necessary for their own sake.

Indeed, before the American Civil War, it seems that the vast majority of American political leaders subscribed to this view. In October 1854, Abraham Lincoln enquired as to what those who were fighting against slavery should do about the Negroes:

Free them, and make them politically and socially, our equals? My own feelings will not admit of this; and if mine would, we well know that those of the great mass of white people will not. Whether this feeling accords with justice and sound judgement, is not the sole question, if indeed, it is any part of it. A universal feeling, whether well or ill founded, can not be safely disregarded. We can not, then, make them equals. (See Franklin 1965: 53)

In many ways this is an extraordinary statement from a political leader who was seen as a champion of the Negro, and yet seemed to be reflecting what most Americans thought in the 1850s. And it turns out that this statement has been used by those wishing to argue for separation of the races more than a century after it was originally formulated. You can see a lot going on in the mind of Lincoln here, where his understanding of justice and his gut instinct seemed to be at odds, and his acute political antennae which tell him that most American citizens at that time would share his gut instinct.

If you want to understand unconscious attitudes to people from different ethnic backgrounds, then one might need to start with political and social thinking from just over a century and a half ago in the US and other great intellectual centres of modern thought. We need to start by reminding ourselves of what people were quite prepared to say openly and publicly for political effect and then to understand how these views may have burrowed underground in the meantime.

In the same volume, Paul B. Sheatsley reviews the evidence for White attitudes towards the Negro from a historical perspective. He begins by arguing that if we want to understand such attitudes towards the Negro in the latter decades of the nineteenth century, or even during the period after the First World War, we have to rely on largely impressionistic evidence (or presumably on political statements like those of Lincoln, who clearly understood the views and opinions of his target audience). He says that if we want to get a better perspective on these attitudes and how they change, then we really need to begin in the 1930s, when public opinion research really began in the US. What follows next is one of those shocks that you sometimes receive when you read historical documents.

> It tells much about white attitudes towards the Negro that, during the seven years from 1935 to 1942, only four questions bearing even indirectly on the subject seem to have been asked by the national public opinion polls of that time. Three of these questions, dealing with opinions about the 'lynching bill' then before Congress in 1937, are practically irrelevant because the results simply show that most Americans thought people should not be lynched and the question itself said nothing about race. (Sheatsley 1965: 303)

It is, of course, extraordinary from a contemporary perspective to think about race and lynching as two concepts that somehow naturally fit together, so that you might 'indirectly' have to draw on one to provide some insight into the other. But what does this survey of public opinion polls show? It shows that from the 1930s on through to the publication date of the book in 1965 that there is a general softening of attitudes. When White participants were asked questions such as: 'If a Negro with the same income and education as you moved into your block, would it make any difference to you?' and 'Generally speaking, do you think there should be separate sections for Negroes on streetcars and buses?', there was a significant change in the response to these sorts of questions in that period.

Between 1942 and 1963 there did seem to be a genuine shift in attitudes; thus in 1942 only 35% of White Americans would have felt comfortable with a Negro neighbour, by 1963 it was 64% (the trend was even more marked for Southern Whites: only 12% would have found it acceptable in 1942 and by 1963 it was 51%). In terms of whether it was acceptable for a Negro to get onto a bus with you, in 1942 42% of American Whites found this acceptable but this had risen to 78% by December 1963. In the case of Southern Whites, only 4% would have found it acceptable in 1942 whereas this had risen to 51% by December 1963. As Sheatsley (1965: 308) succinctly writes: 'By the end of 1963, both forms of integration had achieved majority approval.'

In Gallup polls between the 1950s and 1960s one of the questions asked was 'Do you think the day will ever come in the South when whites and Negroes will be going to the same schools, eating in the same restaurants, and generally sharing the same public accommodations?' In the 1950s apparently only a small proportion of White people answered 'yes' to this question, but by 1963 the proportion had risen to nearly 80%. What these public opinion surveys suggest is that White attitudes were softening. But were they? Or were people merely picking up on the political zeitgeist and the cultural notion that the times really were 'a-changin'', and that it was no longer quite so acceptable to espouse openly racialist views about intellectual and moral inferiority or to express one's beliefs about the role of segregation as somehow operating in everyone's interest? After all, these questions are fairly explicit and attitudes could be read immediately and directly from them. But the big question is how did implicit attitudes change during this time, where the implicit attitude is the great hidden component of the attitude, which might well exert a major influence on so many different aspects of everyday behaviour. What happened to that during these decades of change? And what is the legacy of all this? After all, the 1940s and 1950s are part of the lives of people alive today (or their parents' or grandparents' immediate history). And then we might like to enquire about what was happening in the UK at the same time – a country whose views of ethnicity were shaped by its colonial past, whose experience of dealing with people from the Middle East and the Indian subcontinent and the Far East and South Africa were often in the context of colonial governance, and presumed superiority. How were attitudes formed here and how were they modified over time? And how did people cope with the notion that as the twentieth century progressed it became less and less acceptable to hold certain views and to espouse certain opinions? Did integration and education change everything, or just some things, like what people were prepared to say in public to the opinion pollsters and to the enquiring social scientists, maybe to the electorate, or to public audiences everywhere, and maybe, just maybe, even to themselves?

- It seems extraordinary today that George Washington ordered recruiting officers to avoid recruiting Negroes into the revolutionary army, categorizing them with the dregs of society (including deserters, tramps and suspected enemies).
- Thomas Jefferson clearly viewed the Negro as inferior to Whites 'in the endowment both of body and mind'.
- Dr S. C. Cartwright of the University of Louisiana wrote that the capacity of the adult Negro for learning was equivalent to that of a White infant.
- Some researchers have suggested that if you want to see how White attitudes to Negroes changed in the years before and during the Second World War, then you need to infer these attitudes from people's expressed opinions of the 'lynching bill'.

- Between 1942 and 1963 there seemed to be a significant shift in White attitudes towards Negroes. By December 1963, 78% of White Americans thought that it was now acceptable for a Negro to get onto a bus with them; this was still only 51% for Southern Whites.
- Some social scientists maintain that attitudes did genuinely change in this 20-year period; others say that all that happened was that people learned not to express such openly racist views.
- You might indeed suggest that unconscious attitudes changed little during this period, but you would need better data to be so bold.

5

The nature of prejudice

So could we all indeed have a 'racist' heart, as the title of this book suggests? And could it operate without any kind of conscious awareness? And what other kinds of unconscious or implicit biases may operate in everyday life? What about prejudices based on ethnicity or social class or region or social background or even something like beauty and physical attractiveness? How prevalent are they and how do these operate? I certainly have felt some of these prejudices in my own life so I could imagine how they might operate. But was there really something there or was I just being too sensitive back in the days of my fee paying school when I concluded that the headmaster and some of the teachers were implicitly (or, on occasion, explicitly) biased against me because of my class and my background. Or alternatively, did they simply know that to turn this boy from a rougher than average background into a proper 'academy' boy required a lot of hard work and perhaps some harsh lessons? After all, they did the trick. I did my PhD at Trinity College Cambridge where Kings Edward VII and George VI had studied, and Prince Charles. Prince Charles and I had the same college tutor, but separated by a number of years. 'Never the brightest of students,' my tutor would say in that slightly scurrilous and snobbish Cambridge manner about the young Charles, 'never the brightest'. But later I found that manner turned against me, even after I had left. When I went back to college from my new home in Sheffield, where I was now lecturing, in a brand new suit, to dine with him on High Table the night before I was to receive my PhD, he turned up in a denim jacket, his dark hair slightly tousled in a studied sort of way, and looked at me in that slightly camp manner of his and said, 'You look very prosperous,' and then there was a long dramatic pause before the punchline, and, of course, the put-down, 'in a Northern sort of way'. He then explained that he had other things to do that night (implying that he had much more interesting things to do), but he was sure that I would enjoy dining on my own sandwiched between the other graduands and their tutors who had turned up to dine with their students. But, at least, I had made it to the college of Prince Charles, not to mention the college of Byron and Tennyson, Earl Balfour and Nehru, Francis Bacon, Wittgenstein and Bertrand Russell, Isaac Newton and Lord Rutherford (who had also worked on atomic fission at Manchester for a number of years, leaving a radioactive legacy in the very fabric of the building where I was now working).

I often wondered if my tutor had ever dismissed Charles in that haughty way of his. I thought not, because he always seemed to be a terrible social climber, and his put down of Charles' abilities as a history student was just part of that same social clambering process. But could I have ended up studying there without some of the natural frissons which I experienced at the Royal Academy School (as my father called it)? So what if I became a little self-conscious about my background, or my speech or indeed my toiletry habits, which have been much commented on down the years, shaped in that black hole of a toilet in our backyard. Is this not the natural process of social change and cultural adaptation at work? Is this not what social mobility is all about? A little bit of heartache? A little bit of self-reflexive loneliness? And if I did end up becoming a bit of a rebel at school (after all, if you are sent home for wearing patterned socks, you might as well do something much worse to warrant being sent home, and believe me, I did exactly that), is this not just the natural kickback against the processes that were ultimately going to determine my future?

These questions of implicit as opposed to explicit bias seem to me to be important and difficult issues in psychology and it is important to attempt to work out whether such biases exist or not, what kinds of things they actually are, and how they might influence some of the core processes of everyday life, including the shortlisting of candidates for posts in universities. Such considerations are at the very centre of many of the core areas of psychology, starting of course with the psychology of prejudice, but naturally including the psychology of attitudes, social judgement, impression formation, self-identity, intergroup processes, social interaction, bullying, non-verbal communication, and even social development (I am sure that the real list is even longer than this, but I am sure that you get the point).

But the natural place to start is with the psychology of prejudice because this must surely be at the heart of it. 'Prejudice' is often defined as 'thinking ill of others without sufficient warrant', or sometimes simply as 'rash judgement', which may actually be a little broad because life is full of rash judgements that you would not want to label as 'prejudice'. Gordon Allport, in his classic text *The Nature of Prejudice*, published in 1954, says about the former definition that its advantage is that it combines both the concept of 'unfounded judgment' ('without sufficient warrant') and it hints at an emotional valence involved in the whole process (although it does only hint), or in Allport's words 'the feeling-tone'.

Allport reminds us in his book that prejudice can be positive as well as negative, as recognised in the *New English Dictionary* which defines prejudice as: 'A feeling, favourable, or unfavourable, towards a person or a thing, prior to but not based on actual experience.' This is an important definition because it captures the notion that the 'feeling' is 'prior to' actual experience rather than as a result of experience with the person or object in question. But in this definition the emphasis is all on 'feeling' rather than 'unfounded judgement' and what we need is a definition that has both elements explicitly marked, perhaps combining the dictionary definition with some of Allport's words. Perhaps, the definition could be something like: 'An unfounded judgement and a feeling (that is sometimes hard to articulate), either of which can be favourable or unfavourable, towards a person or thing, without sufficient warrant.'

Allport writes that in order to understand what is contained in these definitions it is important to consider how the term prejudice has undergone something of a transformation in meaning from the original Latin 'praejudicium' ('prae' meaning 'in advance' or 'pre-', and 'judicium' meaning 'judgement'). But, according to Allport, 'praejudicium' may have meant a 'prejudgement', but it was used as the sort of prejudgement (quick judgement) based upon previous decisions and experiences' (in other words, a more or less rational judgement, deriving as it does from appropriate experience, and hopefully, therefore, like most other types of judgement). It was only subsequently that the term in English acquired a meaning of judgement before due examination and consideration of the facts. Any judgement before due examination and consideration is always going to be somewhat premature and probably quick but almost certainly too hasty. Again, it was only through time that the term acquired its emotional valence, capturing the kinds of feelings of favourableness or unfavourableness that accompany such premature and unsupported judgements.

So, going back to my school days, was my chemistry teacher prejudiced against me, did she think ill of me without sufficient warrant? Did she have unfavourable (certainly rather than favourable!) feelings about me because of where I came from? On the basis of the one incident I've described it is quite hard to say because one could say that her response to my disruptive laughter was based on sound judgement and considerable experience of me. Now whether prejudice formed the basis for what she noticed about me in terms of my behaviour in class, in terms of my actions, is a different question altogether, and one that is much harder to answer (and certainly almost impossible to answer on the basis of these kinds of reminiscences). How many other boys and girls laughed inappropriately when she spoke movingly and sincerely about Cambridge? How many others found the word 'scholar' funny? How many others turned up late for the chemistry class after lunch because they had been running at lunchtime so that they would not have to mix with their fellow pupils (or to avoid being rejected by them)? And what about her comments to me about the gutter and where I would end up? Surely this showed a remarkable degree of prejudice against a boy like me from the loyalist ghettos of Belfast? Was this a judgement on her part, a real unfounded judgement full of emotion, or just a comment designed to wound me (or indeed to inspire me(!), because that has been its direct effect, for every time that I find myself weakening, I think of that comment)? Or was it just an insult, all she could think of at that moment in time, and something to be fretted over and regretted with the slow, agonising passage of time?

So prejudice can form the basis for a whole series of judgements, decisions and actions, but it is quite wrong on the basis of someone's negative response to you just to claim that prejudice is necessarily at work. How might prejudice operate in the context of a university where not enough of the top positions are being filled by women or people from differing ethnic backgrounds? The answer is that on the basis of their gender or ethnicity, certain judgements are being made prematurely and hastily without considering all of the facts. Of course, such judgements can be based upon some experience of candidates 'like' the candidate in question, but preferring candidates mainly on the basis of gender or ethnicity would not seem a valid technique (let us not be too delicate or understated here, it would be a ridiculous technique) for making judgements about one candidate solely on the basis of their membership of an impossibly broad category (after all what do two different women have in common, or two Asian men, or two African Caribbean Professors or two White lecturers? Answers on a postcard please, but don't send them to me; you could always post them back to yourself).

But the analysis of prejudice did not start with Gordon Allport. I had read many years earlier the essays of William Hazlitt. There was always something intriguing about the titles of his works, such as *On the Pleasure of Hating* in which Hazlitt (1826) writes: 'love turns, with a little indulgence, to indifference or disgust; hatred alone is immortal'. In this set of essays Hazlitt writes about a wide range of topics that always seemed to have little in common with each other, but maybe these were just things that he had chanced upon or were just currently occupying his thoughts in some way – things like a report of a boxing match between Gas-man and Bill Neate:

> The crowd was very great when we arrived on the spot; open carriages were coming up, with streamers flying and music playing, and the country-people were pouring in over hedge and ditch in all directions, to see their hero beat or be beaten.

Reports of this fight gave way to discussions of 'The Spirit of Monarchy' and a treatise 'On Reason and Imagination'. In this essay and in many others Hazlitt discusses human social judgements and how they pull human beings in one direction or another. His analyses led to his explication of some of the processes of prejudice, and indeed Hazlitt is now credited as really the first writer to offer a working definition of prejudice in an essay first published in 1830.

> Prejudice, in its ordinary and literal sense, is prejudging any question without having significantly examined it, and adhering to our opinion upon it through ignorance, malice or perversity, in spite of every evidence to the contrary . . . Prejudice is the child of ignorance: for as our actual knowledge falls short of our desire to know, or curiosity and interest in the world about us, so must we be tempted to decide upon a greater number of things at a venture; and having no check from reason or inquiry, we shall grow more obstinate and bigoted in our conclusions, according as we have been rash and presumptuous.

As Webster, Saucier and Harris (2010) have pointed out, this is very similar to the working definition of prejudice which was offered by Allport and it could be said that Hazlitt had anticipated what was to come well over a century in advance. What is interesting about Hazlitt's definition is that it combines a range of processes to support the pre-judgement. 'Ignorance' does seem to be given extra weight in the process because Hazlitt does emphasis that 'Prejudice is the child of ignorance', but he clearly does not rule out 'malice' or 'perversity'. Of course, it has to be remembered that, when Hazlitt was writing, people lived much more circumscribed and parochial lives and that ignorance of other cultures, countries and places was undoubtedly the rule. Indeed Hazlitt writes:

The less we look abroad, the more our ideas are introverted, and our habitual impressions, from being made up of a few particulars always repeated, grow together in to a kind of concrete substance, which will not bear taking to pieces, and where the smallest deviation destroys the whole feeling. Thus, the difference of colour in a black man was thought to forfeit his title to belong to the species, till books of voyages and travels, and old Fuller's quaint expression of 'God's image carved in ebony,' have brought the two ideas into a forced union, and men of colour are no longer to be libelled with impunity.

In Hazlitt's age it is easy to see how ignorance could have fuelled much of the prejudicial process. People were much less familiar with others from different cultural backgrounds and any generalisation based on the little they had seen or heard might rarely be challenged, but today, of course, things should be very different. But what is interesting about Hazlitt's take on this topic is his attempt like Allport 130 years later to understand the basic processes in terms of ordinary human function. Allport might write with the objectivity of the social scientist, Hazlitt has no such constraints. He is a passionate observer of human behaviour, 'be they engaged in the training for a fist fight':

A yolk of an egg with a spoonful of rum in it is the first thing in a morning, and then a walk of six miles after breakfast. This meal consists of a plentiful supply of tea and toast and beef-steaks. Then another six or seven miles until dinner-time, and another supply of solid beef or mutton with a pint of porter, and perhaps, at the utmost, a couple of glasses of sherry. Martin trains on water, but this increases his infirmity on another very dangerous side.

'or subject to the basic frailties of human reason'.

Prejudice is one of these basic frailties; it is the judgement, a prejudgement without sufficient examination, which is clung to despite any evidence to the contrary. Why do people suffer from prejudice? In his mind, they do so because human beings are prone to generalisation and, often, over-generalisation. Hazlitt (1826) displays his own feelings of anger for such individuals in his essay *On the Pleasure of Hating*. 'I hate people who have no notion of any thing but generalities, and forms, and creeds and naked propositions, even worse than I dislike those who cannot for the soul of them arrive at the comprehension of an abstract idea.' He quotes from the memoirs of Granville Sharp (see Hoare 1820) who, from his travels in Africa, reports the eloquent argument and moral reasoning of Naimbanna, a young African Chieftain, who said:

> If a man should rob me of my money, I can forgive him; if a man should shoot at me, or try to stab me, I can forgive him; if a man should sell me and all my family to a slave-ship, so that we should pass all the rest of our days in slavery in the West Indies, I can forgive him; but (*added he, rising from his seat with much emotion*) if a man takes away the character of the people of my country, I never can forgive him.

When Naimbanna was asked why he would not forgive such people (despite his Christian views) his reply was:

> If a man should try to kill me, or should sell me and my family for slaves, he would do an injury to as many as he might kill or sell; but if any one takes away the character of Black people, that man injures Black people all over the world; and when he has once taken away their character, there is nothing which he may not do to Black people after. That man, for instance, will beat Black men, and say, 'Oh, it is only a Black man, why should not I beat him?' That man will make slaves of Black people; for, when he has taken away their character, he will say, 'Oh, they are only Black people, why should not I make them slaves?' That man will take away all the people of

Africa if he can catch them; and if you ask him, But why do you take away all these people? He will say, 'Oh! They are only Black people – they are not like White people – why should I not take them?' That is the reason why I cannot forgive the man who takes away the character of the people of my country. (See Hazlitt 1826)

Hazlitt's comments on the young man's arguments reveal his own feelings at this point:

I can see even more real light and vital heat is thrown in to the argument by this struggle of natural feeling to relieve itself from the weight of a false and injurious imputation, than would be added to it by twenty volumes of tables and calculations of the pros and cons of right and wrong.

So, prejudice is overgeneralisation from ignorance or from limited experience to something much more general, which has a huge impact on the target group considered as a whole, and once this is done, as the young Chieftain notes, other actions can flow that much more naturally. In the words of Naimbanna, it is worse than other negative actions no matter how violent or immoral (or indeed morally depraved) against the self or against one's family because it opens up the possibility of something much more serious and something much more widespread and ultimately much more morally repugnant.

So why in Hazlitt's opinion do prejudicial thoughts arise at all? He makes a number of important observations in this regard. His first observation is that prejudice in part derives from 'egotism', in that,

we see a part, and substitute it for the whole; a thing strikes us casually and by halves, and we would have the universe stand proxy for our decision, in order to rivet more firmly in our own belief . . . we would be lords of the understandings and reason of others; and (strange infatuation!) taking up an opinion solely from our own narrow and partial point of view, without consulting the

feelings of others, or the reason of things, we are still
uneasy if all the world do not come into our way of
thinking.

In other words, prejudice allows us to hold and potentially
express an opinion about many aspects of the world, even
aspects that we do not know and understand; we are not left
blind and dumb, but in a position to feel something, maybe
even to say it, even though it may be based on very little.
And then Hazlitt makes perhaps his most interesting observation. He begins by noting that not all prejudices may be
false, but he does point out that 'it is not an easy matter to
distinguish between true and false prejudices'; he goes on to
write:

Prejudice is properly an opinion or feeling, not for which
there is no reason, but of which we cannot render a
satisfactory account on the spot . . . the feeling of the
truth of anything, or the soundness of the judgement
formed upon it from repeated, actual impressions, is one
thing; the power of vindicating and enforcing it, by
distinctly appealing to or explaining those impressions,
is another.

Here Hazlitt sets up a clear distinction between implicit
process based around 'feelings' and explicit processes where
feelings can be and are translated into words. Hazlitt seems
to naturally assume that much of prejudice is implicit,
based on some, mainly very little, experience which is over-
generalised and never properly examined in the cold light of
reason and argument. This analysis, of course, predates
much of what was to come much later in psychology and the
social sciences, not just with Allport but in the decades after
Allport. Hazlitt locates prejudice in the implicit domain, in
the domain of the actions we carry out without conscious
thought:

Without the aid of prejudice and custom, I should not be
able to find my way across the room nor know how to
conduct my self in any circumstances, nor what to feel

in any relation of life. Reason may play the critic, and correct certain errors afterwards; but if we were to wait for its formal and absolute decisions in the shifting and multifarious combinations of human affairs, the world would stand still.

Hazlitt posits that the human mind works on two twin tracks, the implicit system, which is fast and unconscious and unreflective, and the explicit system, which is slow and conscious and highly reflective. When you read *Blink: The Power of Thinking without Thinking* by Malcolm Gladwell (2005), you sometimes wonder what all the fuss was about with respect to this particular book. It was the implicit processes of prejudice that were being hinted at that day in the musty room at the university by the Head of Equality and Diversity.

So prejudice is at the very heart of this book and in the light of contemporary psychology we will be examining what types of processes operate here and how rational or ir-rational they are, what kinds of information, if any, under-pins them, how this information is dealt with and processed, and, importantly, how explicit or implicit some of the core judgements and processes are.

Allport's treatise on prejudice was obviously written in a much different era from Hazlitt's (and from our own) and a good deal of what he focuses on was clearly being driven by the particular problems facing the United States of America in the late 1940s and early 1950s. The book is clearly set in a specific historical context just after the Second World War, so clearly issues to do with the Holocaust and the prejudice shown against the Jewish people were still very raw (and 'raw' is the correct word, indeed there is no other word for it). And prejudice against the Jew is examined with the same focus and intensity as prejudice against the Negro, which was seen as a major social problem facing this new country. Allport's book focuses on prejudice generally (although almost exclusively prejudice *against* people rather than prejudice *for* people, as he explicitly notes), and not just racial prejudice, which is clearly what most people think of immediately when prejudice is mentioned. Allport's view is that this is ' "an unfortunate association of ideas", for throughout history human prejudice has little to do with race' (1954: xv). Allport indeed asks himself the question of why there has been so much emphasis on racial prejudice at the expense of all others. He argues that it is 'the simplicity of "race" as much as anything else, which is the significant factor'. Allport (ibid.: xvi) writes:

> . . . 'race' gave an immediate and visible mark, so it was thought, by which to designate victims of dislike. And the fiction of racial inferiority became, so it seemed, an irrefutable justification for prejudice. It had the stamp of biological finality, and spared people the pains of examining the complex economic, cultural, political, and psychological conditions that enter into group relations. For most purposes the term 'ethnic' is preferable to the term 'race'. Ethnic refers to characteristics of groups that may be, in different proportions, physical, national, cultural, linguistic, religious, or ideological in character. Unlike 'race', the term does not imply biological unity, a condition which in reality seldom marks the groups that are the targets of prejudice. It is true that 'ethnic' does not easily cover occupational, class, caste, and political groupings, nor the two sexes – clusters that are also the victims of prejudice.

In other words, racial prejudice is the form of prejudice that most people discuss and point to simply because it is the most obvious, but there are many possible domains of prejudice, of which prejudice on the basis of race is only one. But, of course, there is more to the overriding focus on racial prejudice than sheer visibility alone. Allport cites here the work of the anthropologist Clyde Kluckhohn (1949) who wrote: 'Though the concept of race is genuine enough, there is perhaps no field of science in which the misunderstandings among educated people are so frequent and so serious'. Allport says that one of the main problems in this area is that people confuse racial and ethnic groupings, where race is thought to reflect heredity and ethnicity is thought to reflect social and cultural ties. Allport blames the ideas enshrined in Darwinism, or at least how some of those ideas have been interpreted, in that if Darwinism is about the development of the species then some people have clung to this idea to give some kind of justification or 'sanction for racial antagonism'. Allport mentions the writings of Sir Arthur Keith who suggested that nature took considerable steps to prevent racial integration,

> To make certain that they would play the great game of life as she intended . . . she put them [races] into colors . . . Nature planted love and hate side by side in the tribal heart – but for what purpose? Suppose, for a moment, she had given the tribal heart only a capacity to love, what would have happened? Why, mankind throughout the world would have regarded each other as brothers, clung together, and mingled together. There could have been no separation of mankind into tribes which are Nature's evolutionary cradles . . . no evolutionary progress – no ascent of man. (Keith 1931a: 41, cited by Allport 1954: 108)

So what Sir Arthur Keith is saying, in effect, is that the separation of mankind is absolutely essential for the ascent of man. In his mind, racial antagonism is not to be attacked nor scorned, but celebrated.

But Allport says that another reason for the focus on racial prejudice is that some of the races look quite different. Allport (ibid.: 108) writes: 'It is not an accident that children's textbooks carry a list of supposed races as white, brown, yellow, red, and black. Color seems basic.' The 'advantage' that race has over anything else like class or background or hedonistic values or aspirations is that ' "race" gave an immediate and visible mark . . . to designate victims of dislike', and Allport (1954: 109) reasons that:

> Even a fragment of visibility, however, focuses people's minds on the possibility that everything may be related to this fragment. A person's character is thought to tie in with his slant eyes, or a menacing aggressiveness is thought to be linked to dark color. Here is an instance of

our common tendency to sharpen and exaggerate a
feature that captures attention and to assimilate as much
as possible to the visual category thus created.

Thus it is not visibility per se, but the fact that human
beings, once they have detected difference, have a tendency
to use the basic processes of assimilation and exaggeration
to make those falling within a category more uniform and
those falling in different categories more different.

What Allport is essentially doing in his book is to
explain and outline the basic human cognitive processes
that underpin prejudice (much as Hazlitt had done in the
nineteenth century but using a very different lexicon and set
of philosophical assumptions about the nature of mankind).
The comment has often been made that what Allport did, in
effect, was to 'normalise' prejudice to show that it is the
natural by-product of how human beings understand the
world, through their use of categories, in order to classify
and simplify the world around them. We know how to
respond around dogs or sheep or ducks or goats. We can
recognise them instantly. They do not all look the same, of
course, but human beings can form categories, they can
abstract away from the particular. Alsatians and terriers
look very different but we know that they are both 'dogs'.
They can be playful, they can be man's best friend, but they
can also bark and bite, and should be avoided by strangers
in certain situations. Allport says that something similar is
going on when we see people from different ethnic backgrounds: we categorise and extrapolate, we group together
two human beings with a multitude of differences but often
with one thing in common, and that is skin colour which is
perceived as 'not white', because it is (more than) possible
that this is the first thing we notice.

Allport begins his treatment of prejudice by considering
'the normality of prejudgement'. He starts with the question
'Why do human beings slip so easily into ethnic prejudice?'
His answer is that:

Everywhere on earth we find a condition of separateness
among groups. People mate with their own kind. They

eat, play, reside in homogeneous clusters. They visit with
their own kind, and prefer to worship together. Much of
this automatic cohesion is due to nothing more than
convenience. There is no need to turn to out-groups for
companionship. With plenty of people at hand to choose
from, why create for ourselves the trouble of adjusting to
new languages, new foods, new cultures, or to people of a
different educational level? It requires less effort to deal
with people who have similar presuppositions. One
reason for the gaiety and joy of college class reunions is
that all members are the same age, have the same
cultural reminiscences (even to the old popular songs
they all love), and have essentially the same educational
history. (Allport 1954: 18)

In other words, people like to be in familiar territory
because it is safe and easy. We have more shared history and
we can make more assumptions. All our communications are
played out against and interpreted in the light of this shared
background. He talks about 'automatic cohesion' fuelled by
'convenience'. He continues:

Thus most of the business of life can go with less effort
if we stick together with our own kind . . . We don't
play bridge with the janitor. Why? Perhaps he prefers
poker; almost certainly he would not grasp the type of
jests and chatter that we and our friends enjoy; there
would be a certain awkwardness in blending our
differing manners. It is not that we have class prejudice,
but only that we find comfort and ease in our own class.
And normally there are plenty of people of our own
class, or race, or religion to play, live, and eat with,
and to marry.
    Psychologically, the crux of the matter is that the
familiar provides the indispensable basis of our
existence. Since existence is good, its accompanying
groundwork seems good and desirable. A child's parents,
neighbourhood, region, nation are given to him – so too
his religion, race, and social traditions. To him all these
affiliations are taken for granted. (ibid.: 29)

So the first steps (and it really is two steps rather than one) in the development of prejudice, according to Allport, are the processes of categorisation and separation – of categorising and identifying 'familiar' and 'unfamiliar' and then choosing to stay with what is familiar and comfortable, to be among one's own kind. But according to Allport, the next step is absolutely critical. He writes that:

> People who stay separate have few channels of communication. They easily exaggerate the degree of difference between groups, and readily misunderstand the grounds for it. And, perhaps most important of all, the separateness may lead to genuine conflicts of interests, as well as to many imaginary conflicts. (1954: 19)

So, Allport looks to the basic desire of human beings to be with their own kind as being at the very root of prejudice and then to communication, or lack of it, for providing the next layer. In effect, what he is saying is that prejudice is the natural by-product of some very basic human instinct. Critical to prejudice, he says, are a number of basic processes. First is the process of categorisation and the process of over-generalisation, and then there is the emotional component (which he often seems to think will show itself mainly in hostility, but of course prejudice can be both positive and negative).

Allport outlines the importance of categorisation in our everyday life, he says that we human beings call upon categories endlessly to guide our everyday decision making. 'When an angry looking dog charges down the street, we categorise him as a "mad dog" and avoid him.' The importance of categories is that when we establish them we rapidly place things inside them 'as a means of prejudging the solution'. Again, in Allport's words 'the mind tends to categorise environmental events in the "grossest" manner compatible with the need for action' (ibid.: 21). In other words, categories start out being crude and often stay crude and only later become refined. But one critical feature of categories is that they enable us to recognise and identify any objective personal idea of the world:

Every event has certain marks that serve as a cue to bring the category of prejudgement into action . . . when we see a crazily swaying automobile we think, 'drunken driver,' and act accordingly. A person with dark brown skin will activate whatever concept of Negro is dominant in our mind. If the dominant category is one composed of negative attitudes and beliefs we will automatically avoid him, or adopt whichever habit of rejection is most available to us. (Allport 1954: 21)

The next feature of categories is that there is often a certain feeling 'associated with them'; some categories can be purely conceptual but many have an emotional valence attached to them. The example that Allport uses is one of trees. We know what a tree is, we can identify a tree, we can describe a tree, we can recognise one quickly and instinctively, but we also know if we like trees or not. And it is the same with ethnic categories. Another point that Allport makes about categories is that they 'may be more or less rational' in that a category tends to grow from a 'kernel of truth'. This is true of many types of categories, but Allport recognises that some may be quite irrational and that human beings have a whole series of devices to prevent logic interfering with the formation and maintenance of the category. For example, there is the simple cognitive device of admitting exceptions as in 'Some of my best friends are Jews but . . . There are nice Negroes, but . . .' Allport describes this as a re-fencing device, 'When a fact cannot fit into a mental field, the exception is acknowledged, but the field is hastily fenced in again and not allowed to remain dangerously open' (ibid.: 23).

So the starting point for prejudice according to Allport is the separation between people and the need to belong. This sense of belongingness is crucial. In Allport's words: 'A child's parents, neighbourhood, region, nation are given to him – so too his religion, race, and social traditions. To him all these affiliations are taken for granted. Since he is part of them, and they are part of him, they are good' (ibid.: 29). A core part of understanding prejudice is to understand the multiple affiliations that human beings have. The list of in-groups of which we are a member are family, the place we grew up, our childhood friends, our school, our college, our profession, our religion, our sex, our sexual orientation, our hobbies, our political party, our holiday preferences, the bands we like, the concerts we attend, the books we read, the way we style our speech, where we sit in an officious room, the socks we wear (deliberately and provocatively, or not). Perhaps even that. Of course, some groups are more important to us than others. Allport writes: 'We have broadly defined an in-group as any cluster of people who can use the term "we" with the same significance' (1954.: 37). I recently heard a commentator on the radio commenting on the 2010 World Cup, that when a team like England plays badly, the comment tends to be 'we played badly'; but if a band at a concert plays badly it would be very unusual to say 'we played badly', suggesting that somehow football and support of a national football team evokes a sense of inclusiveness that the appreciation of music might not. Of course, the fact that one is a member of a large array of in-groups does not necessarily mean that we are psychologically attached to each of these in-groups equally. Sherif and Sherif (1953) introduced the concept of 'reference groups' to deal with this issue: 'those groups to which the individual relates himself as a part, or to which he aspires to relate himself psychologically'. In other words, a reference group is a group to which any given individual really wants to be a part. Of course, many in-groups can also be reference groups but there can be notable exceptions. You may be forced to live with a particular group and yet grow to dislike it intensely. Kurt Lewin has called this 'self-hate' and this self-hate can produce an odd psychological tension.

In many senses growing up, my in-group was the Protestant working class community of Belfast, but my reference group was not easily made available to me. It wasn't immediately obvious to me that I wanted to be like the boys from the Academy and the most obvious alternative would have been other boys who similarly fell between cultures (boys who managed to pass the Eleven-Plus and the interview who were from working-class communities).

But what I discovered was that these tensions drove me to find some other reference group eventually:

> To a considerable degree all minority groups suffer from the same state of marginality, with its haunting consequences of insecurity, conflict, and irritation . . . The situation is particularly clear in the case of the Negro. Negro culture is almost entirely the same as white American culture. The Negro must relate himself to it. Yet whenever he tries to achieve this relatedness he is likely to suffer rebuff . . . If we follow this line of thinking we see why all minority groups, to some degree, occupy a marginal position in society with its unhappy consequents of apprehension and resentment. (Allport 1954: 38)

But of course it is not just Black people who suffer apprehension and resentment in this way and it is not just people from different ethnic backgrounds who are rebuffed when they try to change reference groups; it is something that many people of all ethnic backgrounds have experienced.

Growing up in north Belfast in the late 1960s and early 1970s I didn't see many 'coloured' people or people from different races or much by way of ethnic diversity. I saw my first Sikh in my street when I was about 11, I think. He was selling brushes door to door and we ran after him as much out of excitement and curiosity as out of belligerence. God knows what he made of us with our clattering feet and our incomprehensible harsh guttural shouts at this dark man in a turban. Comments about colour and ethnicity were, however, directed at people on TV. My mother would say that 'Blacks could be very arrogant', 'Mike and Bernie Winters were wee Jew boys' (always 'wee Jew boys') and 'Jews always have the money' (presumably somebody had to have all the money, and it wasn't us). In my primary school there were no children from a different ethnic background and there were also no Catholics. In my secondary school there were some Jews, including Solomon and all the boys that lived in the big houses on the Antrim Road and they travelled back together in an amiable and cohesive group (and a group of which I was very jealous, partly because of their wealth and partly because of their obvious social bonds), but as far as I know there was only one Catholic in the whole school at that particular time. I was invited only once to a party on the Antrim Road and I brought some of my friends from the corner and we blatantly walked out with some records under our arms, by way of thank you. 'Let the wee rich boys try to stop us', my friend said. (I am sure that the 'Jew' word was never mentioned, it was their money that we resented.) We were not gracious guests.

When I travelled to England for my summer holidays to live at my Uncle Terence's house in Chippenham (he had moved from Belfast because of what he said was anti-Catholic discrimination in the Protestant-dominated Civil Service that had marred his chances of promotion) I suddenly started hanging around with boys from an African Caribbean background, and suddenly, things seemed very different. I became friends with boys called Simroy and Leroy and I came back to Belfast with reggae records, with titles like 'Reggae up your Jeggae' and 'Tighten Up', in a curious West Country slight skinhead/black fusion. But my prejudices, if indeed I have any (and it is up to me to find out if I do or do not), may have been laid down in those early formative years in those dismal grey streets of Belfast with my all White friends.

On my street, colour wasn't a big issue, but religion was. Now whether you can actually tell a Catholic or Protestant by how they look is a sensitive issue, but there were many of our neighbours who said that they could, just by looking. 'You can always tell a Taig [a Roman Catholic],' they would say, 'no matter how much they try to disguise it' (and I am sure that many Catholics also thought that no matter how hard they tried, Protestants could not disguise their own awful 'genetic' heritage). I may have believed that there was a slight and subtle physical difference until, one day I received some news that probably constituted one of the biggest shocks in my life and changed my view on this topic for all time. Kevin Rock told me that my Uncle Terence was a Taig. Kevin was a Catholic who lived two doors up from me at the time (the family later moved when someone fired a shot into their house through the front window during the

Troubles). He told me that he had seen my Uncle Terence going into chapel one Sunday morning. He also said that the St Christopher in my Uncle Terence's Ford Anglia wasn't an accident, nor a slip of memory in failing to remove it from the previous owner (as I always maintained, because I had noticed it, a St Christopher in the car was one of those little tell-tale signs of Catholicism that you always noticed), but a deliberate religious symbol there to protect him and his Catholic superstition. I stood shaking on the street as a few unexplained things, like why Terence didn't go to our church with the rest of us, slotted into place. I was also told much later in life by my mother that my Uncle Terence hadn't been allowed into my Uncle Jack's house for nearly 40 years. Jack was a staunch loyalist and married to my mother's other sister, my Aunt May. It was only after I heard this that I realised why my Uncle Terence wasn't there the afternoon of my father's funeral as we all sat round the wooden table at my Uncle Jack's house. He wasn't allowed to be there because of his religion, despite being my father's most loyal friend (and a sort of surrogate father for me after my father's death).

Big Terry was the man about our house, my father was far too soft; that's what they all said, it was always the same expression they used, men were either 'hard', which was what you had to be around here, or 'too soft' meaning 'too lenient'. My Uncle Terence lived at the top of Ligoniel and he taught me how to fish with my hands in the streams above Ligoniel on warm summer nights, standing on wet, slippery stones tickling the bellies of the trout. The top of the Ligoniel Road was the more Catholic part, although for years I didn't put two and two together and work out that he might have been a Catholic. It was inconceivable. He would pay me sixpence to sing that Protestant anthem, the Sash, right into his face, and my father and mother would laugh. I never saw the joke, but a joke it must have been. 'The Sash my father wore.' I would sing it so close that I would be spitting right in his face. 'IT WAS BORN IN DERRY, AUGHRIM, ENNISKILLEN AND THE BOYNE.' *And my uncle would let out a big cheer after each place name as if he had personally been at each of these places and fought on the right side in each conflict, the winning side, the Protestant side that is. (I should perhaps add that I sang the wrong words of this most Protestant of all anthems for many years. It should have been 'WORN IN DERRY, AUGHRIM', etc. not 'BORN IN DERRY, AUGHRIM' as I sang it. I always think that my version made more sense and my uncle tellingly never corrected me.)*

Years later when the Troubles were raging and almost any Catholic could, in the right circumstances, become a legitimate target in Murder Triangle (the new name for my neighbourhood), I became more than proud of him when he was home for my brother's funeral (a funeral without my brother's body, which lay in the mountains of Nepal). He said that he wanted to take me for a drink because I had no father to go out with me that night, and that going for a drink on the night of a funeral was a very Irish thing to do. My mother warned us about going out. Nobody went out anymore around here, she said, unless they had to. Both public houses had been burned to the ground because they had been owned by Catholics; there were now only loyalist drinking clubs, segregated, sectarian, violent, ugly places. All the shops at the 'turn-of-the-road', including the greengrocer's, the video-shop, the dry cleaners, the snooker room, the pub, before it was burnt to the ground, had witnessed at least one murder, except perhaps the chemists. That was spared murder for some reason. One of my friends from St Marks had recently been shot dead in the snooker hall. The graffiti, down the road in the Catholic Ardoyne, read 'Freddie Reynolds snookered'. His name was Bill; they didn't even know his right name and they murdered him. 'They'll recognise your Uncle Terry; they'll know he's a Catholic,' said my worried mother. 'A lot of paramilitaries drink in there; that's where all the godfathers hang out.' But we went anyway, past the metal grilles and the security cameras and the obese security guard on the door, with his balaclava no doubt back at home in his top drawer. Big Terry walked in and nodded their way; he knew them all, and they knew him, and they all knew that he was a Taig and that Taigs are just not welcome here. Taigs take their lives into their own hands when they come into a place like this, if they ever manage to get in that is. But it was Big Terry the boxer who walked in, a hard man of the old school, sleeves rolled up in the street; none of this cowardly nonsense with hoods and

knives and guns, it was toe to toe stuff with him, Big Terry, the
local man. They all wanted to buy the Fenian bastard a lot of
drink that night on his first night back home and slap him on
the back. 'Good to see you, Big Man,' they all said. And I stood
there watching the Godfathers of the Organisation, as they
liked to call themselves, come and pay homage to a man, the
kind of which they would never be in a million years. And I
was very proud of my Uncle Terence that night, the Catholic,
the Fenian bastard, my surrogate father.

Being a Roman Catholic or a Protestant in the Northern
Ireland of the Troubles, or before, required a form of care
and attention in the way that being prejudiced on the basis
of 'race' does not. It was not obvious, it was the subtle things
that you had to look out for: the school badge, the direction
some individual might be walking down a road, a glimpse of
men seen from the back surreptitiously crossing themselves
as they went past the chapel on the bus, the St Christopher
on the dashboard of the car, the key ring with the unfamiliar
religious symbol. You had to be on your toes with this sort of
prejudice, it was more subtle; you could be mixing for years
with someone before you twigged that they were a Taig or a
Prod, but sometimes it could lead to the same awful conclusion. But you got the same visceral response when you finally
discovered the truth. I ended up with odd conflicting
emotions about my Uncle Terence, which I could not control
or change. I loved him dearly but suddenly some of the
emotional connotations of Catholic were transferred onto
him, like discovering that he was a rapist or a murderer.
There was a slight negative feeling there, which I couldn't
displace; it was beyond volition.

People were killed in Northern Ireland because of their
religion and because of prejudice. In the United States
Negroes might have been lynched for decades for merely
glancing at a White woman; in Belfast people were killed for
crossing themselves while passing a chapel, or not (as the
case might be). Of course, there are those who will rightly
point out that the Troubles in Northern Ireland was a political conflict in which two communities, the Nationalists and
the Unionists, had different political agendae and different

political goals and ambitions, but many of the acts carried out needed more than mere political aspiration. When you heard the details you could tell that. They essentially required prejudice where extreme biases in thinking could take over and the normal emotional responses of life could be distorted in ways that are even now with this short passage of time hard to understand (see also Beattie 1992, 1998, 2004).

I would ring my mother over the years that I was away and she would keep me up to date with what had been happening back home, and she would tell me who else from around here had been arrested or who had been gunned down in the street and who had survived. 'Were you a friend of so-and-so?' she would ask, 'or was it your brother?' 'It was me,' I would answer. 'Oh, yeah, he was a very quiet wee boy but he's just got life. He did more murders than Billy the Kid; that's what I heard anyway. And do you remember his brother, Davy, the good looking fella? I think that he's a bit older than you; anyway, they tried to murder him last week coming out of the wee club. The car drove right up beside him and they just opened up.'

It was odd having these brutal events relayed to you by your mother, who now talked about bombs and bullets as part and parcel of her daily life. She had developed some of the vocabulary for reporting the events. 'Do you remember George Walmsley?' she would ask, and you knew what was coming next; it was never going to be a story about success or good fortune, it was always going to be a story about despair and probably death; that's how it was around here. 'Well,' she began, 'he was gunned down by the IRA as he left the Orange Hall in Ligoniel. I knew George from when I was a wee girl. He was a lovely, quiet man. He was coming home early because he was worried about his mother's health. She had just lost her husband; I told you about that at the time, but you probably can't remember it, you were probably too busy to listen. They don't know whether George was hit by gunmen from a car or by a sniper.'

An invisible enemy was killing her Protestant neighbours. The killers were a sinister and anonymous group. The locals from the mill village of Ligoniel who were Catholic and who had lived there for generations were trustworthy – 'dead on', in her words – but some of the new ones that they'd moved up to Ligoniel in more recent years from elsewhere were not. 'Some of them are a right bad bunch. I've got old neighbours who are Catholic who come to see me week in week out, and that's what they say about some of these newcomers from Ardoyne or West Belfast.'

It made her angry when she heard representatives of Sinn Fein saying that the violence of the IRA, unlike that of the UDA and the UVF, did not have a sectarian element to it. 'What do they call it then?' she would say. 'It's all sectarian; there's no other word for it. How can Gerry Adams say that it's not sectarian? Why are they targeting people like George Walmsley or Billy Younger? He knows that it's a lie.' She had lived there all her life, but she knew victims on both sides, and she would store up little incidental details to tell me, little details that captured the reality of the violence around her. 'Did you hear about your man being shot in Clifton Street? He was a Catholic. They'd had a wee party in their house and then they went outside for a snowball fight; he was shot when he was walking to his home with all the snow in his hair and on his coat. He was trying to get back up off the ground when his family found him. It must have been awful to watch. It was like if you've ever seen a dog hit by a car, the way that they try to get on their feet again. And you can see in their face that they know that they're dying, that fear, even auld dogs know it, so imagine what it's like for a human being. It's terrible what they do to ordinary people in this town of ours. And imagine being shot dead because you'd gone outside for a wee snowball fight. How terrible is that? If he'd stayed in that night and just watched the snow fall, he'd be alive today.'

It was hard to look at the houses and the streets and the entries around here in the same kind of way, knowing what had gone on. 'You know that pub near the pet shops in Gresham Street where you used to sell your guinea pigs?' she said, 'well your man just ran in and shouted "Alright, all the Prods get to one side and all the Catholics get to the other". And then he opened up. They killed five men in there, men just out having a quiet wee drink; three of them were Catholic, and two of them were Protestant. It was just indiscriminate murder, *and,' she added, 'the gunman was a Protestant. We're always shooting our own. Our lot can be just as bad as theirs, and a lot stupider.'*

I once interviewed a member of a Protestant paramilitary organisation for a television programme and he explained to me how during the Troubles he had been involved in killing a Catholic. His broad justification was that he was engaged in a 'war on the IRA' (who, he said, had themselves first declared war on the Protestant people of Ulster). We stood in a garden near to my home in north Belfast on a wet, grey summer night, with a party going on in the house, as he described in great detail a 'hit' on the enemy that had gone slightly wrong. He stood in the great white light of the television camera, in clear confessional mode. It is as if TV can sometimes elicit the greatest of confessions; it may be the white light of the TV lights and the reminder of the interrogation room that does it, I'm not sure; perhaps it's the expectancy of the response and the embarrassment of not answering when you're on the telly; maybe it's as simple as that. I cued his confessions and the language was telling (but the actions of his small hit squad that night were equally telling).

'Well, we missed the target that night and that was the next target that came. Instead of going home empty-handed we took him out of the picture.'
They were short, sharp sentences that already seemed strange in their fluency and their construction. The Troubles were always a strange conflict because neighbours butchered neighbours. If it was a war, it was a very odd, psychological war, where friend and foe had to be carefully constructed in everyday thinking with a careful use of language. Not careful in the sense of being conscious and sentient but careful in the sense of its functionality. Careful language that had to remove the human element, no longer a neighbour that you might recognise but a 'target', no longer emotional words like 'murder' or 'killing' but 'taking him out of the picture'. There were few pauses in the account.

'We weren't really looking for this one. We were looking for another one who was in the IRA. And then this other guy came along.'
This was a tale of a hapless victim. This was a story about the 'other guy', not the one they were looking for. This was just some other poor mug who came along.

'It was denied that this one was in the IRA, but the way I see it is that throughout the Troubles if the British Army or the RUC shoot somebody then they always say that the victims were killed in active service and that they are lieutenant colonels or rank or they're volunteers in the IRA, but when the Loyalists hit one of them, and we've got a full dossier on them, it's denied, and I believe that it's all a cover-up to make the Loyalists look as if they are just hitting ordinary Catholics.'
In other words, it would not matter what information emerged after the murder, this 'other guy' was still probably in something or other, no matter how much it would be denied, he was guilty of something, he deserved it. They, the Government, the intelligence services, the security forces were out to make the Protestant paramilitaries look bad.

I asked if this was someone that they definitely had intelligence on, rather than merely a random Catholic.

'That was a random because we missed the one we were looking for. So this guy came along and we just wiped him out.'
How can you wipe out an innocent individual? The Sioux wiped out General George Custer at the Battle of the Little Big Horn. The Germans in 1916 wiped out most of the 36th Ulster Division at the Battle of the Somme. But you don't wipe out one individual. That's not how it works. You can pick off an individual, you can kill them, you can murder them, you can even assassinate them, but you can't wipe them out.

'I know it's sad.'
And there was this awful eerie smile as he 'confessed' his emotional response to what he had done. But why did he smile here? Perhaps it was the release of tension on his part, or perhaps it was an oddly pleasurable memory, or perhaps

he was trying to build a connection with me, trying to get me (old misery guts) with the tape recorder to lighten up. Smiles sometimes look very odd, and this one did. An ethnologist called van Hooff in 1972 had suggested that while laughter had evolved from the 'relaxed open mouth' display associated with play fighting in primates, the smile had evolved from the silent bared teeth display of fear. In other words, the evolutionary origin of certain smiles may have been in fearful defence. Perhaps my confessional terrorist might himself have felt that moment of fear as he made his bland comment on the emotional significance of the event in question.

'But that night I felt like he had to go, he just had to go. You see, we'd taken the chances of hijacking the car, going way up the Shankill with the guns in the car. We weren't going home empty-handed.'
And here was the careful language of terrible action, the perpetrator, the terrorist, having no choice, none at all. Once the terrorist sequence is started, the conclusion becomes inevitable.

'Because if we had been caught we were getting big time, so he had to go, instead of us going home empty-handed.'
And ditto.

'Cambrai Street is between the Shankill and the Crumlin. He came from the Crumlin to go across to the Shankill and we let him get to the ramps on Cambrai Street and moved out in front of him and shot him.'
So this is how this other guy became a victim: he drove across one particular street in the wrong direction. If he had been going in the other direction, from the Shankill rather than from the Crumlin, they would have assumed that he was a Protestant (although what he would be doing going to the Crumlin remains unclear, perhaps he would just have been taking a shortcut) and let him go, probably with an armed escort.

'He was in a car, his ten-year-old son was with him, but I can put my hand on my heart and say that I didn't see the child.'

And here we see some emotion again. Old Hacksaw (so-called because he was sent to administer a punishment shooting to some young local tearaway but rather than shoot him, he sawed some of the young man's fingers off instead. 'I got a reputation as a bit of a softy after that,' said my informant, 'that's why the nickname "Hacksaw" stuck.') threw a sorrowful expression and shook his head before moving on.

'The child was sitting on the passenger side down, but apparently the child was hit in the leg but we didn't see the child. The next day when I heard about this I wasn't worried about the father, but I was interested in the child; but when they gave it out that the child was only grazed I said, "Well, that's happy days the child is alright", but I wasn't worried about the da because that was one less to worry about.'

And then came the excuses, about not personally pulling the trigger, the endless reattributions of personal responsibility, the explanations that it was like your father asking you to do something, about the buzz and the excitement that interferes with your thinking, about the inevitability of killing a Taig, once you have started the 'mission'.

'Three of us went out to do the job, a driver and two gunmen. I was the driver; they both shot him. Two of us got done for it; one was never caught. We believed that once we came back from a shooting you weren't allowed to speak about it. It was loose talk then. If you were caught talking about it then you got it, so it had to be secret. If me and you and somebody else went out tonight once we had done that mission and went back, the only ones who knew were the Commander and nobody else, and that was as far as it went. You have to do what you're told; it's like if your father tells you to do something you have to do it, but it's more stricter than your father. It's hard to describe because if I don't do what I'm told then I'm putting your life in danger. And if I do something drastic while you're with me the consequences could be we could be captured or else shot dead. The adrenaline is flying through you; you're really keyed up. Capture is the last thing on your mind when you are out on a mission like that. You see, I've a gun in my hand. If somebody tries to stop us we have to shoot our way out.

To the best of my knowledge, I have never met anyone who has lynched a Negro or beaten a Pakistani to death, but I have seen the destructive power of prejudice in my own home town and it makes me shudder. I had heard directly and without any real spontaneous emotion from this para-military member how someone could be murdered at will because they were going along a particular street in the wrong direction. This pattern of movement held some clue as to which neighbourhood they might live in and there-fore it gave some hint as to their religious affiliation. And remember this human being was still a Christian, some observers might think that we are splitting hairs here in religious terms when we are talking about Protestants and Catholics compared to killings based on other religious differences. But because of some great psychological divide this family man accompanied by his young son became, in an instant, an object, 'a random', a 'legitimate target', simply because the gunmen could not go home empty-handed. He had to be 'wiped out', 'destroyed', 'taken out of the picture' because that was 'one less to worry about'. Language can direct us to think in particular ways, and the language here was the language of objectification, literally turning a living, breathing, sentient human being into an object, and then the language of necessary catastrophe and ethnic cleansing, 'wiping out' as necessity. Objectification followed by catastrophisation.

But how can people learn to think like this about our fellow human beings? Is there more to the whole thing than Allport was making out? Surely there is more to the whole process than categorisation and separation and the break-down of communication between groups? Surely to God there is more to the whole thing than that?

Susan Fiske (2005) thinks there is, in her re-evaluation of Allport's classic legacy. She argues that in the 50 years since the publication of Allport's book, research has clearly demonstrated the ubiquitous nature of categorisation in everyday life. Indeed, we now know that categorisation is more or less automatic, supporting Allport's view that: 'The human mind *must* think with the aid of categories ... We *cannot possibly avoid* this process . . . [that] results *inevitably* in prejudgments' (Allport 1954: 20; italics added). Fiske (2005: 39) writes:

> Social psychologists and their lay audiences have been shocked by how rapidly categories cue in group advantages to us and match out group stereotypes to *them*. For example (Gaertner and McLaughlin 1983), White participants, primed with the words 'Whites' or 'Blacks', then had to distinguish words from non-words. Compared to 'Blacks', the prime 'Whites' speeded decisions about White stereotypic words (*ambitious, smart, clean*). This result and others like it showed the rapid, apparently unavoidable impact of race, age, gender, and even literal 'us–them' categories on prejudgement.

Fiske also reviews the evidence that after initial categorisation people do engage in 're-fencing' in order to allow exceptions to the categorisation or stereotype, just as Allport had suggested. Again she suggests that Allport was right when he wrote that 'all sorts of psychological elaboration' make people 'easily exaggerate the degree of difference between groups, and readily misunderstand the grounds for it' (Allport 1954: 19). Fiske points to work on attribution theory, which originated after Allport's time, as applied to an individual's perception and explanation of group success and failure. People tend to attribute 'an outgroup failure to their inherent, dispositional features, but their success to a random fluke ... the opposite logic holds for ingroup outcomes' (Fiske 2005: 40).

But it is not just the basic processes of attribution that operate with the more-or-less automatic categories of ingroup and outgroup, it is human memory itself. Of course, people may remember exceptions to any given rule; nevertheless, according to Fiske (ibid.: 41),

> memory operates with a stereotype-matching advantage under many conditions: when the expectancy is strong and prior, discrepancies are minimal or ambiguous, other tasks interrupt, and the observer acts under cognitive

overload (see Rojahn and Pettigrew 1992; Stangor and McMillan 1992), all features of daily life.

So far then, so good. Fiske clearly finds evidence to support Allport's 'cognitive' view of prejudgement and prejudice. But what she and others have done in the past half century is to elaborate the other half of the domain of prejudice, namely what drives all of this cognitive effort in the first place. As Fiske notes, Allport clearly did believe in motives underlying prejudice, but the vast majority of his book was devoted to the detailing of the elaborate cognitions or thought processes that seem to be connected to it. Fiske tries to restore the balance: 'Motives and emotions matter as the motor that translates cognitions into actions. Cold cognitions may steer behavior, but hot biases energize it' (Fiske 2005: 42).

Fiske uses what might be called an evolutionary perspective to identify five basic motives underpinning prejudice namely: 'group belonging, understanding, controlling perceived threat, enhancing self and trusting ingroup others.' These processes are core to the basic pattern of human survival:

> People survive and thrive better within an ongoing ingroup that presumably shares their goals, defining the group and setting it apart from other groups that have different and therefore competing goals. Emotional prejudices follow from those presumed outgroup goals (Fiske and Ruscher 1993) which often mystify, inconvenience, annoy, and frustrate the ingroup. (ibid.: 42)

The first thing people want to know about another person or group (from an evolutionary perspective) is whether this other person is a friend or foe and whether this friend or foe is competent or not (i.e. how big a threat it really is) and this basic two-dimensional space defined by 'warmth' and 'competence' is pertinent to mapping out a diverse variety of outgroups. So, according to Fiske, we have high warmth/low competence groups (e.g. older people, disabled people), low warmth/high competence groups (e.g. rich people, professionals), low warmth/low competence groups (e.g. poor people, those on benefits) and high warmth/high competence groups (e.g. people like us and our allies). Fiske writes that each of these groups attracts different but ambivalent reactions in that:

> The nice but dumb ones are pitied and receive help but also neglect, whereas the smart but cold ones are envied and receive affiliation but also attack. Of course, some groups are simply despised, and these are the low competence/low warmth ones who receive disgust and contempt. They also receive both active harm (attack) and passive harm (neglect). (2005: 43)

Fiske says that it is only the high warmth/high competence group (people like us) that inspire 'pride and admiration, as well as both help and affiliation'.

But belongingness is only the start of the basic motivational process for prejudice. Clearly, in Fiske's terms, you can see how the processes already start to connect to basic human emotion and the 'hot biases' that drive the mechanisms of prejudices. The second motive, according to Fiske, is 'understanding':

> Social sharing among ingroup members – gossip, rumor, opinions, stories, media – contribute to consensus in stereotyped beliefs and prejudices. The most easily communicated traits constitute the core of most stable stereotypes (Schaller and Conway 2001). The knowledge that their prejudices and stereotypes are shared gives people social permission to express their biases, reinforcing their own and other people's stereotypes and prejudice. (ibid.: 44)

The third motive is controlling perceived threats, where such threats can be either physical or symbolic. Here Fiske writes:

> A variety of perceived threats to ingroup values and economic status create intergroup anxiety, which fuels prejudice . . . Ingroup control is fundamental in that

threats to the ingroup operate as threats to self. People treat the ingroup as an extension of self, protecting it as they do the self. (ibid.: 45)

Clearly perceived threats can result in strong emotions including anger and fear, and research demonstrates that emotional prejudice predicts discriminatory behaviour much better than cognitive beliefs and stereotypes (see Talaska, Fiske and Chaiken, 2008). Related to controlling and perceived threats is the enhancement of self to make oneself and one's own group seem better than others. The fifth of these core motives is what Fiske calls trusting ingroup others. She writes:

We trust ingroupers because they are convenient, and outgroup members are a strain. Recent research documents how true this is . . . Whites often go into interracial interactions with concerns about appearing prejudiced, and the more they do so, the more anxiety they feel and the less they enjoy the interaction. (2005: 47)

This body of research fills in much of the detail of an area suggested by Allport but not really developed. This is the irrational, emotional side of prejudice, crude and primitive but somehow comprehensible in brute evolutionary terms. Here we have the kind of motivations hinted at in Hacksaw's discourse: friend or foe, threats to self, war, only trust the gang, life or death, the hot biases that underpin both the cognitions and Hacksaw's attempt to take the emotions back out of his apparent thinking through his use of language. Finally, Fiske reminds us of other recent research in psychology, specifically from brain imaging studies which demonstrate the physical basis of irrational judgement. Here we find evidence of:

activation of the brain's amygdala (vigilance alarm) during presentation of pictures of unfamiliar faces from a racial outgroup, in comparison to faces from the observers' own group (Hart, Whalen, Shin, *et al.* 2000). In effect, the brain's burglar alarm habituates faster to members of the ingroup. This differential amygdala response correlates with implicit evaluation of racial groups (Phelps, O'Connor, Cunningham, *et al*. 2000). (Fiske 2005: 49).

In other words we now know a great deal more about how automatic and emotional processes activated in primitive parts of the brain may play a role in the complex cognitions that underpin everyday social life, including evaluation, judgement, memory and even the ubiquitous drawing of categories here, there and everywhere. Human beings are thinking organisms, but there is another, darker, side to them.

- William Hazlitt was the first to define prejudice as 'prejudging any question without having significantly examined it.'
- Hazlitt thought that prejudice was 'the child of ignorance'.
- In 1954 Gordon Allport stressed that prejudice involves both 'unfounded judgment' and 'a feeling-tone'.
- Naimbanna, a young African Chieftain, said that prejudice is worse than someone trying to kill you, or rob you, or sell you into slavery because with prejudice 'that man injures Black people all over the world; and when he has once taken away their character, there is nothing which he may not do to Black people after'.
- According to Allport, there are many forms of prejudice, but racial prejudice is often focused upon just because it is so visible.
- According to Allport, prejudice results from prejudgement and derives from the fact that we are most at home with people like ourselves.
- Categorisation and separation are, according to Allport, crucial for the development of prejudice.
- Some categories grow from a 'kernel of truth' but some are irrational.
- People have simple strategies for maintaining the categorical distinctions in the face of any logic 'When a fact cannot fit into a mental field, the exception is acknowledged, but the field is hastily fenced in again and not allowed to remain dangerously open'.

- People often say things like say 'there are nice Negroes, but . . .'. This is an example of such re-fencing.
- Religious prejudice often requires more work than racial prejudice because you have to look for more subtle signs of religious affiliation.
- To act on prejudice you often need to draw upon the transformational power of language to help make sense of your life and experiences and to justify the present and the past.
- Language, with the aid of prejudice, can transform a person into a thing, with a neighbour suddenly becoming 'a target' or 'a hit', and the killing of a neighbour becoming an act of subtraction ('one less to worry about').
- Some psychologists have argued (from an evolutionary perspective) that the first thing people want to know about another person is whether this person is a friend or a foe and whether they are competent or not (i.e. how big a threat they really are), and this two-dimensional space defined by 'warmth' (friend/foe) and 'competence' (big threat/little threat) is crucial to understanding our emotional and cognitive responses to a range of other social groups.
- Prejudice involves both emotion and cognition, bound together in complex ways.
- Emotion often precedes cognition. We may have a feeling state that sets up a predisposition to act. Our cognitions may sometimes allow us to deal with these feelings in rational, or seemingly rational, ways.
- There is a greater response from the alarm system of the human brain, the amygdala, to images of people who come from different racial groups to ourselves.
- Some processes connected to prejudice may have deep origins.

PART II

A pipeline to the soul?

6

The times they are a-changin' (or not, as the case may be)

It was suggested earlier that between the 1940s and 1960s there was a major shift in White attitudes towards Blacks. It seems that in 1942 only 35% of White Americans would have felt comfortable with a Negro neighbour, by 1963 it was 64% (the trend, I pointed out, was even more marked for Southern Whites, only 12% of whom would have found it acceptable in 1942 and by 1963 it was 51%). In terms of whether it was acceptable for a Negro to get onto a bus with you, in 1942 42% of American Whites found this acceptable but this had risen to 78% by December 1963. In the case of Southern Whites, only 4% would have found it acceptable in 1942 whereas this had risen to 51% by December 1963. As Sheatsley (1965: 308) succinctly writes: 'By the end of 1963, both forms of integration had achieved majority approval.'

In Gallup polls between the 1950s and 1960s one of the questions asked was 'Do you think the day will ever come in the South when whites and Negroes will be going to the same schools, eating in the same restaurants, and generally sharing the same public accommodations?' In the 1950s apparently only a small proportion of White people answered 'yes' to this question, but by 1963 the proportion had risen to nearly 80%.

These in many ways are extraordinary figures, and it may be that as the years rolled by people genuinely did become less prejudiced in terms of both their behaviour and their underlying attitude. But there is a second possibility; namely that people stayed prejudiced but, in the meantime, they had learned to disguise their prejudice and not express it in surveys, to be more guarded, to keep it closer to their chests. Inside, they knew how they really felt about Blacks or Arabs or Jews or the Irish or the plebs on the street, they just didn't say it anymore (to researchers, at least). And then there is a third possibility, where again prejudice did not go away but instead of it simply being denied it was pushed downwards, down into some deep recesses of the psyche. In other words, it stayed in place but somehow had to be buried, and lie there alongside other core values that clashed with it, and any 'accommodation', such as it was, had to be dealt with psychologically.

This aforementioned second possibility (we will leave the third possibility to the next chapter) has given rise to much methodological and theoretical effort. Many of the early researchers into racial attitudes, no matter how determined, in the end really gave up, admitting that they had not yet managed to get their hands on the genuine racial attitudes of their participants and that all they ever ended up with were somewhat sanitised versions of how their participants really felt. The researchers ended up feeling that as soon as their participants saw the words 'Negro' and 'White', they somehow remembered to clamp their mouths tightly shut (while simultaneously biting their lip) lest the truth come tumbling out, and they revealed far, far too much. This, in a sense, was one of the core challenges that psychologists in this area faced – how to probe the real attitude of their respondents.

The 1970s saw a new era in attempting to measure racial attitudes and Edward E. Jones from Duke University and Harold Sigall from the University of Rochester were at the vanguard of this, publishing their well-known article, 'The Bogus Pipeline: A new paradigm for measuring affect and attitude', in one of the leading psychological journals, *Psychological Bulletin*. They began their article clearly laying out their stall:

> Many psychologists for many years, beset with the vexing difficulties associated with inferring true feelings from behavior, must have had fantasies about discovering a direct pipeline to the soul . . . Wouldn't it be nice if

THE TIMES THEY ARE A-CHANGIN'   101

people really did wear their hearts on their sleeves?
(Jones and Sigall 1971: 349)

This is the problem that Jones and Sigall tried to deal
with and their solution was to attempt to convince people
that they had 'a machine' which was some sort of lie detection device that could measure their participants' real attitudes towards a person or an issue. In other words, these
psychologists tried to persuade people that they had a
machine that could see right into the soul. The psychology
underpinning their approach is very simple, 'no one wants
to be second-guessed by a machine'; nobody wants to be
discovered hiding or disguising their true feelings when a
machine can catch them out. They argue that the self-report
rating scales that had been used from the 1920s through to
the 1960s were all flawed for a number of different reasons.
First, what they term 'the generosity effect.' People tend to
be very generous to those that they are judging, they rarely
use the 'negative halves of scales like generous–*stingy*, wise–
foolish, or friendly–*hostile*'. Experimental participants do
not want to appear, in their words, 'odd or extreme and
choose a moderately positive rating as a "place to hide" on
the scale'. Next there is the old familiar 'evaluation apprehension', which is that participants understand the social
desirability aspect of each of their responses, and in the case
of racial attitudes (and other equally sensitive topics) 'the
subject will try to respond as he thinks a mature and rational
person would'. Then there is the issue of 'experimenter
demand' where experimental participants try to please the
experimenters, and then the problem of 'thoughtlessness', in
which the authors say that some participants simply don't
take the trouble to make careful judgements. And finally
they note the problem of the 'halo effect' when some broad
evaluative judgement affects other specific judgements in
ways that might not be warranted.

As the basis for their new research Jones and Sigall
reviewed the evidence for possible physiological indicators
of attitudes. They cite the work of Rankin and Campbell
(1955) who observed a significant relationship between
galvanic skin response (GSR) and differences between

participants responding to contact with White versus Negro experimenters. These researchers found that contact with different races impacted on some core physiological responses (although this study has been sometimes hard to replicate, see Porier and Lott 1967). Westie and DeFleur (1959) found that when their experimental participants viewed pictures of Negroes and Whites on a screen in front of them, their prejudiced participants showed a greater GSR, but a lower pulse rate, to slides depicting Negroes. In other words, there is some evidence, according to Jones and Sigall, which suggests that our attitude impacts on aspects of our physiological response.

What Jones and Sigall did with this basic physiological work was not to try to use this research to get a glimpse into people's hearts and minds, rather they tried to build a new 'measure' based upon the *plausibility* of this early research. The specific device they used in their study was an electromyograph (EMG). The most important aspect of the working of the EMG in their research was the *story* the participants were given about it. It was explained to participants that it was

> a physiological monitoring device . . . able to measure both the amplitude and direction of emotional response . . . when the subject held the steering wheel, and electrodes were attached to her forearms, the EMG would pick up her tendency to turn the wheel to any point on the scale. She was told that she actually did not have to turn the wheel, that the EMG screened out *gross* muscle movements and recorded the 'first, undistorted' reaction. (Jones and Sigall 1971: 349, 359)

Sigall and Page (1971) then used this 'bogus pipeline' to reveal people's real attitudes. Their participants were asked to think about either 'Americans or Negroes' and they were read 22 trait descriptors which they had to mark on a scale from −3 (completely uncharacteristic) to +3 (completely characteristic) either with the EMG machine apparently being used to monitor their responses or not. What the researchers found was that the Americans were described more favourably in the condition where the EMG machine was apparently being used, but with Negroes exactly the opposite was found – Negroes were described less favourably when the EMG machine was 'in operation'. In other words, people seem to provide different responses on self-report questionnaires when they believe that the experimenters know how they feel already. When the participants thought that they were being monitored by a 'lie detection device' they were more favourable to the American targets and much less favourable to the Negro targets than when they thought they were not being monitored.

Some of the specific results are quite illuminating. Thus, the trait descriptor 'lazy' was reported as 'uncharacteristic' of Americans in the EMG condition and 'uncharacteristic' in the non-EMG condition. So, participants consistently said that they thought Americans were 'not lazy' and this seemed to be true even when they thought that this lie detection device was going to give the experimenter a gateway into their soul. However, the trait descriptor 'lazy' was offered as 'uncharacteristic' of Negroes in the non-EMG condition, but 'characteristic' in the EMG condition. In other words, the participants rated both Negroes and Americans as 'not lazy' when there was no 'lie detector', but when there was a 'lie detector', suddenly their response changed. The experimenters argue that the proposition 'Negroes are lazy' is something that ordinarily the experimental participants did not want to report and they only did report this when they felt that the experimenter already knew how they felt because of the lie detector.

So what are the overall conclusions from this classic study? Perhaps the most obvious conclusion is that:

> the bogus pipeline measures operated like a lie detection device in facilitating scrupulously truthful reporting. To embrace this alternative is to accept the assumption that subjects do not typically tell us the truth when they report their attitudes and feelings about sensitive matters, or those where private feelings might be expected to differ from a socially respected norm. (Jones and Sigall 1971: 362)

However, to their credit Jones and Sigall do think about alternative explanations, including the possibility that the introduction of the physiological measurement with the EMG prompts participants to focus on the affective or emotional aspect of their attitude to the target categories (American or Negro).

> The resultant response may therefore differ from the verbal rating that is equally honest, but that reflects different dimensions of the attitude being measured . . . People may have a kind of id-ego conception of their attitudes. They may assume that their ugly, negative feelings are buried in the autonomic nervous system and are expressed only in off-guard moments. (ibid.: 363)

This alternative explanation, of course, would suggest a very different plan of action for future research. If you accept the first explanation then you need some measure like the bogus pipeline to expose attitudes in highly sensitive areas. If you accept the second explanation then you may instead like to focus on exploring the complexity of the structure of attitudes and how the affective and cognitive aspects fit together, and whether some psychologists are indeed right when they consider that attitudes may have an ugly 'id' and a more rational and socialised 'ego' that somehow reside together uncomfortably in the human mind.

In a real sense the bogus pipeline research was the intellectual precursor of Greenwald's Implicit Association Test (IAT) and in the IAT both research foci reconnect with a vengeance.

- In the 1970s, psychologists tried to dig a pipeline to the soul by lying to their participants; they told them that they had a 'lie detector' which could reveal their true feelings.
- When White participants were attached to this 'lie detector' they reported that Negroes were lazy. When they were not attached to this 'lie detector', they didn't say this.
- This could be very significant if you are trying to determine people's real attitude towards people from different ethnic backgrounds.

7

The inner conflict

But what happens if the problem with the measurement of prejudiced attitudes is not just about self-presentation? What happens if it is not just about respondents wanting to be more politically correct? What happens if the whole thing is not just about people disguising their real underlying attitudes; attitudes which they have access to and indeed know only too well? What happens if prejudiced attitudes are complicated things with various different components?

Allport acknowledges this possibility in his opening to his chapter on 'Inner Conflict' in his classic book. He writes,

> The course of prejudice in a life seldom runs smoothly.
> For prejudice attitudes are almost certain to collide with
> deep-seated values that are often equally or more central
> to the personality. The influence of the school may
> contradict the influence of the home. The teachings of
> religion may challenge social stratification. Integration
> of such opposing forces within a single life is hard to
> achieve. (1954: 326)

He contrasts this sort of individual who may make uncomfortable attempts to integrate colliding attitudes with the out-and-out bigot, whose attitudes seem perfectly reconciled, who seems to have no such problem. The example he cites of 'prejudice without compunction' is a telegram sent by Governor Bilbo of Mississippi to the Mayor of Chicago in 1920. Chicago, in Allport's words, was facing 'a surplus of Negro migrants who had come to Chicago looking for work during the First World War.' The mayor, it seems, had enquired whether some of them could possibly be sent back to their Southern homeland. The response from Governor Bilbo is clear and to the point and shows no evidence of any difficulty in expressing underlying attitudes:

Your telegram, asking how many Negroes Mississippi can absorb, received. I reply, I desire to state that we have all the room in the world for what we know as N-i-g-g-e-r-s, but none whatever for 'colored ladies and gentlemen.' If these Negroes have been contaminated with Northern social and political dreams of equality, we cannot use them, nor do we want them. The Negro who understands his proper relation to the white man in this country will be gladly received by the people of Mississippi, as we are very much in need of labor. (Quoted first in Young 1933, see also Allport 1954: 326)

Or consider the words of Lord Chesterfield, who in his letters to his son was keen to offer some paternal advice, including living one's life by reason rather than by prejudice. Lord Chesterfield, nevertheless, has this to say about women:

Women, then, are only children of a larger growth; they have an entertaining tattle, and sometimes wit; but for solid reasoning, good sense, I never knew in my life one that had it, or who reasoned or acted consequentially for four and twenty hours together . . . A man of sense only trifles with them, plays with them, humors and flatters them, as he does a sprightly, forward child; but he neither consults them about, nor trusts them with serious matters; though he often makes them believe that he does both; which is the thing in the world that they are most proud of . . . Women are much more like each other than men; they have in truth but two passions, vanity and love: these are their universal characteristics. (Strachey 1925: 261)

It turns out that many people are (thankfully) not like Governor Bilbo of Mississippi or Lord Chesterfield. Although what proportion of people fall into the Bilbo and Chesterfield category (the out-and-out bigot) does remain to be properly determined. According to Allport's own research, only ten per cent of participants in his research in the late 1940s and early 1950s could write about their attitudes towards minority groups in the US and express prejudice openly and without feelings of guilt and conflict (but it is important to point out that these estimates are based entirely upon a sample of college students who are clearly not representative of the population as a whole, see Sears 1986). The vast majority of the college students Allport tested had strongly ambivalent feelings that could cause them some distress, so that they would get angry at themselves for these feelings. They would call themselves 'hypocrite', 'intolerant' and 'narrow-minded'. But they would often appear stuck, unable to change and hardly able to face up to their intolerance. They would write about the split between 'my reason and prejudice'. They would say that they 'try to lean over backwards to counteract the attitude'. But ultimately recognising that they were powerless: 'it is remarkable how strong a hold it has on me'. They may be conflicted in attitudinal terms but they stayed eloquent to the end. 'My compulsive prejudice is putting up a fight against its own elimination.' It is almost too eloquent sometimes (in my opinion) to be taken as a clear reflection of how such conflicted attitudes feel. These are after all college students, who were studying psychology, trying hard in essays to convey the experience, and maybe even a little too hard at times. But they are valuable nonetheless in their own way. Allport comments on these revealed experiences, 'Defeated intellectually, prejudice lingers emotionally' and later: 'Self-insight, however, does not automatically cure prejudice. At best it starts the individual wondering.'

So what are the implications of this inner conflict on the experience and realisation of prejudice? According to Allport (1954: 332),

> when inner conflict is present, people put brakes upon their prejudices. They do not act them out – or they act them out only up to a certain point. Something stops the

logical progression somewhere. In New York City, as E.B. White has pointed out, there smoulders every ethnic problem there is; yet the noticeable thing is not the problem, but the remarkable control.

Allport says that such prejudice may be expressed when in the safe bosom's of one's own family but not in the presence of member of the target group; prejudice may pop out in the bar or the club but not on the street or the station; in other words, where one feels safe and protected, both psychologically as well as physically. But Allport maintains that 'such marked contrast in *situational* behaviour would not occur unless there were *inner conflict* in the person harbouring prejudice' (ibid.: 334).

So, as a psychologist, Allport maintains that most human beings are conflicted when it comes to prejudice, and much of everyday life is dedicated to a battle in which people try to control or master it. He then identifies four ways that people use to handle these unruly and 'contrary impulses' – repression (denial), defence (rationalisation), compromise (partial resolution) and integration (true resolution). Repression, according to Allport, is so powerful because the alternative, actually admitting that there is an issue 'is to accuse oneself of being both irrational and unethical. No one wants to be at odds with his own conscience. Man has to live with himself' (ibid.: 334). Evidence of repression appears in many forms, but one of the most common is 'I am not prejudiced, but . . .'. To Allport, 'Psychologically, the mechanism is one of affirming virtue so that the subsequent lapses will pass unnoticed' (ibid.: 335). But, he argues that repression rarely 'stands alone' and needs defensive rationalisations to back it up.

Defensive rationalisation, according to Allport, is all about 'selective perception' and 'selective forgetting'; this is where the individual consciously or unconsciously (but in most cases probably unconsciously) sees or finds 'evidence to bolster a categorical overgeneralisation' and then remembers it clearly but forgets counter-examples. Individual examples are stored in memory to support the overgeneralisation; details are noticed that would otherwise never have been noticed. For example, the Jewish student who borrows the bus fare and never returns it (tight), the Black student walking slowly to the lecture theatre (lazy), the Irish student play fighting in the Student Union (belligerent). Newspapers and the media are scoured for further support, and they are a rich vein, not just because of the amount of material to be selectively read but because of their own explicit or implicit biases.

But there are other 'defensive tricks' (Allport's term) which are available as well. There is bifurcation, which seems to represent differentiation within a category, but it is a differentiation based upon questionable criteria. 'I am not prejudiced against Negroes; some are good. It is only bad niggers that I dislike.' So what, asks Allport, is a 'bad nigger'? Is it a Black person who flatters the White man's self-esteem? 'The bifurcation is based on what does and what does not seem to threaten one, not on the merit of individuals' (ibid.: 336). Another defensive trick is 'rationalisation by making exceptions' as in 'Some of my best friends are Black, but . . .'. As Allport (ibid.) says: 'If one makes a few exceptions, then one can justify holding the remaining portion of the category intact'. The essence of this kind of statement is that if you have good friends that fall into the category then what you are about to say that is very negative (signalled by the 'but') cannot be put down to prejudice.

Then, according to Allport, there is evidence of inner conflict in 'alternation'. 'When one frame of reference is invoked, one set of subsidiary attitudes and habits comes into play; when a contrary frame is invoked, a quite opposite set of dispositions is activated' (ibid.: 337). In other words, human beings deal with this inner conflict by not being consistent with themselves. Sometimes they display prejudice and sometimes they do not; it depends upon the situation and who they are surrounded with, the inconsistency can be in what they say, or between what they say and their actual behaviour and Allport says that this is perfectly normal and understandable. Indeed he says, 'it is the rigid consistency of the fanatic (whether of a bigot or a crusader for equal rights) that is regarded as pathological in our society' (ibid.).

Allport maintains that the fact that we have multiple roles to play in everyday life assists in this process of not being consistent. Different roles demand different behaviours (Allport uses the rather curious, and stereotypic example here of being at church and being in a Pullman smoking car, two situations that elicit and reinforce different sets of values). But you can imagine many other diverse roles that pull people in different directions – university lecturer, parent, son, sports competitor, shop customer, football fan, bystander, neighbour, interviewer, interviewee, customer in bar, customer in posh restaurant – when it comes to behaviour towards other human beings who fall into racial, ethnic or other categories. Allport finishes his comments on alternation with the quixotic, 'To be a conformist under diverse sets of conditions is almost unavoidably to compromise one's integrity as a person' (ibid.: 338). Here, he makes clear the logical necessity of a degree of alternation in everyday life. But the critical point is to what degree this alternation is allowable. If people are aware of an inconsistency in underlying values they may find this very troubling and it may lead to a journey to resolve this (hopefully by getting rid of 'racial bogies' and 'traditional scapegoats'). Allport himself is not necessarily that optimistic about how easy this is to achieve. 'Perhaps few people achieve integration of this type; but many are fairly far along the road . . . Such resentments and hatred as they have are reserved strictly for those who actually threaten basic value systems. Only a personality organised in such a manner can be fully integrated' (ibid.: 339).

And this is how Allport finished his treatise on 'inner conflict', but the treatment always seems to me to be first, well ahead of its time but, second, also a little schematic. All he really says, after all, is that some inconsistency is unavoidable and that people repress and rationalise much of the time. Some achieve consistency eventually but how and why remains unclear. So how does the inner conflict feel? How does it work? Are we necessarily aware of all our inconsistencies? What are the mechanisms of change? How are the inconsistencies represented in the human mind? Are we inconsistent at all or do we just say things for good social reasons, to be part of a group, to fit in, to form coalitions, to offset blame, to build our own self-identity (see for example, Potter and Wetherell 1987)? Allport may have begun the questioning process, but ultimately, in my opinion, he himself provides no substantial answer to many of the questions he raises. Perhaps we needed more agreement about the relative importance of each of the questions he raised and much more data. Perhaps that's the problem with being a genuine intellectual pioneer like Allport; you need time for other researchers to catch up.

Of course, the consensus (and the data) eventually arrived and Allport's classic text was put to a critical evaluation by a set of distinguished scholars some 50 years after its original publication. They began by acknowledging that *The Nature of Prejudice* really 'was the foundation for the social psychology of prejudice' (Hazlitt, interestingly, is never mentioned in this festchrift).

> Contemporary prejudice researchers and scholars regularly refer back to this work not only for apt quotations but also for inspiration . . . Indeed, any student of prejudice ignorant of Allport would be rightly considered illiterate . . . Yet half a century after its publication, *The Nature of Prejudice* remains the most widely cited work on prejudice. The scope and endurance of its influence has been nothing short of remarkable. (Dovidio, Glick and Rudman 2005: 1)

Each of Allport's core concepts is dissected by contemporary eyes and Patricia Devine has the responsibility for re-examining Allport's concept of inner conflict. One of her comments is telling when she responds to the basic question, as to whether Allport has been supported or not by 50 years of research – 'it is worth noting that Allport offered his analysis of inner conflict and speculations concerning strategies for resolving it largely without the benefit of empirical data. This fact makes re-examination of his analysis and speculations an interesting exercise' (Devine 2005: 337). But despite the fact that Allport produced little by way of empirical data to support his analysis, Devine concludes that Allport was, more or less, spot on:

one could argue that his ideas and suppositions were nothing short of prescient. In reading Allport's 'Inner Conflict' chapter, one can't help but be impressed with Allport's presaging of many of the major themes explored by subsequent generations of scholars. Allport's insight about both the origins and the nature of inner conflict were right on target. (ibid.: 337)

Devine then presents each of Allport's claims juxtaposed with what subsequent generations of psychologists had discovered on the subject. So, for example, when Allport had suggested that people suppressed evidence of the racial bias, Dovidio and Gaertner (2004) had found that these negrophobics became 'activated' whenever White people interact with Black people and that

the conflict between the simultaneously-activated prejudiced and egalitarian views causes aversive feelings, such as discomfort, unease, and sometimes fear. Aversive feelings can motivate people to avoid future interactions with Black people in order to avoid evoking negative emotions. (Devine 2005: 330)

When it comes to defensive rationalisation Devine points out that subsequently psychologists had found numerous examples where people can simultaneously hold quite discrepant views; for example, that some Blacks can do extremely well, but most Blacks are extremely lazy. Contemporary psychologists call this 'subtyping' (Rothbart and John 1985). The role of subtyping is to use a form of categorical thinking that leaves the broad stereotype intact. Similarly, contemporary psychologists have found a great deal of evidence for the alternation in beliefs that Allport describes in that 'people vacillate between their egalitarian values and their prejudiced beliefs based on situational factors that make one or the other salient (Devine 2005: 331). Katz and Hass (1988) called this ambivalent racism, which is defined as a simultaneous possession of positive and negative attitudes towards Black people.

But what Allport never did was to detail the subsystems that might be responsible for these ambivalent attitudes and we had to wait for further developments in psychology generally before we were provided with a basis for them. The developments came with the work of Anthony Greenwald, who provided a new way of construing attitudes in terms of implicit and explicit attitudes. This led Devine and others to reconceptualise Allport's concept of inner conflict as 'a struggle between automatic and controlled processes'. According to Devine (2005: 333),

> whether people are consciously prejudiced or not, they are vulnerable to the automatic activation of the cultural stereotype of African Americans. This type of automatic stereotype activation is a legacy of our common socialization experiences and occurs without people's consent or bidding. The model assumes that adoption of non-prejudiced beliefs or values does not immediately eliminate automatic prejudiced responses. Importantly, the model does not presume that people who adopt egalitarian values hide from or deny automatic biases; instead, the biases are recognized, viewed as unacceptable, and motivate corrective efforts . . . In developing this analysis, I argued that eliminating 'as a first response' requires overcoming a lifetime of socialization experiences, which, unfortunately, promote automatic prejudice (Devine 1989). I likened the process of overcoming prejudice to the breaking of a bad habit in that people must make a decision to eliminate the habit and then learn to inhibit the habitual response.

Devine thus attempts to extend Allport's model in the light of what we are now learning about the subsystems of the human mind. There are a couple of major assumptions underpinning her particular analysis. One is that people are aware of their racial or ethnic biases; she says quite explicitly that biases are 'recognized, and viewed as unacceptable'. And second, the cause of the negative implicit bias is the 'automatic activation of some cultural stereotype'. In other words, the implicit attitude reflects a cultural bias that has been internalised at the level of the individual. One might argue that this makes problematic the diversity of people's implicit bias, because if it is some broad cultural understanding that is being internalised, why is there such divergence in this? What is the contribution of individual experience in the acquisition of this cultural knowledge and how might specific life experiences impact on this whole process? Devine's analysis itself raises many unanswered questions but it does allow Allport's views to be reconceptualised in modern terms. It also allows us to delve into the analysis of the unconscious automatic processes in a way avoided by Allport, and it allows us to rethink how to go about 'breaking the prejudice habit'. Devine (2005: 337–338) sums up in the following way:

> the contemporary literature has a number of strengths not evident in Allport's chapter. For example, the contemporary literature has provided much more detailed theoretical analyses of the disparity between one's reason and one's prejudice and the modern conceptualizations of this conflict have been subjected to empirical tests. Indeed, some of the most exciting developments have come from fleshing out the process issues involved in 'breaking the prejudice habit.' Because Allport did not speak to automaticity, he did not anticipate these advances.

To understand prejudice we need to think more carefully about automatic processes, and in order to do so we need to consider in detail the whole nature of the concept of the attitude and to ask if core aspects of this could possibly be unconscious, and if they are, how then can they be measured?

- Some people are out-and-out bigots but most people are not.
- Most people have ambivalent feelings about race that can cause them some distress and many people suffer from an 'inner conflict'.

- Human beings have four main ways of dealing with these 'contrary impulses': *repression, denial, defence and rationalisation*.
- Repression is very common because, in Allport's words, 'No one wants to be at odds with his own conscience. Man has to live with himself'.
- People often use selective perception and selective forgetting to find 'evidence' to 'bolster a categorical overgeneralisation'. All counter-examples are conveniently forgotten.
- Allport also says that many people alternate in their beliefs.
- Contemporary psychologists call this 'ambivalent racism', which is defined as a simultaneous holding of positive and negative attitudes towards Black people and other racial or ethnic groups.

8

How much of our attitude is unconscious?

The concept of 'attitude' is, of course, one of the most important concepts in psychology. It would seem to be the natural first step in the analysis and prediction of behaviour, some form of analysis of 'predisposition to act'. Allport (1935: 798) himself wrote, 'The concept of attitude is probably the most distinctive and indispensable concept in contemporary social psychology. In fact several writers ... *define* social psychology as the scientific study of attitudes.' And perhaps the single most significant contributor in the evolution of the concept of the 'attitude' was Allport himself. Allport was repelled by the way that psychoanalysis dug far too deeply for the root causes of human action, while more behavioural approaches, he thought, just skimmed the surface and did not go deep enough. It was Allport who gave early social psychology much of its distinctive feel, and led it carefully away from where it might have ended up in the endless psychoanalytic depths.

What is fascinating about Allport, the man who steered social psychology on its course for the 75 years since his book on attitudes came out, is that he liked to give us glimpses into his own life, so that we might understand why he chose one scientific course rather than another. And there is one particular autobiographical nugget that stands out from all the others. As a student, he tells us, he visited Freud in Vienna, and that one chance visit changed him and changed the future course of psychology. What happened there was basically that dramatic (in a highly personal sort of way). He liked to tell the story of the encounter as evidence of the psychoanalytic tendency to read too much into every-thing, without first considering the more obvious and the more parsimonious explanation. And this story has been repeated and reproduced many times. Over the years, it has moved away from being a private story of an embarrassing moment in a young man's life to become something of a parable about psychoanalysis and the emergence of the science of social psychology and its retreat from what Allport himself liked to call 'psychoanalytic excess'. But the events described were clearly critical in Allport's develop-ment and therefore were critical to the development of the discipline of social psychology.

It begins with Allport's visit to Austria in 1920. Allport had arranged a meeting with Freud in his office in Vienna. Freud was at the height of his fame, and Allport was then just 22 years old, having just recently graduated with a Bachelor's degree from Harvard but nevertheless with the forwardness and confidence, no matter how shaky, to write to the great man to set up the visit. In Allport's own words 'I wrote to Freud announcing that I was in Vienna and implied that no doubt he would be glad to make my acquain-tance. I received a kind reply in his own handwriting inviting me to come to his office at a certain time.' On entering Freud's office, Allport was greeted with the famil-iarity of the room, known even then, and an expectant but uncomfortable silence that seemed to open up and engulf them both. Here he was in front of the great man, but he found himself just staring down at the red patterned Berber rug in the famous inner office, the matted walls painted deep red, the walls laden with pictures of dreams with all their iconic and provocative symbolism, and fragments from antiquity buried deep in the earth for centuries now released like suppressed memories brought back into consciousness; the whole room reeking of decayed cigar smoke. The heady, stale smell of success that almost made Allport choke.

Allport coughed briefly. The bookshelf behind Freud's desk acted as a reminder to all who entered the room of Freud's own great intellectual journey with books by Goethe, Shakespeare, Heine, Multatuli (Eduard Dekker) and Anatole France, the dramatists, philosophers and poets, who had recognised the power of the unconscious. Allport noted each of these books in turn, he had never heard of a number of the authors, they were outside his realm. He felt intimidated. And in that silence when he dared to lift his head, he had the opportunity to scrutinise some of the other pictures hanging around the room, 'Oedipus and the Riddle of the Sphinx', where Oedipus stands, wearing a traveller's cloak with a petasos cap hanging over his shoulder, addressing the woman-headed winged lion. Oedipus's right hand is extended in gesture, open and dynamic. Allport could see the famous couch covered with velvet cushions and a patterned Qashqa'i rug with the three linked octagons symbolising, to some of Freud's followers at least, the uterus contractions during parturition. But the three linked octagons merely acted as a reminder to Allport of the id, the ego and the superego and the holy trinity of the psyche and the neat packaging of psychoanalytic ideas into a list of three. A list of three like some cheap advertising slogan which sells all products, 'A Mars a day helps you work, rest and play', or 'Coke – delicious, wholesome, thirst quenching', first coined in 1909, but certainly around in Allport's time. Allport had noticed that there are always three in the list, always three, when you want to sell big time that is (and 'wholesome' indeed!). And Allport noticed the plush green armchair where Freud would sit behind his patients while they engaged in free association. Allport was drawn to the expression of Doctor Charcot in the famous painting by Andre Brouillet of Doctor Charcot at work at the Salpêtrière, with the hysterical female patient in full seizure displayed before the staff and medical students. Freud himself had been a student in the audience many years before and the painting may have reminded him of those happier carefree days, or it may have acted as a symbolic reminder of the power of the mesmeric great teacher who had pioneered the use of hypnosis and the effects he was having on his enchanted and captivated audience and on the frozen, hysterical female patient who was helpless in front of them all, with only the great Doctor Charcot or Freud himself capable of understanding her malady. It just made Allport uncomfortable in the extreme; it was all a bit too showy for him, it went against his own implicit beliefs.

In the days before Harvard, Allport had been a shy, studious boy, often teased by his school friends for having just eight toes as a result of a birth defect. He had a veneer now of Harvard sophistication, of the new international academic in the making, but silences like this made him more uncomfortable. It reminded him of who he had been; maybe of who he was. He knew better than most that personality never really changes. He needed to say something, so he thought that he would make an observation, a psychological observation of something that he had just witnessed. He described how he had watched a small boy of about four on the tram car on the way to Freud's office who was terrified of coming into contact with any dirt. He refused to allow this particular man on the tram to sit beside him because he thought that the man was dirty, despite his mother's cajoling and reassurance. Allport studied the woman in question and noted how neat and tidy she was, and how domineering in her approach to her son. Allport hypothesised that the dirt phobia of the young boy had been picked up from his mother, someone who needed everything neat and tidy and in its correct place. 'To him [the boy] everything was *schmutzig*. His mother was a well-starched *Hausfrau*, so dominant and purposive looking that I thought the cause and effect apparent.'

Freud looked at Allport carefully for the first time, with his 'kindly therapeutic eyes', and then asked, 'And was that little boy you?' Allport blinked uncomfortably and said nothing, appalled by Freud's attempt to psychoanalyse him on the spot. Allport himself knew that his observation was driven by the desire to fill the silence, his desire to display to Freud that as a psychologist he, the young man from Harvard, never stopped observing, and his desire to connect with the great man, maybe even his need for belonging through this essential connection. These were all manifest and clear motives, maybe at different levels, but all open to the conscious mind, which should be obvious to all. What it was not was any unconscious desire to reveal his own deep-seated uncertainties and anxieties resulting from problems in potty training back in Montezuma, Indiana. Allport tried to change the subject but the damage had been done.

> I realized that he was accustomed to neurotic defenses and that my manifest motivation (a sort of rude curiosity and youthful ambition) escaped him. For therapeutic progress he would have to cut through my defenses, but it so happened that therapeutic progress was not here an issue. (Allport 1967: 7–8)

Allport later wrote that the 'experience taught me that depth psychology, for all its merits, may plunge too deep, and that psychologists would do well to give full recognition to manifest motives before probing the unconscious'. This was a clear example, in his mind, of the 'psychoanalytic excess' that he liked to detail, although needless to say psychoanalysts ever since are not necessarily convinced by his argument. Faber writing in 1970 suggested that Freud got it exactly right, that Allport had:

> practiced a kind of deception in order to work his way into Freud's office. The deception lay in his implied claim that (1) he genuinely wanted to meet Freud as a human being and as an intellectual rather than as an object, and (2) that he (Allport) himself was worth meeting as a human being and as an 'intellectual'. (Faber 1970: 62)

Faber believes that Freud saw through this deception quickly and that by asking Allport whether he was the little boy in the story he was in fact indicating to Allport that he knew that he was a 'dirty little boy' and that by putting this question to him, Freud was merely trying to restart the conversation in an honest and straightforward way. Elms (1993) attributed even greater analytic power and clarity of thinking to Freud in this meeting. Allport's childhood was characterised by 'plain Protestant piety' (Allport 1968) with an emphasis on clear religious answers to difficult theological and personal questions and an upbringing in an environment which doubled as a home and as a hospital and which was run by Allport's physician father. According to

Elms the question had such a marked effect on Allport because he 'was still carrying within him the super-clean little boy' brought up in that literal and metaphorical sterile Protestant environment where patients were to be avoided as sources of infection and possible danger.

But Allport was convinced of his own explanation for the event and was determined to do something about this psychoanalytic excess. This meeting encouraged Allport to develop something different, a different sort of approach to the human mind, an approach that stayed with us for some 60 years before anyone really dared challenge it in a systematic way. An approach based around conscious reflection and the power of language to uncover and articulate underlying attitudes, to bring attitudes into the open where they could be studied and analysed objectively and scientifically. This was to characterise the new social psychology that held sway for the next half century or more and gave us our core methods and techniques in social psychology. But was it the whole story?

- Allport avoided probing the possible unconscious components of an attitude because Freud tried to psychoanalyse him when he visited Freud in Vienna when he was just 22 years old. Allport never got over this experience and commented on it on many occasions.
- There is nothing in Allport's early definitions of attitude which excludes a possible unconscious component; it is just that Allport didn't like going there, for his own reasons.

9

Measuring the unconscious

Allport made genuine advances in many areas of psychology, not least in the area of prejudice, as we have already seen. In order to develop his science of personality, Allport began by going through the dictionary and identifying every single lexical item that could be used to describe a person. His trawl pulled in 4,500 trait-like words. In these lexical descriptors, the words used in everyday life, he saw the start of a new scientific theory of personality, rooted in the stuff of everyday life, in the words that we use consciously and deliberately to describe other people. It was four years later, in 1924 at Harvard, that Allport began what was in all likelihood the very first course on Personality in the United States – 'Personality: Its Psychological and Social Aspect'. It is the kind of course that could well fit into the modern psychology curriculum. He went on to develop theories and write books on prejudice, the psychology of rumour and the concept of the self, developing the careers of many outstanding social psychologists including Jerome Bruner, Stanley Milgram, Leo Postman, Thomas Pettigrew and M. Brewster Smith. Another of his students was Anthony Greenwald. Given Allport's stance on Freud's fixed attentional gaze on the unconscious, it is highly ironic that Greenwald is best known for taking one of Allport's core concepts, the attitude, and detailing the unconscious or implicit aspects of it; indeed he challenged the whole basis for identifying and measuring it.

Allport himself viewed the concept of the attitude as the central plank of the new psychology. He defined it as 'a mental and neural state of readiness organized through experience, exerting a directive or dynamic influence upon the individual's response to all objects and situations with which it is related.'(1935: 810). In other words, an attitude is an internal state of mind affected by what we do, which affects our behaviour towards the world around us. In 1935 Allport announced proudly that this concept of the attitude was social psychology's 'most distinctive and indispensable concept' (ibid: 798). Its importance should be clear – it should have a major impact upon our behaviour (but of course it is not the only factor and, in 1991, Ajzen argued that the subjective norm, or how you think others will behave, plus the level of perceived behavioural control, in other words the control you have over the particular behaviour, are also crucial).

Of course, there is nothing in Allport's formal definition which formally excludes a possible unconscious component to the attitude (see also Greenwald and Banaji 1995: 7). Indeed, Doob, another great scholar of attitude, working in the years shortly after Allport, had defined an attitude as 'an implicit, drive-producing response considered socially significant in the individual's society' (Doob 1947: 136), and in 1992 in an article in which he looked back at the early development of social psychology, he wrote that in the 1940s, and earlier, the notion of attitudes operating unconsciously was quite acceptable to many researchers.

But when you read this early work of Allport with fresh eyes, I think that you could go much further than this. I think that in Allport's classic (1935) chapter, and despite what happened to him in Freud's office, he initially displays considerable awareness of the unconscious dimensions of an attitude and great sensitivity to this unconscious aspect. When he talks about the early German experimentalists from the Wurzburg school, he points out that they believed that attitudes were:

neither sensation, nor imagery, nor affection, nor any combination of these states. Time and again they were studied by the method of introspection, always with meagre results. Often an attitude seemed to have no representation in consciousness other than a vague sense of need, or some indefinite or unanalyzable feeling of doubt, assent, conviction, effort, or familiarity. (Allport 1935: 800)

Some psychologists (e.g. Clarke 1911) clearly thought that attitudes were represented in consciousness through 'imagery, sensation and affection', but Allport himself seemed to hold quite a different view. Thus he wrote that

The meagreness with which attitudes are represented in consciousness resulted in a tendency to regard them as manifestations of brain activity or of the unconscious mind. The persistence of attitudes which are totally unconscious was demonstrated by Muller and Pilzecker (1900), who called the phenomenon 'perseveration'. (Allport 1935: 801)

So in this classic chapter, Allport not only displays explicit recognition of the significance of the unconscious dimensions of an attitude, he also praises Freud's contribution to this concept, and specifically applauds him for endowing attitudes with 'vitality, identifying them with longing, hatred and love, with passion and prejudice, in short, with the onrushing stream of unconscious life (ibid.: 801). This all came from a man who had been personally put off by Freud's attempt to psychoanalyse him in his office some 15 years previously.

But his chapter has a historical timeline underpinning it and as we get towards the middle and end of the chapter the unconscious is mentioned less and less, and by the final section the focus has moved away entirely from the unconscious to the conscious – in effect, to what can be measured with the greatest ease. He seems impressed by Likert's research which looked at White people's attitudes to 'Negros' and the fact that scales could be used to determine 'the amount of favor or disfavor toward the rights of the Negro'. The 'Likert Scales' were measurement devices that pick up on conscious thoughts, sometimes thoughts that maybe we are not that happy with, but conscious thoughts nonetheless. Allport seems in awe of the work that had been done on intelligence testing, despite the fact that there was still huge disagreement about what 'intelligence' actually was. He wrote admiringly about the domain of intelligence, 'where practicable tests are an established fact although the nature of intelligence is still in dispute' (and, of course, he is alluding here to the huge debate then raging about how to define the concept of 'attitude'). These intelligence tests yielded vast amounts of quantitative data which in his view was clearly of practical value to an emergent nation. He saw the same practical application for attitude measurement and he concluded with some pride that:

> The success achieved in the past ten years in the field
> of the measurement of attitudes may be regarded as one
> of the major accomplishments of social psychology
> in America. The rate of progress is so great that
> further achievements in the near future are inevitable.
> (1935: 832)

As soon as he found himself in the domain of intelligence testing and Likert the unconscious dimension of the attitude seems to have been forgotten and it remained forgotten for a significant period of time. Allport wanted to measure attitudes with precision and reliability so he went for introspective paper and pencil type tests. He clearly had his own objection to hypothesising scientifically about unknown and unknowable forces affecting our lives through the unconscious, and given Allport's influence on the developing field of social psychology the focus turned away from the unconscious to the conscious, and therefore to self-report type measures. It stayed there for the next half century and more.

So, perhaps not surprisingly, it is important to measure attitudes towards ethnicity in the tradition of Gordon Allport and the great experimentalist social psychologists who have documented our attitudes for decades, using Likert Scales to reveal consciously held attitudes. But I was not intending to restrict it to that. The new research by Greenwald and others saw to that.

- Early on in his career Allport did seem to recognise that core aspects of an attitude could be unconscious.
- Allport, however, wanted precision and reliability in measurement so he focused on self-report measures of attitudes.
- Allport's views have dominated the field of attitude measurement in psychology for a very significant period.

10

A new way into our unconscious attitude

The new approach to understanding and measuring underlying attitudes was developed by Anthony Greenwald. He
developed a powerful argument that we should reconceptualise what we mean by an attitude in the light of new research
in cognitive rather than social psychological research
(the principal domain for this type of work). He cited the
conclusion of Myers (1987) who had come to the view that
the models of the attitude-behaviour relationship only
really worked by 'limiting the scope of the attitude concept.'
Thus,

> Our attitudes predict our actions (1) if other influences
> are minimized, (2) if the attitude is specific to the action,
> and (3) if, as we act, we are conscious of our attitudes,
> either because something reminds us of them or because
> we acquired them in a manner that makes them strong.
> When these conditions are not met, our attitudes seem
> disconnected from our actions. (Myers 1987: 45)

Greenwald (1990: 256), clearly not a man to mince his words,
wrote – 'Myer's conclusion is decidedly embarrassing as a
summary of the predictive power of social psychology's
major theoretical construct'. What he did in the remainder
of this short paper was to review new research in cognitive
psychology on unconscious cognitive processes to provide a
new theoretical basis to the work on attitudes. The fully
formed Gordon Allport, the psychologist who had rejected
Freud's attempt to bring the role of the unconscious even

into his brief meeting with his younger self, would have turned in his grave. One consequence of Greenwald's devastating review was to 'call into question the appropriateness of the presently most favoured techniques of attitude measurement' (ibid.: 256). The rest as they say is history.

Greenwald started with Myers' conclusion. Myers' paper was in many people's eyes a devastating summary of the attitude-behaviour relationship but one bit of the conclusion was wrong according to Greenwald, and that was his third conclusion. Greenwald claimed that some of the most reliable and robust findings of attitudes predicting behaviour are exactly in those domains where the actor is not focusing attention on the attitude. One example of this, used by Greenwald, is the halo effect. The halo effect is the tendency to make new positive (or negative) judgements about a person when a positive (or negative) attitude towards that person already exists. In a famous study Landy and Sigall (1974) found that male participants judged the quality of a poor essay more favourably when the female author was attractive than when she was unattractive. This seemed to occur without any attentional focus on the underlying attitude. The fact that a photograph of the author was in the folder with the essay itself was designed to be almost coincidental. Greenwald did not attempt to excuse himself here. He used an example from his own life as an academic to illustrate that implicit attitudinal forces are in constant operation in our everyday lives:

> As a manuscript reviewer, I often cannot help noticing an initial warm, positive reaction when I review a manuscript that cites my work favourably (or maybe just cites it at all), and sometimes I notice the opposite – a colder reaction when some of my work that might have been cited is not mentioned. I know that these reactions interfere with the way my work as reviewer should be done, but it is difficult to avoid these reactions – and it is difficult not to do the review by searching for virtues that will justify the initial warm reaction, or for flaws that will justify the initial cold reaction. (Greenwald 1990: 257)

This was the phenomenon that he was trying to pin down and understand – this initial reaction full of emotional overtones well under the radar of consciousness but ultimately controlling our behaviour. Nobody, but nobody, escaped his gaze. With Eric Schuh and Katharine Engell, Greenwald analysed the citation patterns for authors whose names were selected from the 1987 Social Sciences Citation Index on the basis that they could be classified unambiguously as Jewish or Anglo-Saxon in origin. They found that Jewish-named authors cited 6 per cent more authors with Jewish names than did Anglo-Saxon authors, and conversely Anglo-Saxon authors cited 7 per cent more authors with Anglo-Saxon names than did Jewish authors. His conclusion was that 'Social scientists (who are widely regarded as being relatively free of prejudice) might display ethnic prejudices' (1990: 258). Even his friends and colleagues were not safe from his emerging theoretical perspective. This was putting colleagues on the spot just as pointedly as did Freud exactly 70 years earlier.

Greenwald saw an emerging pattern in all of this.

The subject is in a situation that requires a response to some object; attitude towards an attribute of the object influences the response, and it does so without the subject's being aware that an attitude is being activated. These situations amount to indirect memory tasks for which the response has an evaluative component. (ibid.: 259)

Greenwald's goal was to elucidate the processes underlying implicit cognition and to demonstrate why they were critical to a reformulation of how we thought about attitudes and how we should measure them.

For Greenwald and Banaji (1995: 4–5), 'the signature of implicit cognition is that traces of past experience affect some performance, even though the influential earlier experience is not remembered in the usual sense – that is, it is unavailable to self-report or introspection'. In this paper he provides a simple example of implicit cognition in operation. Consider an experiment where the participants have to generate a complete word in response to an incomplete letter string (a word stem or a word fragment). The words that the participants generate here are more likely to be words that they have been 'casually' exposed to earlier in the experiment than words that they have not been exposed to. Greenwald and Banaji (1995: 5) write that: 'This effect of prior exposure occurs despite subjects' poor ability to recall or recognise words from the earlier list.' In other words, even though the participants do not recognise certain words as being on a list that they had seen previously, these words have been 'primed' in their memory and come out more readily than words that had not been primed.

Similar to this is the experimental work he had already conducted on what he called 'detectionless processing', one of the main areas of implicit cognition, where stimuli of which people have little conscious awareness can be demonstrated to have an impact on behaviour. In detectionless processing, he demonstrated that words can be processed in terms of meaning, and therefore have an impact on our subsequent thoughts, even in situations where the words are presented below the threshold of conscious perception. What the participants in his study had to do was to decide whether each of a series of target words meant something good (e.g. fame, comedy, rescue) or bad (stress, detest, malaria). One half second before each of these target words were presented, a priming word was presented briefly to the non-dominant eye. The priming words themselves were either good (happy, joy, peace, love, excellent, pleasant) or bad (evil, grief, sad, gloom, ugly, horrid). The priming word was followed a matter of milliseconds later by a pattern mask (a complex visual stimulus) which interferes with the perception of the word that precedes it such that participants were unable to report what position the priming words were on a computer screen (i.e. whether they were to the left or right of a fixation point). So even though the participants seemed to have little conscious information about the priming words and did not know even where these words had been presented, these 'invisible' words affected processing of the subsequent target words, such that target words that were preceded by a congruent prime (for example, a positive target word preceded by a positive prime, or a negative target word preceded by a negative prime) were identified significantly more quickly than target words that were preceded by an incongruent prime (see Greenwald, Klinger and Liu 1989). In other words 'invisible' words (with extremely brief presentations followed by a pattern mask) can influence the workings of the human mind. Suddenly, the unconscious was back in vogue.

Sometimes priming can have very practical (and important domestic) consequences (Beattie 2011a). There seems to be evidence that if you want someone to clean up around the house then one way to do this is to ensure that they are primed with a vague hint of citrus (Holland, Hendriks and Aarts 2005). The smell should not be too strong and not too obvious; this slight smell, it seems, can unconsciously influence someone's thoughts, plans and actions. It will make them think more readily of cleaning products. If asked what they are going to do in the day, they are more likely to think of cleaning as one of their activities and if left alone, they will be more likely to clean up after themselves. What this smell does is to bring certain associations to mind to guide their behaviour in certain directions. Holland *et al.* cite the classic research by Bargh, Chen and Burrows (1996) who gave people a list of five words out of which they had to make a grammatical four word sentence in a 'scrambled sentence test'. There were lists of words such as –

1 Shoes gave replace old the.
2 Sky the seamless grey is.
3 Should now withdraw forgetful we.
4 Us bingo sing play let.
5 Sunlight makes temperature wrinkle raisins.

So the experimental participants might end up with:

1b. Replace the old shoes.
2b. The sky is grey.
3b. We should now withdraw.
4b. Let us play bingo.
5b. Sunlight makes raisins wrinkle.

In their study, Bargh *et al.* effectively primed their participants with words associated with being elderly, embedded in each of the original lists:

'old'
'grey'
'forgetful'
'bingo'
'wrinkle'.

The participants thought they were just doing a language task but what Bargh was actually doing was unconsciously priming them to think about being old. The researchers then asked participants to walk down a hallway by the laboratory and somewhat incredibly they found that those people who had been primed in this way, walked more slowly as a consequence than those who had not been primed.

The question that Holland and his colleagues then asked was 'Can we cue people unconsciously to clean using a similar priming technique?' They tested their idea with a number of experiments. In the first experiment, they used a lexical decision task where people have to decide whether a string of letters on a computer screen is a real word or not. Participants have to press a 'yes' or a 'no' key and the researchers measure the time in milliseconds to press the key. The researchers looked at the effect of a slight hint of citrus (the smell of a cleaning product) in the experimental cubicle on this lexical decision task, in which the participants had to decide whether a string of letters was a real cleaning-related word or not. The participants were also asked what they thought the study was about and whether they noticed any particular smell in the cubicle (and if so, what the scent was).

They found that participants in the 'citrus smell' condition responded faster to the cleaning related words than the participants in the control condition (with a mean latency of about 590 milliseconds in the smell condition compared to 620 milliseconds in the control condition for the cleaning related words). The latency to identify the non-cleaning related words was the same in the two conditions.

This significant difference occurred without them consciously being aware of the smell of the scent. In a second study, again participants entered either a cubicle smelling slightly of citrus or a control cubicle which did not. This time they were merely asked to write about what they were planning to do that day. Again, extraordinarily, when they did this in the cubicle which smelt slightly of citrus, they were more likely to list a cleaning activity as one of their planned activities. Indeed, they were three times more likely to mention cleaning as part of that day's plans than when they were in the control cubicle.

So it looks as if the merest hint of citrus affects our thinking and our plans, but does it influence our actual behaviour? The researchers tested this in a third experiment. They brought their participants into the cubicle as before and then they were taken into a separate room where they sat at a table and were given a crumbly biscuit to eat. A hidden video camera recorded their every movement. What the researchers found was that when the participants had been exposed to the smell of the cleaning fluid, they were more likely to sweep up the crumbs that fell onto the table than when they had not been exposed to the smell. In other words, exposing someone to the slight smell of a cleaning product affects the accessibility of their thoughts, their action plans and also their actual behaviour, and all of this seems to happen without any conscious awareness of the citrus smell. This is priming at work. Kahneman (2011: 53) describes the implications of this in the following strong language: 'priming is not restricted to concepts and words. You cannot know this from conscious experience, of course, but you must accept the alien idea that your actions and emotions can be primed by events of which you are not even aware.'

But let's return to Greenwald. The article that Greenwald wrote with Mahzarin Banaji in 1995 is in many senses of the word a classic paper. It has been cited by social scientists over 1,200 times. The thesis of the paper articulated Greenwald's view of the unconscious in determining our behaviour. It successfully links the growing body of research on implicit cognition with the research on attitudes and behaviour. It argued that:

> Recent work has established that attitudes are activated
> outside of conscious attention, by showing both that
> activation occurs more rapidly than can be mediated by
> conscious activity . . . and that activation is initiated by
> (subliminal) stimuli, the presence of which is unreportable.
> (Greenwald and Banaji 1995: 5)

Greenwald was keen to demonstrate the role of implicit processes in a whole series of domains. He employed the 'false-fame procedure' in an attempt to find experimental evidence for implicit stereotyping, including sex-role stereotyping which associates gender with achievement. The method is simple yet it produces highly significant results. It was based on a procedure used by Kelley and his colleagues (Jacoby, Kelley, Brown and Jasechko 1989) to uncover implicit memory. In the Kelley studies, participants would read a list of both famous and non-famous names on day 1. The next day the same participants were presented with previously seen non-famous names from the first list or new non-famous names that they had not seen before mixed in with previously seen and new famous names. The question that they were asked was 'Is this person famous?' The researchers hypothesised that although the non-famous names should fade from memory over the 24-hour period (from day 1 to day 2), the fact that they have seen some of the non-famous names before on the first list might lead them to the conclusion that some of these names were actually famous. And that is exactly what they found; there was a higher false-alarm rate for the previously seen non-famous names than for the new ones. Some non-famous names had quite literally 'become famous overnight' all because of the extra exposure and the resulting familiarity. This was a demonstration of a significant unconscious influence on memory.

What Greenwald and Banaji did next was to introduce gender into this simple paradigm. They asked what happens if you use a set of male and female names here and consider gender as a principal variable. They found that the false-alarm rate for (previously seen) non-famous names was significantly greater for male than for female names. In other words, the participants were more likely to assume that the male names

were famous (because of the familiarity due to repeated exposure) when they were not actually famous, compared with
female names. So, the authors concluded that this was clear
evidence for implicit gender stereotyping in everyday life
where maleness is associated with achievement.

In their summing up in this article, they concluded that:

> considerable evidence now supports the view that social
> behaviour often operates in an implicit or unconscious
> fashion. The identifying feature of implicit cognition is
> that past experience influences judgment in a fashion
> not introspectively known by the actor. The present
> conclusion – that attitudes, self-esteem, and stereotypes
> have important implicit modes of operation – extends
> both the construct validity and predictive usefulness of
> these major theoretical constructs of social psychology.
> Methodologically, this review calls for increased use of
> indirect measures – which are imperative in studies of
> social cognition. (Greenwald and Banaji 1995: 4)

In other words, this review article was arguing for a
major reconceptualisation of how we should view both attitudes and social behaviour more generally. And then, of
course, if we accept the argument about the role of implicit
or unconscious factors in controlling both our attitudes and
our behaviour then we must accept that we will need a new
methodology for studying some of these processes. A new
methodology which does not involve self-report and which is
sufficiently sensitive to detect some of the very rapid
processes involved. The development of a new methodology
was crucial here because Greenwald recognised that some of
what he was saying had been said before.

> Implicit social cognition overlaps with several concepts
> that were significant in works of previous generations of
> psychologists. Psychoanalytic theory's concept of cathexis
> contained some of the sense of implicit attitude, and its
> concept of ego defence similarly captured at least part of
> the present notion of implicit self-esteem . . . At a time
> when the influence of psychoanalytic theory in academic

psychology was declining, its conceptions of unconscious phenomena that related to implicit social cognition were being imported into behaviour theory (Dollard and Miller 1950; Doob 1947; Osgood 1957). The New Look in Perception of the 1950s focused on several phenomena that are interpretable as implicit social cognition. The developing Cognitive approach to these phenomena can be seen in Bruner's (1957) introduction to the concept of perceptual readiness. (Greenwald and Banaji 1995: 20)

But the punch line came next.

Importantly, the psychoanalytic, behaviourist, and cognitive treatments just mentioned all lacked an essential ingredient, that is, they lacked reliable laboratory models of their focal phenomena that could support efficient testing and development of theory. The missing ingredient is now available . . . (ibid.)

- Social scientists (who are usually regarded as being relatively free of prejudice) display ethnic prejudice in their pattern of citations, being more likely to cite authors from the same ethnic background as themselves.
- Implicit cognition, where traces of past experience affect behaviour, even though the influential earlier experience is not remembered, is easily demonstrated.
- In the 1990s, the unconscious came back into vogue; the research on implicit cognition gave us a new way of thinking about the concept of attitude.
- It is now not quite so embarrassing for social scientists to say that social behaviour often operates in an implicit or unconscious fashion.
- You can make someone more willing to clean a house by making sure that there is a vague hint of cleaning fluid in the background, where the smell is *not* consciously noticed.

11

By-passing the conscious mind

The missing ingredient was introduced in 1998 in an article published in the *Journal of Personality and Social Psychology*, which Anthony Greenwald co-authored with Debbie McGhee and Jordan Schwartz. The basic premise behind the Implicit Association Test (IAT) is that when categorising items into two sets of paired concepts, if the paired concepts are strongly associated, then participants should be able to categorise items faster into these category concepts. Greenwald introduced the new method with a thought experiment. Imagine being shown a series of male and female faces and having to respond rapidly by saying 'hello' to the male face and 'goodbye' to the female face. Then you are shown a series of names and this time you say 'hello' to the male name and 'goodbye' to the female name. Greenwald *et al.* (1998) reported:

> In that experiment subjects gave a response on a computer keyboard with the index finger of the right hand to words that named pleasant things and to names of flowers. With the left hand they were to respond to another two categories – words that named unpleasant things and insect names. This was a very easy task. Then we made one minor change: We switched hands for the flower and insect names. Now subjects had to give the same response to pleasant words and insect names and a different response to unpleasant words and flower names. Immediately the task became hugely difficult. The slowing on a response-by-response basis was on the order of 300

milliseconds, which was a magnitude of impact nobody could have expected. We certainly did not expect it. I was the first subject in the experiment. When I experienced the slowing I found to my surprise that I could not overcome it – repeating the task did not make me faster. If I tried to go faster, I just started making errors when I was trying to give the same response to flower names and unpleasant words. This was a mind-opener.

The very first paper reporting the IAT provided psychologists with a much sought after method to measure unconscious, implicit attitudes; but perhaps even more than that, it uncovered something that was extremely unsettling for Greenwald and colleagues, and no doubt for anyone who read the paper. In today's society, many people (who have not read this book) like to think that race is no longer a significant issue. America has, after all, now got its first Black president (although several years in, his popularity seems to be fading fast, as does the American electorate's view of his religion and background. Obama has had to publicly discuss his mother's Christian but non-practising background for the first time because more and more of the American people believe that he is a Muslim by birth). But surely the times of racial prejudice and stereotype are far behind us all in the West? The IAT revealed that this is not necessarily the case. It revealed that people were consistently faster at categorising Black and White names and pleasant and unpleasant words when the target categories were grouped 'White'/'pleasant' and 'Black'/'unpleasant' than when they were grouped 'White'/'unpleasant' and 'Black'/'pleasant', suggesting that the former concepts are more strongly associated than the second set of concepts. When compared to explicit measures, the majority of White college students who took part in the study reported that they had no racial preference between White and Black, with some even saying they had a preference for Black. However, the IAT revealed that only one of these students showed a preference for Black, consistent with their stated explicit attitudes. The remaining participants all showed a White preference, suggesting that the concept 'White' had positive associations, whereas 'Black' had negative associations. As such, Greenwald argued that the IAT was able to successfully reveal underlying implicit attitudes.

In the first web-based experiment of its kind, Project Implicit measured implicit attitudes towards a range of social groups, including an implicit measure of racial attitudes. The project collated 600,000 tests between October 1998 and December 2000, allowing for replication of the race IAT on an enormous scale using both White and Black participants, again with surprising results. It found that White participants tended to explicitly endorse a preference for the concept White but implicitly they demonstrated an even stronger preference for White names and faces. Black participants, on the other hand, demonstrated a strong explicit preference for the concept Black yet, remarkably, in the IAT, Black participants demonstrated a weak implicit preference for White names and faces.

You can try this test for yourself by going to: www.projectimplicit.com

According to Nosek, Banaji and Greenwald (2002), who provided this overview of the IAT results, the preference shown for White by both White and Black participants is indicative of the American culture in which Black Americans are still often depicted in a negative light. The result is that these negative associations have penetrated into underlying racial attitudes and stereotypes, leading to the creation of automatic evaluations which show an implicit preference for White over Black people. For people who show strong explicit endorsement of racial indifference, the prospect that they may implicitly hold the very attitudes they strongly condemn can be a worrying thought (see also Gladwell 2005). As Fyodor Dostoevsky wrote in his *Notes from the Underground* (1864/1972: 55):

Every man has some reminiscences which he would not tell to everyone, but only to his friends. He has others which he would not reveal even to his friends, but only to himself, and that in secret. But finally there are still others which a man is even afraid to tell himself, and every decent man has a considerable number of such things stored away. That is, one can say that the more decent he is, the greater the number of such things in his mind.

This implicit bias has been found in other cultures against other minority groups. Thus, in Germany the proportion of German students who take longer to associate Turk with 'good' than German with 'good' is in the region of 75 per cent (Fiedler and Bluemke 2005), suggesting in the words of the authors 'almost consensual implicit prejudice', although as Fiedler, Messner and Bluemke (2006: 78) point out 'the vast majority from this population would verbally assert themselves not to be prejudiced at all, and many of them would actually be in contact with Turkish friends'. Other research has shown that White Americans have negative implicit attitudes towards Latinos (Uhlmann, Dasgupta, Elgueta *et al.* 2002) and towards Asians (Son Hing, Li and Zanna 2002).

However, the research has also suggested that implicit attitudes can be changed. In 2001, Dasgupta and Greenwald found that by exposing participants to pictures of a range of admired Black Americans, such as Martin Luther King, and disliked White Americans, such as Al Capone, the pro-White effect usually found in the race IAT was substantially reduced, immediately after and even 24 hours after the initial exposure (although 24 hours is not that long in the grand scale of things). Whilst this was only a temporary modification, there is the possibility that being consistently exposed to exemplars of admired Black people (particularly in the media) could lead to more permanent changes in underlying implicit attitudes.

At present there are something like 15 versions of the IAT online at Project Implicit, as shown in Table 11.1:

Table 11.1 Versions of the IAT online at Project Implicit

Ethnicity		Social
Race IAT	Age IAT	Gender–Science IAT
Asian IAT	Religion IAT	Gender–Career IAT
Arab–Muslim IAT	Sexuality IAT	Obama–McCain IAT
Skin-tone IAT	Weight IAT	Presidents IAT
Native IAT	Disability IAT	Weapons IAT

For a measure of unconscious processing, engaging on the IAT is an oddly self-conscious process. I am strangely anxious every time I do it, maybe because I think that this may reveal the uncomfortable truth about me. It is a quick test, almost too quick and the computerised IAT flashes the results up at you without embarrassment or pause after the completion of each test. You sit nervously by the screen prepared to view your own prejudices and biases, secretly hoping that none will be revealed. Or at worst, hoping to see just a slight prejudice in your reaction times and error rates, and the expression 'Your data suggest a moderate preference for X over Y'. I sat all of the tests that I thought might help produce a reasonable psychological profile for myself, one after the other like a set of challenges (as shown in Table 11.2).

It turns out that I either had no preference or a whole series of moderate preferences, except when it came to weight where I had a strong preference for thin people compared to fat people. Is this plausible? Can I find any evidence from my own life that the implicit attitudes revealed by this test do have any substantive or actual behavioural implications? I think that the answer with respect to my one strong prejudice is probably yes. However, the behaviour is not to do with actual discrimination against fat people but

Table 11.2 **My personal IAT results**

	Preference
Race IAT	Your data suggests a moderate automatic preference for European American over African American
Skin-tone IAT	Your data suggests a moderate automatic preference for light skin over dark skin
Weight IAT	Your data suggests a strong automatic preference for thin people compared to fat people
Sexuality IAT	Your data suggests a moderate automatic preference for straight compared to gay people
Age IAT	Your data suggests no automatic preference for Young compared to Old

behaviour directed against myself, and not dieting but something else. I have always been a compulsive runner, and compulsive here means compulsive, every day without fail, in any country no matter how inconvenient or difficult – through the centre of Tokyo at 5.00 am because the flight back to the UK was to leave early, along a motorway in Sweden in the middle of the night in a snowstorm without a clue as to which direction led back to the centre of Gothenburg, along the Pacific Coast Highway in California, just off the plane and suffering from jet lag, with no pavement for protection and with wide gaudy red and yellow trucks almost brushing my legs. I was a child with a chubby face, never fat, but I am sure that strangers might have thought that I was fat because of my face ('you had a face like the moon when you were a baby', my mother used to say proudly 'like the moon', and she would smile broadly whenever she said, as if the memory made her happy) and I like the way that running makes my face look lean. I refuse to go on television unless I have a run first (many television producers will vouch in frustration for this fact). But my one compulsion runs deeper than mere misplaced vanity; more rooted I am sure in my unconscious mind. This compulsion started when I was at school. I would run every day and twice on a Tuesday and a Thursday (and there may have been other reasons for running every lunchtime at school, as I alluded to earlier). I started when I was 13. A lot happened that year – I broke my arm doing judo, which meant that many sports were for a long while out of bounds and my father died unexpectedly of some heart-related condition. I never understood what he died of, it was never properly explained to me as a child; I am not sure that my mother properly understood what had happened anyway, except that it happened during an operation. I suppose that this made the fear more intense, the fear of life being interrupted in a sudden and unexpected way. I might have a similar congenital weakness, so I decided to get fit, and run and run to make my heart stronger and stronger. I never stopped. Running, we all know, can be very addictive.

But I have another image from that one life-changing year, as well. An image that has never faded or been diminished by time, an image that has been silent and never discussed until it was written down. An image, nevertheless, that has haunted me.

On the night of my father's funeral, after we had laid him to rest in Roselawn Cemetery with the wind lifting the dirty green carpet used to cover the wet clay grave, we were in my aunt's house for the sandwiches and tea because our own house (a two up two down in north Belfast) wasn't big enough. Everyone was there, drinking quietly, the quiet, subdued sobbing made worse by the image of the coffin juddering down into its final position, everyone except my cousin Myrna, that is, who inexplicably had gone to work that day. Nobody had explained why. Life at the time seemed to be full of things that were never properly explained, at least to a 13-year-old boy. My cousin walked in right in the middle of the wake. She seemed to cling to the doorframe, not entering just standing there, staring at us all, and I can picture her now, an image etched on my mind forever, an emaciated grey ghost, already dead in the eyes and the mouth. I had heard, overheard, that she had got some kind of eating disorder, anorexia nervosa, 'slimmer's disease', my mother called it, but I hadn't seen her for months, as the slimmer's disease took hold. She avoided seeing relatives. But there she stood in the silence and the sadness, and everyone looked at her and nobody said a thing, as if she looked normal and healthy and was just late for the funeral. I think she walked slowly past us all into the kitchen to stand alone, the place where food is prepared and eaten, but not for her.

She died a couple of weeks later of pneumonia and was buried in the row opposite my father, which is handy from the point of view of people bringing flowers to either grave. Her mother, my Aunt May, a sweet, lovely woman with a giggly, girly voice, always said that what triggered the anorexia was a chance remark from a doctor at work during a routine medical examination, a remark that she was a little over-weight. From that day on, my aunt always said, she never ate properly again.

It sounds almost ridiculous that such a life-threatening disorder could be triggered in this way but years later I supervised a postgraduate student who analysed the social construction of anorexia in the families of sufferers and it was extraordinary the number of interviewees who pointed to a similar 'chance remark' as the cause of the whole thing. Anorexia is a complex disorder with cultural, personality and biological factors all implicated in its ontogenesis but human being like to identify a single cause that they can pick out and say 'if only that hadn't happened . . .' This single cause is usually something fairly random (so that any random family could potentially be affected) and external to the family itself (so that no blame could be attached to the family itself). The PE teacher who commented that Tracy was too fat to be any good at games, the boyfriend who said that Jane's bum was too big for her skinny jeans, the doctor who quipped that his patient could do with losing a little weight. It was always things like that. It reminded me of what Friedrich Nietzsche (1871/1962: 62) wrote,

> To trace something unknown back to something known is alleviating, soothing, gratifying, and gives us moreover a feeling of power. Danger, disquiet, anxiety attend the unknown, and the first instinct is to eliminate these distressing states. First principle: any explanation is better than none.

My family, and many other families, had found an explanation, one which stressed the power of the word, of the chance remark (and I suppose by implication, the dangerous power of the carelessness of those in authority). Nobody ever disputed my aunt's account, and it became the true version of what had become of my beautiful cousin, and I sometimes think that in that awful year of my life my weight prejudices were probably laid down forever.

Of course, this story may tell you why weight is an important issue for me but why have I ended up with an anti-fat prejudice, why not an anti-thin prejudice? After all, it was not the fact that Myrna was a few pounds overweight (maybe more, maybe less) that killed her. Well maybe it was the implicit message in the story. The implicit message being that if you are overweight then you can be killed by a chance remark, the unconscious message being that being fat makes you too sensitive to others' insensitivity, the unconscious theme being that being fat means that others can control your life, and even your death. My compulsive running may just reflect my unconscious desires to escape from my father's destiny, but it may also reflect this deep-seated desire to put myself out of harm's way from chance remarks (and thereby make myself less vulnerable in life). It may be core to my psychological make-up and mean that I have an implicit and unconscious bias against fat people, who have not made the effort to shield themselves in this way. Of course, the fact that my implicit attitude actually does connect to some core behaviours in my everyday life, namely my determination to run, is very encouraging from the point of view of my current academic concerns. It is also, of course, more than a little depressing for me.

The big question is whether the IAT gives us more insight than the measures of explicit attitudes? The beauty of the IAT is that because it measures automatically activated associations it is resistant (some have argued 'immune') to faking (see Greenwald, Poehlman, Uhlmann and Banaji, 2009). Would it, therefore, help us to understand and predict actual behaviour more effectively? The focus on behavioural prediction was, of course, inevitable from the inception of the IAT and 'plagued' the IAT very early on (in the eyes and words of some of the core researchers). Banaji (2001: 132) commented that 'tolerance' was needed if this question is to be answered, 'Pushing fast and furiously to "show me what predicts" may be counterproductive. One first needs to understand the construct before asking what it may or may not predict.'

Greenwald *et al.* (2009) conducted a meta-analysis on the predictive validity of the IAT and concluded that, in general, when the IAT and explicit attitude measures are combined, they are together better predictors of behaviour than either measure alone. However, when attitudes are 'socially sensitive', and where social desirability concerns are inevitably present (as in attitudes to race, age, gender or the environment) then explicit measures are very poor predictors of behaviour and in these situations the IAT would appear to be a much better predictor of behaviour than explicit measures. From the meta-analysis conducted by Greenwald *et al.* (2009), the overall conclusion would seem to be that the IAT does significantly predict behaviour (although the actual level of prediction can be modest at times). But as Gregg (2008: 765) has commented: 'the behaviours documented are often quite specific, so it is striking that general implicit associations predict them at all. Moreover, the IAT outstrips self-report in forecasting instances of discrimination and prejudice. Hence, it offers some genuine diagnostic advantages.'

To probe attitudes to people from different ethnic backgrounds I needed to devise a new more robust IAT. The reason was that on a PC it allows much more accurate and controlled measurement than the on-line versions, which form part of Project Implicit. And the problem with the on-line versions is that you do not know who is filling them in or under what conditions. There is, of course, nothing like hands-on experience to allow you to see the complexities and the issues associated with any phenomenon, so I approached the next phase of my work with more than a little anxiety. Was it going to reveal our racist heart or something about how difficult it is to expose our most innermost feelings? Was my new robust test even going to reveal that I myself was something of a racist, despite all of my protestations?

> - I have one strong implicit bias and that is to do with weight.
> - This seems to have a pervasive influence over my own life; indeed it may direct a lot of how I spend my free time.
> - This latter point, however, could be nothing more than a post-hoc rationalisation.

PART III

The project itself: are we implicitly racist?

12

A new test of implicit ethnic bias

I started with a measure of explicit attitudes, as Allport would have liked, to provide a measure of conscious predisposition. In order to assess the explicit attitudes towards people from different ethnic backgrounds my team and I developed two separate measures. One was a computerised Likert Scale and the second was what is called a 'Feeling Thermometer' to assess explicit 'feelings' towards White and non-White (or Minority Ethnic) people. The Likert Scale (see Figure 12.1) gives a very simple measure of explicit attitude. I could not help noticing that the scale that we finally agreed on had that very odd lexicon of 'White' and 'non-White'; it almost sounded discriminatory to begin with, as if it defined the whole diversity of mankind (and womankind) with the label of not being something, but my team argued strongly that this was the way to start and that people who are from ethnically diverse backgrounds are often seen as being 'non-White', from a White European point of view. If 'non-White' does hint at a vague and slightly sinister residual category then presumably this should be picked up in the self-report attitudes.

We also used a 'Feeling Thermometer' (see Figure 12.2), which asked people to rate how warm or cold they felt towards White and non-White people. From the two ratings on the Feeling Thermometer a Thermometer Difference (TD) score can be calculated, so for example, someone with a very positive feeling towards White people might tick '5' meaning 'very warm' to White people and '1' meaning 'very cold' to non-White people, which would

Please pick the statement you agree with by pressing the
corresponding number on the computer keyboard:

1. I strongly prefer non-White people to White people
2. I moderately prefer non-White people to White people
3. I like non-White people and White people equally
4. I moderately prefer White people to non-White people
5. I strongly prefer White people to non-White people

Figure 12.1 **A computerised version of the Likert Scale for measuring explicit attitudes towards White and non-White people.**

Please rate how cold or warm you feel towards non-White people by pressing the corresponding number on the computer keyboard:	Please rate how cold or warm you feel towards White people by pressing the corresponding number on the computer keyboard:
1 = very cold, 2 = cold, 3 = neutral, 4 = warm, 5 = very warm	1 = very cold, 2 = cold, 3 = neutral, 4 = warm, 5 = very warm
1 2 3 4 5	1 2 3 4 5

Figure 12.2 **A computerised version of the Feeling Thermometer for measuring explicit attitudes towards White and non-White people.**

yield a TD score of + 4. On the other hand, someone who had a very positive feeling towards non-White people might tick '5' meaning 'very warm' towards non-White people and '1' for White people, thus producing a TD score of – 4.

Implicit Association Test

Next we created our own new 'ethnic' Implicit Association Test (IAT), which would be used to probe implicit attitudes towards White and non-White people by comparing the categories of White and non-White and the attributes 'good' and 'bad'. 'Non-White' here would cover people from quite different racial or ethnic backgrounds including African Caribbean, African, Pakistani, Chinese and Middle Eastern. To get an idea of how the IAT works, you might like to try the following example, just focusing on the critical trials. All you have to do is put the pictures and words that appear down the middle of the page (see Figure 12.3) into the categories that appear on the left hand side ('White or Good') or the right hand side of the page ('Non-White or Bad') as quickly as you can. The theoretical assumption is that the more closely the concepts 'White' and 'good' are associated in the mind the easier it is to assign any pictures or words to that pair of categories. On the other hand, if the concepts 'White' and 'Bad' are more closely associated in the mind then the easier it should be to assign pictures or words to that paired category (see Figure 12.4). In the real test, items are assigned to the categories (or paired categories) on the left by pressing a key to the left of the keyboard ('Z'), or to the categories on the right by pressing a key to the right of the keyboard ('M'). However, for the examples included here you can just tap either the left-hand side of the page or the right-hand side of the page. As in the experiment itself, you must try to do this as quickly as you can, without making mistakes. For example, the first item 'Awful' fits into the category on the right-hand side of the page 'Non-White or Bad' because the word 'Awful' clearly represents the concept 'Bad', so tap the right-hand side of the page. The underlying psychological reasoning here is that if you unconsciously hold negative associations towards non-White people then this assignment should be relatively easy. The second item, a photograph of a young white female goes in the category 'White' so here you should tap the left-hand side of the page ('White or Good'). If you unconsciously hold positive associations towards White people then this assignment should be relatively easy. The

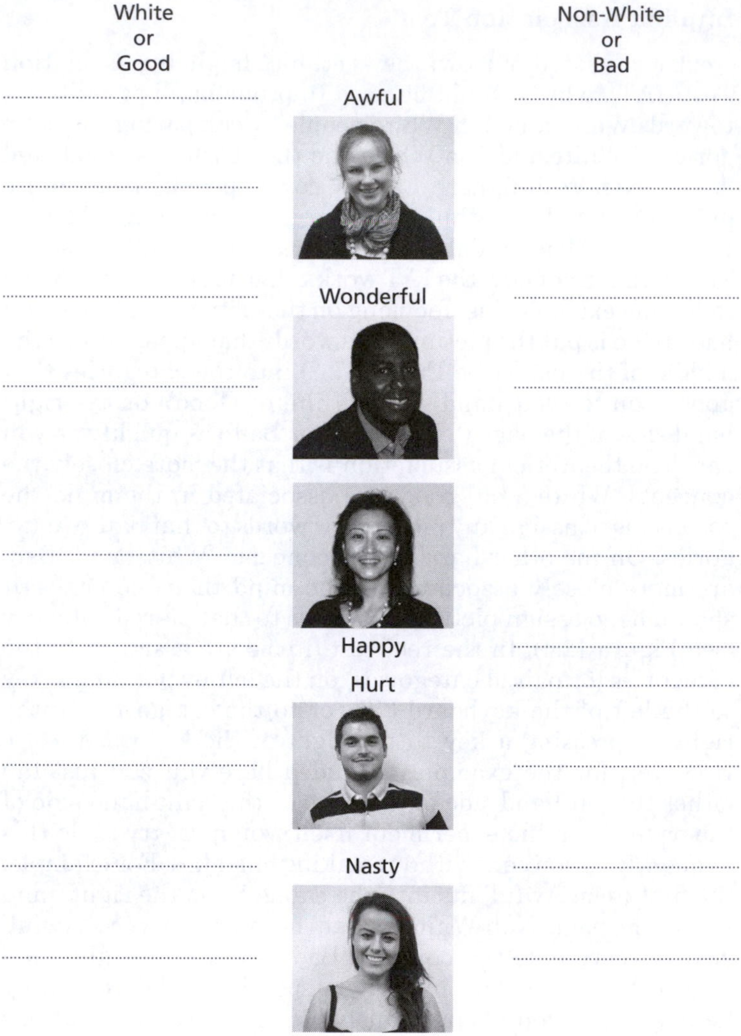

Figure 12.3 Sample IAT procedure.

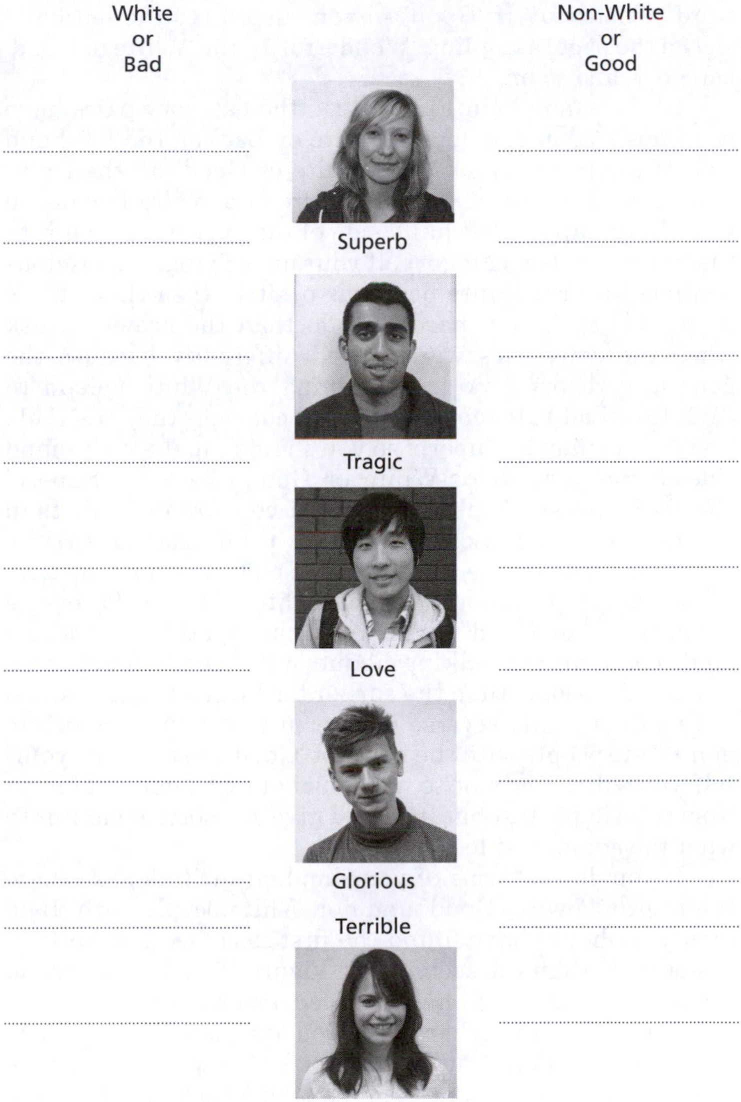

White
or
Bad

Non-White
or
Good

Superb

Tragic

Love

Glorious

Terrible

Figure 12.4 **Sample IAT procedure: reversed associations.**

word 'Wonderful' is 'Good' so you should tap the left-hand side of the page, assigning 'Wonderful' to the 'White or Good' category, and so on.

In the example in Figure 12.4, the category pairs have been reversed and we have 'White or Bad' on the left-hand side of the page versus 'Non-White or Good' on the right-hand side. The first item is a picture of a White female, so you should tap the left-hand side of the page assigning it to the 'White or Bad' category. If your underlying unconscious attitude towards White people is positive then this will be (relatively speaking) harder to do than the previous task when the categories were paired differently because the generic category you are assigning the White person to ('White or Bad') also covers words or concepts that are 'Bad'. The second item is 'Superb' so you should tap the right-hand side of the page ('Non-White or Good') because 'Superb' clearly is 'Good'. Again this should be more difficult than before if you unconsciously do not think that non-White people are 'Good'. The third item is a picture of a young non-White male so you should tap the right-hand side of the page ('Non-White or Good'), which will be relatively speaking (and again we are talking about milliseconds here) more difficult for people than the earlier task when the categories were paired in the reverse manner if they do not associate non-White people with the concept 'Good'. So try it for yourself; you will not be able to work out your own implicit biases from this simple test but it should give you some insight into what the actual test feels like.

If you do (in terms of your implicit attitude) associate White people with 'Good' and non-White people with 'Bad' then you should have found the first task (see Figure 12.3) easier to do than the second (see Figure 12.4). In the second example, you may well have noticed a slowing in your reaction time. If, on the other hand, you associate White people with 'Bad' and non-White with 'Good' then you should have been faster when categorising items in Figure 12.4 than the items in Figure 12.3.

Table 12.1 shows the blocks of trials used in the IAT (with the critical comparison trials outlined in bold).

The computerised versions of the seven trials are shown

Table 12.1 IAT practice trials and critical trials (critical trials in bold)

Block	Number of trials	Stimuli	Items assigned to left-key response (Z key)	Items assigned to right-key response (M key)
B1	20	Pictures	'White'	'Non-White'
B2	20	Words	'Good'	'Bad'
B3	20	Pictures and words	'Good or White'	'Bad or Non-White'
B4	**40**	**Pictures and words**	**'Good or White'**	**'Bad or Non-White'**
B5	40	Pictures	'Non-White'	'White'
B6	20	Pictures and words	'Good or Non-White'	'Bad or White'
B7	**40**	**Pictures and words**	**'Good or Non-White'**	**'Bad or White'**

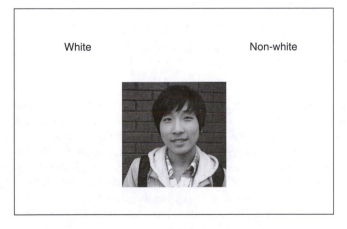

Figure 12.5 First trial (block B1): 'White' vs. 'Non-White'.

in Figures 12.5 to 12.9. They show what it looked like from the participants' point of view on the computer screen in our new IAT.

The D score (or Difference score) is the critical measure used in the IAT. This is a statistical measure which

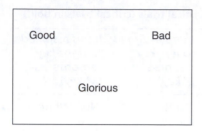

Figure 12.6 Second trial (block B2): 'Good' vs. 'Bad'.

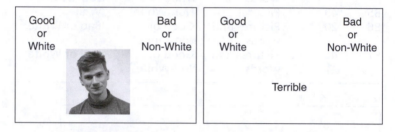

Figure 12.7 Third and fourth trials (blocks B3 and B4): 'Good or White' vs. 'Bad or Non-White'.

calculates both the difference in the latency, or time taken to respond, in the critical trials and the error rate. The main point to remember here is the more positive a person's D score, the more positive their implicit attitude to White people. Anything between 0 and either 0.2 or −0.2 indicates a more or less neutral implicit attitude towards the concepts of 'White' or 'non-White'; anything between 0.2 and 0.5 indicates a slight attitudinal preference towards 'White' and anything between −0.2 and −0.5 indicates a slight attitudinal preference towards 'non-White'; anything between 0.5 and 0.8 indicates a medium attitudinal preference towards 'White' and anything between −0.5 and −0.8 indicates a medium attitudinal preference towards 'non-White'. Anything greater than or equal to 0.8 indicates a strong implicit attitude towards 'White'; anything less than or equal to −0.8 indicates a strong implicit attitude towards 'non-White'. These values

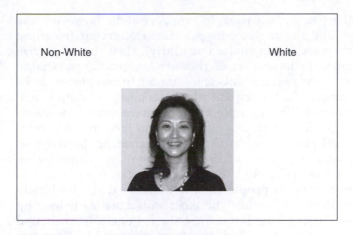

Figure 12.8 Fifth trial (block 5): 'Non-White' vs. 'White'.

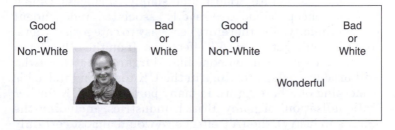

Figure 12.9 Sixth and seventh trials (blocks 6 and 7): 'Good or Non-White' vs. 'Bad or White'.

are assumed to be the key benchmarks across a whole series of domains in which the IAT has been applied.

The selection of the particular images for the IAT is extremely important. According to Bluemke and Friese (2005), the type of images selected can dramatically alter any possible IAT effect sizes. The research, after all, is based on the idea that that when the stimulus (e.g. a face) and target concept (e.g. 'Good' or 'Bad') are congruent (meaning that they are evaluated similarly), the effect size will generally be greater as they are more readily associated with one another and therefore are easier to categorise. If, however, the stimuli and the target concept are incongruent (meaning that they are not evaluated similarly), then the effect size will generally be smaller as they are less readily associated with one another, and therefore harder to categorise. Take the example of a participant who has a positive implicit attitude towards White people and a negative attitude towards Black people. Given this rationale you have to be careful about selecting images that may either be positive or negative, independent of the variable you are considering (in this case ethnicity). For example, if you were to use images of famous people then it is likely that (the highly iconic) Princess Diana, who most would see as belonging to the category 'Good' (because she is generally evaluated very positively), would yield a very strong IAT effect size (which indicates a stronger association between the concepts 'White'/'Good' and a weaker association between the concepts 'White'/'Bad'). Put simply, 'Princess Diana' and the concept 'Good' are readily associated, independent of her ethnicity, and therefore very easy to categorise, therefore we would get a big IAT effect size. If on the other hand you used an image of someone like Margaret Thatcher (who still produces mixed feelings in the UK today and indeed is something of a hate figure in many parts of the UK for her 'rationalisation' of many British industries, including the mining industry), the IAT effect size would almost certainly decrease (suggesting a weaker association between the concepts 'White'/'Good' and a stronger association with the concepts 'White'/'Bad') as 'Margaret Thatcher' and the concept 'Good' are much less readily associated (in many people's eyes; although in certain sections of the Home Counties, her natural political territory, it would, I am sure, be the exact opposite) and will therefore be harder to categorise. If a picture of Barack Obama was used in the IAT then the general tendency in the Race IAT to find a pro-White bias may be significantly reduced as Barack Obama is (or was before, and just after, the US Presidential Election, and after Osama Bin Laden's assassination) generally evaluated positively, so here we may find a weaker IAT effect (suggesting a weaker association between the concepts

'White'/'Good' and 'Black'/'Bad' and a stronger association with the concepts 'White'/'Bad' and 'Black'/'Good'). 'Barack Obama' and the concept 'Bad' are less readily associated and therefore harder to categorise. If a Black person such as O. J. Simpson were used instead then the pro-White bias would probably return (suggesting a stronger association between the concepts 'White'/'Good' and 'Black'/'Bad') as 'O. J. Simpson' and the concept 'Bad' are still fairly readily associated, in many people's minds. Many people do seem to think after all that a guilty man walked free.

The importance of the selection of the images was shown in a study by Govan and Williams (2004) who found that when they used famous Black people who were evaluated positively and famous White people who were evaluated negatively, the pro-White IAT effect was actually eliminated. This highlights both the importance of careful stimulus selection and the need to pre-test exemplars in some way to avoid influencing the magnitude of the IAT effect unintentionally one way or another; as Govan and Williams (ibid.: 364) concluded: 'If the goal of the research is to demonstrate the magnitude of an attitude, then the selection of stimulus items could be crucial.' For this reason, a great deal of care was taken in the selection of photographs used in the development of our new Ethnic IAT, as outlined below:

- A large corpus of photos were collected from the internet to include White people and a range of non-White or Black and Minority Ethnic people (African, African Caribbean, Pakistani, Chinese, Middle Eastern) representing a range of ages and including both males and females.
- A number of photos were then removed based on image quality, pose and facial expression.
- The remaining photos were then rated by a number of judges for attractiveness on a scale from 1 to 10, where 1 means extremely unattractive and 10 means extremely attractive.
- From these ratings only the photos that were judged to be in the middle range of the scale (with a mean rating between 3 and 7), and comparable in terms of attractiveness from

one ethnic group to another, were retained (the actual photos shown in this book are not those used in the experiment itself because of issues to do with permissions with photos sourced from the internet).

- The remaining photos were then divided into two groups of 10 White and 10 non-White people, ensuring that the photos included people from a range of ages and included an equal number of males and females.
- Finally, the overall ratings for the photos in the White and non-White condition were compared to ensure they were similar so that one group was not judged to be more attractive overall than the other.

A number of Race IATs such as those presented online at Project Implicit do not use full natural-looking profile photographs (see Figure 12.10); rather they use morphed photos or photos of only a section of the face. The morphed faces in the Weight IAT look unnatural in the extreme. The Skin Tone IAT uses drawings that have been shaded in to change skin tone. The Race IAT uses photos of real faces taken very close to the face. The faces are unsmiling and they look threatening. It is also very difficult to determine the gender of the person featured. Using actual photos of people rather than, say, names or morphed faces would seem to hold greater ecological validity and be of more general applicability to everyday life (particularly compared to morphed faces, as there does often seem to be something inherently strange about them), and it makes intuitive sense for the stimuli used in the IAT to represent the kinds of faces/images that we are used to seeing.

These were some of the considerations that formed the basis for our new 'Ethnic' IAT. We ran this IAT on a sample of 130 participants, including staff from a major British university, researchers, university and college students and members of the public more generally. We also took measures of explicit attitude (from the Likert Scale and the Feeling Thermometer) to compare with measures of implicit attitude (the 'D' score). So the question is: how did these self-report and implicit measures compare? And was there any evidence whatsoever of an implicit ethnic bias?

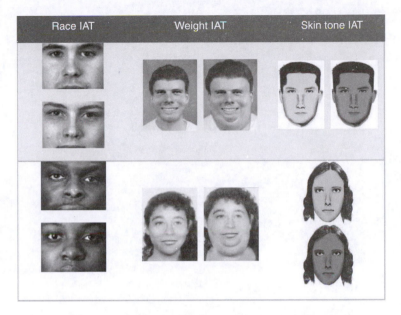

Figure 12.10 **Examples of stimuli sets used in Project Implicit.**

- The selection of the images for the Implicit Association Test (IAT) is crucial when you are trying to measure implicit attitudes.
- The Race IAT on Project Implicit has used rather odd-looking images.
- Our new Ethnic IAT uses images of people from different ethnic backgrounds in the 'non-White' category.
- This was done for good reasons.

13

New data on possible implicit ethnic biases

The mean explicit and implicit attitude scores are shown in Table 13.1. The mean Likert score from our new study was 3.18 (which indicates more or less a neutral explicit attitude; '3' remember translates as 'I like non-White and White people equally'), the mean Thermometer Difference (TD) score was 0.31 (which again indicates more or less a neutral explicit attitude towards ethnicity), but critically the mean Difference (D) score (from the Implicit Association Test; IAT) was 0.74 (technically this is a moderate pro-White implicit attitude, but approaching the normal cut-off of 0.8, which would translate as a strong implicit attitude towards Whites).

The actual distribution of explicit and implicit attitude measures is displayed in Figures 13.1 to 13.4. It should be immediately apparent that in the self-report measures (Figures 13.1 and 13.2), the vast majority of participants are right in the middle of the scale; they report essentially a neutral attitude, both in terms of preference for (Likert

Table 13.1 **Mean explicit and implicit attitude scores**

	Mean	*SD*
Likert score	3.18	0.54
TD score	0.31	0.78
D score	0.74	0.90

D = IAT Difference; SD = Standard Deviation; TD = Thermometer Difference

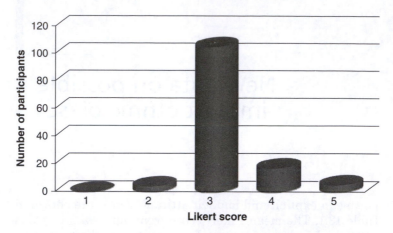

Figure 13.1 Distribution of Likert scores towards White and non-White targets.

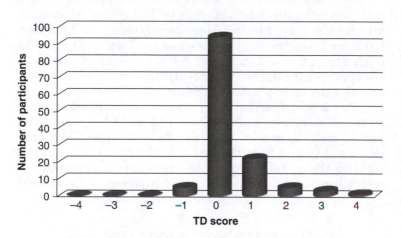

Figure 13.2 Distribution of Thermometer Difference (TD) scores towards White and non-White targets.

score) or feelings about (Thermometer Difference score; TD) White and non-White people.

The distribution of the D scores from the IAT, however, looks very different (see Figures 13.3 and 13.4). You can see quite clearly from the distribution of D scores that there is a

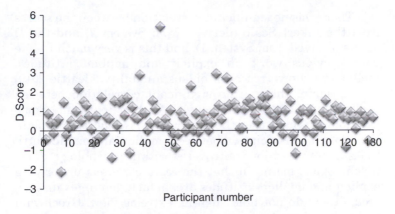

Figure 13.3 **Distribution of Difference (D) scores from the IAT.**

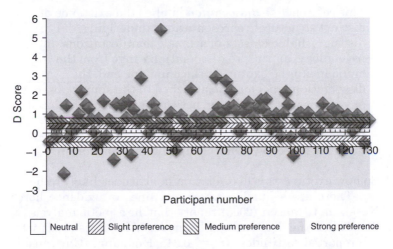

☐ Neutral   ▨ Slight preference   ▨ Medium preference   ▨ Strong preference

Figure 13.4 **Distribution of Difference (D) scores in relation to D score effect sizes.**

large set of D scores above the 0.8 mark indicating a strong preference for Whites (and a small set of isolated individuals with a strong preference for non-Whites). There are relatively few D scores in the neutral band (−0.2 to 0.2). In other words, the results from the IAT seem very different to the results that come from the self-report measures.

There was no significant correlation between the scores from the Likert Scale (derived from System 2) and the D scores (derived from System 1), and this is very much in line with previous work on explicit and implicit attitudes, including my own research on sustainability (Beattie 2010) where, again, there is no significant correlation between explicit and implicit attitudes to carbon footprint. Some psychologists have used the concept of *dissociation* to explain this. Possible dissociation between implicit and explicit attitudes is now a major controversy within psychology. Some psychologists maintain that the *representations* underlying explicit and implicit attitudes are, in fact, genuinely dissociated, others do not hold such an extreme view. Greenwald and Nosek (2008: 65) discuss this in the following terms;

> This reference to *dissociation* implies the existence of distinct structural representations underlying distinguishable classes of attitude manifestations. In psychology, appeals to dissociation range from the mundane to the exotic. At the mundane end, the dissociation label may be attached to the simple absence or weakness of correlation between presumably related measures. At the exotic end, dissociation may be understood as a split in consciousness, such as mutually unaware person systems occupying the same brain.

So how exotic is this dissociation in attitudes likely to be?

There are a number of critical lines of evidence here. Nosek and Hansen (2008) report that in a meta-analysis of 81 studies the IAT was only moderately correlated with self-reported attitudes ($r = 0.24$; Hofmann, Gawronski, Gschwendner, Le and Schmitt 2005) and, in a study of 50 attitude domains, Nosek (2005) found that the strength of the correlation between the IAT and self-reported attitudes varied from near zero for some attitude domains (e.g. attitudes to thin and fat) to approximately 0.70 in other domains (e.g. pro-choice/pro-life attitudes). So in Greenwald and Nosek's (2008) terms there is clearly, at least, a mundane dissociation between the two constructs. But, in addition, there is the finding that other variables (like, for example, chronological age) can have a well-defined relationship with one of the measures (say, explicit attitude) but no relation with the other (say, implicit attitude). This has been found for things like explicit and implicit age preference. Here, there is a significant correlation between the age of the participant and age preference, in the case of the explicit measure, but no significant correlation in the case of the implicit measure.

Of course, these types of findings of possible attitudinal dissociation do not point to one single interpretation of the data and Greenwald and Nosek (2008) have argued that they are, in fact, compatible with three different interpretations. First, the 'single-representation hypothesis', which maintains that the appearance of a dissociation is really just an illusion and all that is happening is that in explicit self-report measures, participants have the opportunity to modify their real response in their explicit reporting of their attitude. The second 'dual-representation hypothesis' is the real dissociation claim, and this maintains that implicit and explicit measures of attitude have structurally distinct mental representations of attitudes and they are genuinely dissociated (see Chaiken and Trope 1999; Wilson, Lindsey and Schooler 2000). This hypothesis seems to be favoured by many in this area. Thus:

> Abundant theory, and some evidence, point to the human mind being divided into two largely independent subsystems: first, a familiar foreground, where processing is conscious, controlled, intentional, reflective and slow, but where learning occurs rapidly; and second, a hidden background, where processing is unconscious, automatic, unintended, impulsive and fast, but where learning occurs gradually . . . This dual-process model is appealingly neat. It recalls Freud's model of the mind, but with the inner sex maniac replaced by a dull but efficient zombie. (Gregg 2008: 764)

In this hypothesis the implicit attitudes (part of system 1) operate automatically and unconsciously (and have unconscious representations) while the explicit attitudes (part of system 2) operate consciously and with deliberate thought (and have an underlying representation which is quite different). The third 'person vs. culture hypothesis' is that explicit measures capture the attitudes operating within a person while implicit attitudes represent the more general influence of what is known about a particular thing in a particular culture. Nosek and Hansen (2008) argue, however, that the evidence from variations in the level of correlation in the IAT and self-reported attitude across individuals largely rules out the third hypothesis and that the IAT does not merely reflect the evaluative judgement of the culture as a whole. Their conclusion is that the data demonstrates that the IAT is an individual difference measure and is associated with individual-level thoughts, feelings, and actions. But that still leaves two major hypotheses; one hypothesis (the single-representation hypothesis) is that there is one underlying representation for both implicit and explicit attitudes; the second is that implicit attitudes have their roots in the unconscious (dual-representation hypothesis) and explicit attitudes have their roots else-where. The first hypothesis might suggest that when we report our attitude we may be aware of what we really feel but we modify our verbal response particularly in sensitive domains (like race, attitudes to obesity and attitudes to green issues which we might like to exaggerate to make ourselves look good). The second hypothesis suggests that the implicit attitude is grounded in the unconscious; we are unaware of this attitude and may well be puzzled by the slowness of our reaction times and our high error rate when we sit in front of the computer screen as we complete the IAT.

But what we observed in this new domain of ethnicity (and quite unlike the research on sustainability) was that the TD scores and the D scores from the IAT were significantly correlated. In other words, an implicit attitude might well be associated with a vague 'feeling' of 'warmth' or 'coldness' towards the target, which can be, and is, reported. So how does this sit with the single representation hypothesis? According to this model there is just one representation, but social desirability prevents its expression. Why wasn't it preventing its expression in the Feeling Thermometer? It may be more fruitful here to acknowledge that although the

Likert and the Feeling Thermometer are both self-report measures they really do focus in on different things, after all 'stated preference' for different ethnic groups and 'feelings' towards different ethnic groups are not the same thing. And it would seem that implicit attitude might connect to feelings but not stated preference.

It is also interesting and informative to plot the self-report measures and the implicit scores against each other. Figure 13.5 shows the distribution of Likert scores plotted against the D score for each participant and Figure 13.6 shows the distribution of TD scores plotted against the D scores. What these two figures reveal is that there is a general tendency to express neutral attitudes (with the majority of people scoring 3 on the Likert Scale and 0 on the Feeling Thermometer) in self-report measures but the distribution of D scores of these individuals with neutral self-report scores actually indicates a clear preference for White over non-White with positive D scores (≥ 0.2) and many D scores well over 0.8.

If we look at the explicit and implicit attitude scores by gender (75 females and 55 males), there is very little variation in the self-report measures by gender, but the implicit scores show a much larger difference (see Table 13.2). For

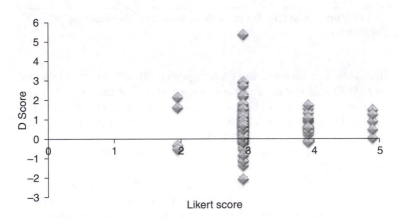

Figure 13.5 Likert scores plotted against IAT Difference (D) scores.

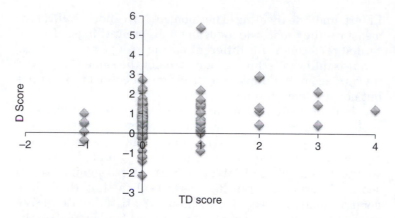

Figure 13.6 **Thermometer Difference (TD) scores plotted against IAT Difference (D) scores.**

Table 13.2 **Mean explicit and implicit attitude scores by gender**

	Female		Male	
	Mean	SD	Mean	SD
Likert score	3.20	0.55	3.15	0.52
TD score	0.32	0.68	0.29	0.90
D score	0.69	0.95	0.79	0.84

D = IAT Difference; SD = Standard Deviation; TD = Thermometer Difference

females, the mean Likert score was 3.20, the mean TD score was 0.32 and the mean D score was 0.69. For males, the mean Likert score was 3.15, the mean TD score was 0.29 and the mean D score was 0.79 (very close to the critical 0.8 for a strong pro-White attitude). However, it is important to point out that these gender differences in D score were not statistically reliable.

Figure 13.7 shows the distribution of female Likert scores and Figure 13.8 shows the distribution of male Likert scores, Figure 13.9 shows the distribution of female TD scores, and Figure 13.10 shows the distribution of male TD scores.

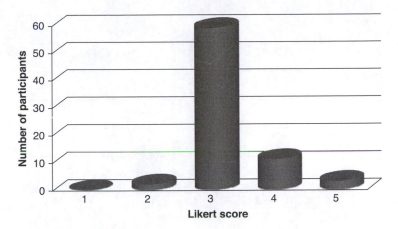

Figure 13.7 Distribution of Likert scores of our female participants towards White and non-White targets.

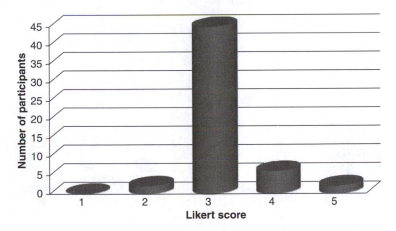

Figure 13.8 Distribution of Likert scores of our male participants towards White and non-White targets.

Finally, Figures 13.11 and 13.12 show the distribution of female D scores and male D scores. All of these figures seem to show a common pattern of self-report attitudes that are essentially neutral and measures of implicit attitude that are not.

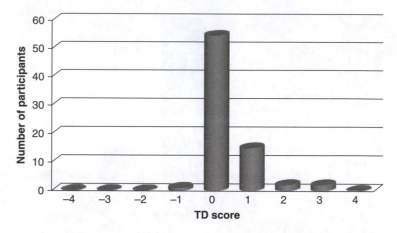

Figure 13.9 Distribution of Thermometer Difference (TD) scores of our female participants towards White and non-White targets.

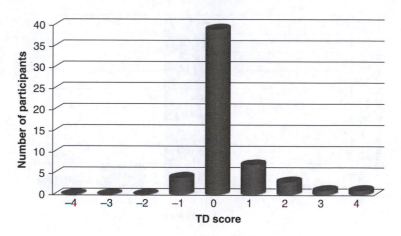

Figure 13.10 Distribution of Thermometer Difference (TD) scores of our male participants towards White and non-White targets.

Gender did not appear to influence implicit attitudes in a statistically robust way. The ethnicity of our participants, however, did (see Table 13.3). Whilst the explicit measures are again quite similar, especially in the case of the Likert measures, the scores for the implicit attitude were very much

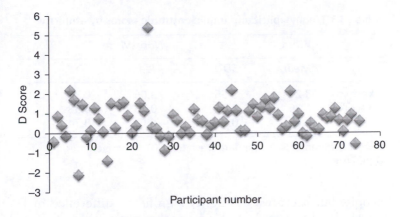

Figure 13.11 **Distribution of IAT Difference (D) scores of our female participants towards White and non-White targets.**

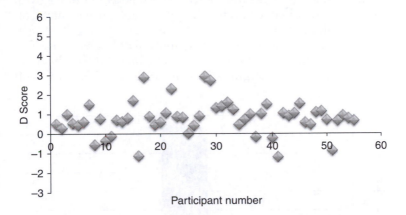

Figure 13.12 **Distribution of IAT Difference (D) scores of our male participants towards White and non-White targets.**

influenced by the ethnicity of the participant. For White participants, the mean D score was 0.87, indicating a strong preference for Whites. For non-White participants, however, the mean D score was −0.01, which indicates no preference either way. There was no significant difference in either the Likert or the TD scores between White and non-White

Table 13.3 **Mean explicit and implicit attitude scores by ethnicity**

	White		Non-White	
	Mean	*SD*	*Mean*	*SD*
Likert score	3.20	0.56	3.05	0.38
TD score	0.36	0.82	0.05	0.38
D score	0.87	0.86	−0.01	0.74

D = IAT Difference; SD = Standard Deviation; TD = Thermometer Difference

people, but there was a highly significant difference in D scores. In other words, one's own ethnicity might not affect one's indicated 'preference' for 'Whites' or 'non-Whites' or one's self-reported feelings about Whites and non-Whites (which remain essentially neutral irrespective of one's own ethnicity) but it does significantly impact on measures of one's implicit attitudes.

Figure 13.13 outlines the distribution of Likert scores for White participants and Figure 13.14 outlines those of the non-White participants. Figure 13.15 outlines the distribution of

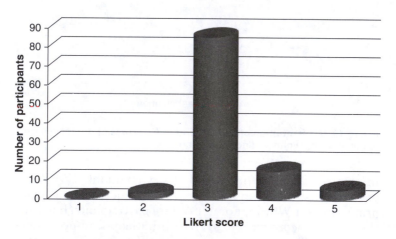

Figure 13.13 Distribution of Likert scores for White participants towards White and non-White targets.

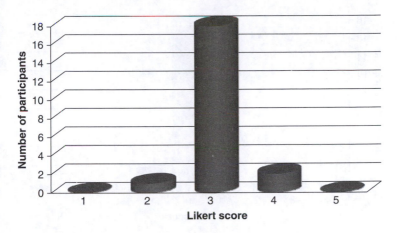

Figure 13.14 **Distribution of Likert scores for non-White participants towards White and non-White targets.**

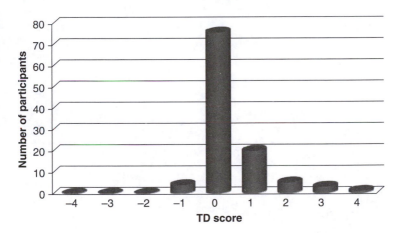

Figure 13.15 **Distribution of Thermometer Difference (TD) scores for White participants towards White and non-White targets.**

TD scores for White participants and Figure 13.16 outlines those for non-White participants. Finally, Figure 13.17 outlines the distribution of D scores for White participants and Figure 13.18 outlines the distribution of D scores for non-White participants.

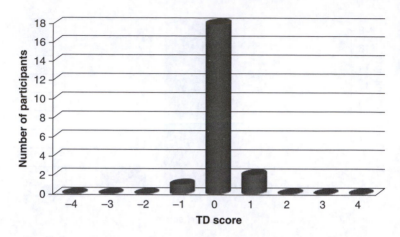

Figure 13.16 **Distribution of Thermometer Difference (TD) scores for non-White participants towards White and non-White targets.**

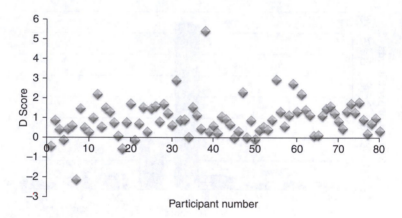

Figure 13.17 **Distribution of IAT Difference (D) scores for White participants towards White and non-White targets.**

Of course, results like this always become more interesting when they allow you to focus on individuals and their own unique responses, which are sometimes in a different direction to their peers. There were four cases which stand out in particular in this particular data set. In Figure 13.19,

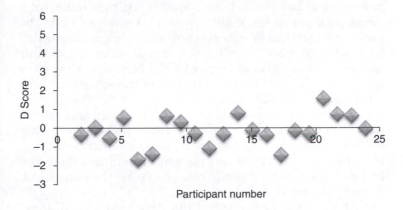

Figure 13.18 **Distribution of IAT Difference (D) scores for non-White participants towards White and non-White targets**

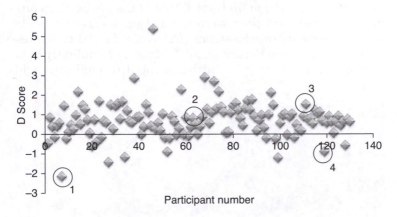

Figure 13.19 **Participants with strong implicit attitudinal preferences at odds with the general pattern (circled).**

the participant marked '1' was White and their self-report measures indicated no preference either way, yet their implicit attitude indicated a strong preference for non-Whites with a D score of −2.12. The participant marked '2' was non-White, and again their self-report measures indicated no preference either way yet their implicit attitude indicated a strong preference for Whites, with a D score of 0.83. The participant marked '3' was also non-White but demonstrated a strong preference for Whites with a D score of 1.54; this participant was again in terms of self-report neutral; and the participant marked '4' was White but indicated a strong preference for non-Whites with a D score of −0.87. This participant again reported neutral attitudes. These, in many ways, were the exceptions to the general rule which suggests that one's own ethnicity can impact on implicit attitudes in that at an implicit level White people appear to favour their own broad ethnic category; non-White people, on the other hand, appear to be neutral.

Another way of looking at this data is to take all those participants who explicitly stated they held neutral attitudes towards both Whites and non-Whites but whose implicit attitude scores actually indicated a strong preference in one or other direction. In total, 53 out of the 130 participants who reported that they were neutral on the Likert Scale actually demonstrated a strong preference for either Whites or non-Whites (see Figure 13.20). Of these, 47 implicitly held strong pro-White implicit attitudes, and 6 implicitly held

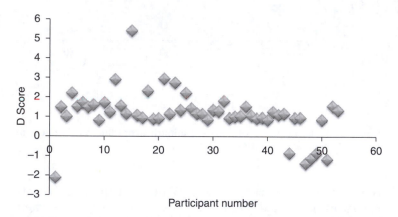

Figure 13.20 Distribution of IAT Difference (D) scores of participants who explicitly stated they were neutral on the Likert Scale towards White and non-White targets.

strong non-White attitudes (4 of these participants were non-White themselves). Therefore, despite over 40 per cent of the participants in this study explicitly espousing exactly neutral attitudes it would appear that, when measured implicitly, they in fact hold very strong attitudes that in the vast majority of cases favour Whites over non-Whites.

A very similar pattern emerged for those participants who explicitly stated they had neutral feelings about White and non-White people (their TD scores). Their implicit attitude scores again indicated strong preferences rather than no preferences. In total, 46 out of the 130 participants who said they were exactly neutral in terms of their feelings actually demonstrated a strong preference for either White or non-White people (see Figure 13.21). Of these, 41 held strong pro-White implicit attitudes, and only 5 held strong non-White attitudes (4 of these again were non-White). In other words, only one of the participants in the sample so far who reported that they were attitudinally neutral about ethnicity (through the TD measure), but who held strong implicit non-White attitudes, turned out to be White.

Therefore, despite over 35 per cent of participants in this study explicitly reporting neutral attitudes and feelings

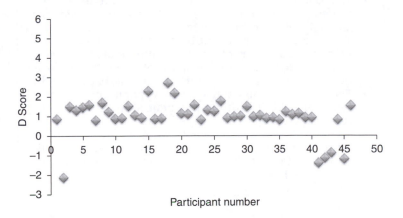

Figure 13.21 Distribution of IAT Difference (D) scores of participants who explicitly stated they were neutral in terms of their Thermometer Difference scores towards White and non-White targets.

about Whites and non-Whites, it would appear that they hold very strong implicit attitudes that in the vast majority of cases favour White people over non-White people. This could potentially have enormous consequences for us all. See also Appendix 1 for some additional considerations.

- We can measure implicit or unconscious attitude by pairing concepts, for example Black and White, with pleasant or unpleasant words and seeing how fast people can assign words or images to the paired categories.
- Measuring implicit attitudes can be quite disconcerting for the person taking part in the experiment.
- Measures of implicit attitude seem more resistant to faking and can be a better predictor of actual behaviour than explicit attitudes in some situations.
- Many previous measures of implicit attitude have used odd looking stimuli which may have affected the results obtained.
- We found that self-report measures of attitude were essentially neutral about White and non-White people.
- The implicit attitude seemed to be moderately pro-White overall and approaching strongly pro-White in the case of the males in our sample.
- The Likert measures of self-reported attitudes (stated preference) towards Whites and non-Whites did not correlate with the measure of implicit attitude.
- The measure of implicit attitude, however, did correlate with the TD scores, in other words, implicit attitude might well be associated with 'feelings' of 'warmth' or 'coldness' towards people from different ethnic backgrounds.
- The Whites in this sample were strongly pro-White in terms of implicit attitude but neutral in terms of self-reported attitude.
- The non-Whites in this sample were neutral in implicit attitude and also neutral in terms of self-reported attitude (but this was a very small, preliminary sample of non-Whites).

14

Am I a racist?

And then, of course, there is me. How do I fit into all this? It is one thing testing other people and hypothesising about the implications of all of this; it is a different matter when you put yourself under the microscope. What uncomfortable truths might lie here in terms of my underlying attitude? Project Implicit had already suggested that I was moderately rather than strongly biased in terms of race, but I could deal with this negative result in terms of what I see as the methodological shortcomings of that particular test and the odd images that the test used. And then again it was only a 'moderate' rather than a 'strong' bias, less pronounced, perhaps less to worry about, more likely to change when the methodological flaws are ironed out. But how would I fare on the new ethnic IAT, with fewer of these obvious methodological issues to protect me? This is an important issue especially because I feel that there may be good psychological reasons, from my own past, why I display the particular strong bias that I do seem to have (the weight bias that has already been picked up). In other words, I seem to be giving some credence to any such results by trying to make personal explanations for them.

In an interesting review article published in 2004, Laurie Rudman from Rutgers University considered the evidence as to where implicit attitudes might originate from. Her view is that implicit attitudes 'stem from different sources and, therefore, should be conceptualised as succinct constructs in comparison with explicit attitudes'. She argues that there are three possible influences on the development of implicit attitudes. The first is that implicit attitudes stem from early experiences in the life of the individual whereas explicit attitudes are shaped primarily by our more recent experiences. She uses, as an example of this, smokers' explicit and implicit attitudes to smoking. She suggests that for the vast majority of people, their first experiences of smoking are largely unpleasant (the taste, the nausea, the cough, the bad breath). However, as people become seasoned smokers, they learn to appreciate other more positive aspects of the experience (the relaxation, the bonding, the 'cool' image, the reduction in hunger pangs). So she suggests that smokers should have implicit attitudes to smoking that are much more negative than their explicit attitudes, and this is exactly what she says the research suggests.

You could imagine this being applied to issues to do with race. She presumably would argue that those early first experiences, the perceptions of difference and perhaps the anxiety associated with this would form the basis for more negative implicit attitudes. On the other hand, the years of happily working together with colleagues from differing ethnic backgrounds would impact upon explicit attitude but would not necessarily override those early first experiences. Of course, both her study and conclusions about smoking and the conjecture about race do contain a lot of assumptions. Is everyone's early experience with smoking necessarily negative? What proportion of smokers do not experience the nausea and physical symptoms early on? Similarly when it comes to race, when does perceived difference in skin colour become a negative event associated with anxiety? Is this hardwired in the human brain? When does perceived difference become 'novelty' instead, and draw us towards the object? How important is the social context in which you see someone different for the first time? How important is the caretaker in providing a suitable evaluation?

Rudman would presumably argue that this social context and the social learning that occurs within it are crucial to the development of implicit attitudes. Thus, she writes:

Much of what is learned early in life is preverbal and taught indirectly. These lessons form the foundation on which later learning is built and may also serve as a non-conscious source for related evaluations and actions. Goodwin and I obtained results consistent with this possibility when we investigated whether early (even preverbal) attachment to maternal caregivers was associated with people's gender-related attitudes (Rudman and Goodwin 2003). First, people raised primarily by their mothers implicitly preferred women to men. Second, people implicitly favoured women if they automatically preferred their mothers to their fathers. By contrast, explicit attitudes towards parents and gender were not related. (Rudman 2004: 79).

So, Rudman suggests, early experience might be critical in the development in implicit attitudes but she says that there are other possible factors as well. She suggests that 'implicit attitudes are more sensitive to affective experiences than are explicit attitudes', and she points to some research which suggests that the measures of implicit attitude are associated with increased activation in the amygdala, which is crucial in the control of emotion. She also reviewed evidence from her own laboratory which showed that White people who volunteered for diversity training showed reduced anti-Black attitudes in terms of both implicit and explicit attitudes. However, a reduction in negative implicit attitudes was connected to emotion-based features such as reduced fear and increased liking, whereas a reduction in negative explicit attitudes was related to an increased awareness of bias and their desire and willingness to overcome their own prejudice. Rudman argues therefore that implicit attitudes are more connected to emotional responses and changes in implicit attitudes require a certain amount of emotional 'reconditioning'. Changes in explicit attitudes, on the other hand, are more in the domain of cognitive motivational factors.

The third type of factor that Rudman points to are what she calls 'cultural biases' and the main piece of empirical evidence that she cites here is the repeated observation that both White and Black people show more anti-Black bias on implicit measures than they do on explicit measures. She suggests that this observation does makes sense in American culture where there is a cultural representation of Blacks that is not as positive as that of Whites, and that this cultural representation has been internalised by all cultures regardless of their colour. She argues that no matter how fair Black people themselves might try to be, they simply cannot overcome this unconscious cultural bias against themselves. But she uses no systematic data here to show where this cultural bias derives from (she assumes we would all recognise it). Some have suggested that it is even woven into the very lexicon of our language, is present in stock phrases and idioms, and that it is a real black mark against you if you cannot see it immediately. Indeed, some argue that every time we say 'get your clothes whiter than white', we are doing another disservice to people of colour. I sit on some decking by my house in the centre of Manchester and try to fill a pure white sheet with some other examples. You can start with some of the compound words and expressions, and you might well conclude that indeed there is something in this claim because more of the terms with 'black' in them seem to have negative connotations. Here are my own individual evaluations in terms of positive (+), negative (−) or neutral (n) for a number of words and phrases that readily come to my mind (hardly systematic I know).

> Blackbird (n) – a nice enough bird (but not very nice)
> Blackboard (n) – depends on your school days
> Blackberry (p) – most people love theirs
> Black hole (−) – a scary place!
> Blackball (−) – not very nice
> Black out (−) – a scary experience!
> Black magic (−) – speaks for itself
> Black sheep (−) – ditto
> Black mark (−) – ditto
> Black Death (−) – ditto
> Blackmail (−) – ditto
> Black cat (−) – the companion of a witch!

And compare these with:

Whitewash (−) – cover up something bad
White witch (+) – a nice witch!
White lie (+) – not such a bad lie!
White magic (+) – good magic!
White elephant (n) – not bad, not good, not relevant!
White knuckle (+) – scary but in a good way
White noise (n) – can be okay (psychologists use it a lot!)
White knight (+) – my saviour!
White feather (−) – symbol of cowardice, and, therefore, not very nice.

Perhaps you could try this exercise yourself and write down some compound words, idioms and expressions to determine how specific or general this argument might be. And these are some of the words and expressions that we use in everyday life, which have been in common usage for a very long time, out of which we construct social meaning and interpret our lived experience. There does seem to be a slight tendency for 'black' to be found in more expressions (that come immediately to my mind at least) with negative connotations than does 'white'. How prevalent this is throughout the English language as a whole remains to be determined.

But what the Rudman article is really telling us is that there is little consensus at the present time as to where these implicit attitudes come from. They could be formed in our earliest experiences, they could derive from the processing of perceived difference by primitive parts of the human brain, they could be inculcated through our broadest cultural understandings, and of course, they could come from all of these, and that is our challenge for the future – to work out what shapes the development of implicit and explicit attitudes and to understand how both types of attitude affect and control our behaviour. And it is clear from all that has been said so far that this is not going to be an easy challenge.

I have, however, good grounds to be optimistic about my own personal psychology, and why I may not have such a strong bias when it comes to ethnicity, at least on the basis of my reading of Allport. When I read Allport's theoretical account I kept thinking that he seemed to be implying that the more happy and contented you are with your own particular background, then, all things being equal (which they never are), the more likely you are to be prejudiced, and presumably vice versa (although this might be a significant inference on my part).

After all, Allport's basic thesis seems to have been that prejudice arises because we like to stay with what is familiar. In his words: 'Psychologically, the crux of the matter is that the familiar provides the indispensable basis of our existence. Since existence is good, its accompanying groundwork seems good and desirable.' And elsewhere he had written:

> Everywhere on earth we find a condition of separateness among groups. People mate with their own kind. They eat, play, reside in homogeneous clusters. They visit with their own kind, and prefer to worship together. Much of this automatic cohesion is due to nothing more than convenience. There is no need to turn to out-groups for companionship. With plenty of people at hand to choose from, why create for ourselves the trouble of adjusting to new languages, new foods, new cultures, or to people of a different educational level? It requires less effort to deal with people who have similar presuppositions. (Allport 1954)

Allport's view is stark and to the point – 'his nation's way of life is *his* way of life – and he cannot lightly abrogate the ground of his whole existence. Such almost reflex preference for the familiar grips us all' (1954: 44). Allport believed, then, in a 'reflex preference for the familiar'; a reflex preference – it sounds almost instinctive.

But what happens if you do not appear to have a reflex preference for the familiar? What happens if you do not think that the familiar is easy, and you do not feel safe and secure embedded within it? What happens if it does not require less effort? Does this protect you from prejudice and implicit biases, now that we have the means to render these visible? I have a personal quibble here with Allport's basic argument. On the basis of my own experiences I think that Allport is somewhat overstating the case about the draw of the familiar. He fails to recognise that the familiar, and by that he means one's familial and cultural background, can sometimes be anything but entrancing. It may appear as alien and strange. And sometimes it is impossible to stick entirely within the familiar because external pressures, of one sort or another (maybe even something like passing the Eleven-Plus) pull you away and it becomes effortful rather than effortless to stay with your own kind. The presuppositions underpinning everyday life become twisted and contrasting. So how do we fold all of this into our understanding of prejudice and where it comes from?

My transition to the school with the 'Royal' in the title had meant that nothing now seemed like safe territory any longer. And I am sure that I am not alone in my sorts of experiences. I could feel the great divide, now on every side. I could feel the prejudice towards me and the prejudice emanating from within me and sometimes it is good and helpful to try to document these things, to fill in the detail of Allport's great sketch, to make it personal, to make it real.

It was my A-level year and I liked to be out of the house by five at the very latest, before my mother got back. The Troubles were now the backdrop to my life; Hacksaw was out in his car driving along looking for potential 'hits'. Tit for tat, tat for tit, and so it went on; you would hear the boom of the bombs at night, as the IRA, in my mother's words, 'tried to blow the arse off Belfast'. If I didn't get out of the house by five there would probably be an argument. My mother slaving away in that mill; and me sitting on my arse watching television before the homework started, the television that didn't work properly. She still worked in the mill, but it was now a thread factory, things had moved on in that part of Belfast, and now she was a thread inspector. She had to check that thread, which came down from great oiled rollers near the dusty ceiling, didn't have too many knots in it. Then she checked the thread for oil stains. Finally, she packed the coiled strands away in little brown speckled boxes, which she assembled herself by slotting sharp corners and long cutting flaps into ready-made slits.

Twelve of the cones in the one box, all of the same colour. You needed quick hands to put the boxes together and a very quick mind to check for knots and flaws. Oil stains on thread could be difficult to detect in a room like that which wasn't very well lit, and knots were impossible sometimes. But she could do all of this and more in a room with one fluorescent strip out, and the other which flickered away in the corner. 'It could give you a fit that light,' she said. 'But I've never had a fit, never in my whole life,' she would say. 'And I sit at a table like the managers themselves up in their offices above the shop floor. I sit on the very same chairs that they use themselves, when they've both done with them. The stuffing might have gone a bit, but they're still good chairs. The girls who work the machines have to stand all day in the same place. They're on their feet for eight, sometimes ten hours when they fancy a bit of overtime.'

The way she talked about the job you could tell that she regarded herself as a cut above the rest. They only had to do one job. Most of them had just got quick hands. She liked to remind me of that, whenever I told her what somebody in the street had said to me. She'd say, 'Don't listen to them, they only work a machine up in the mill. What do they know?' But they earned more than her for working the machines that never stopped during the shift. 'But that work's relentless,' she always said. 'It would make your mind go numb.'

She also collected the Christmas Club money, not only for what used to be the carding room, but for the store room next door as well. You needed to be good with figures for that position, and to be trustworthy. Beyond reproach. The Christmas Club was started in early August, so that half of the year was spent looking forward to a few damp days in December. There was the Christmas Club in the baker's for the cakes for Christmas, the butcher's Christmas Club money for the turkey, but the mill's Christmas Club money was the most important. It was the money you saved for all the rest, the presents for the wee ones. The wee innocent ones who had to have something to look forward to in this part of north Belfast with its bullets and its bombs and its job prospects, which were nil.

For month after month, she kept the money below the bed in the front room in an old shoebox, with all the figures recorded in thick pencil on ripped-out sheets of a shorthand notebook. The cover of the notebook said Chapman's Stationer to the Nation. She had figures running up and down the inside of the cover, the totals underlined. The notebook came from the director of the thread factory's office. It was his little contribution to the well-being of his staff.

'People like to call us millies,' she liked to say, 'but we're not millies any longer. That's the old name. It's not a flax mill any more so how can we be wee millies, wee Belfast millies who work in a mill; we're machine operatives or inspectors in a thread factory. That's our proper titles. People in Belfast used to talk about millies as if we were good things, easy touches, but you can't talk about machine operatives like that, or inspectors. It doesn't sound the same. They can't put you down the same way the way they used to when we worked in the spinning mill. They'd like to, but they can't.'

At least she was trying to make something of herself. That was always the source of the torrent that swept us along night after night. She seemed to believe that we were all made of clay waiting to be sculpted. Earth to be shaped by our own hands. Our own quick hands. But some were just dirt. You could tell who they were. It was hard enough getting by where we lived without mixing with dirt. I had, of course, loftier ambitions than most, but they were vague and ill-defined at that point in time. I was thinking about studying psychology but who was going to advise me about this?

'What the hell is psychology anyway?' my mother would ask when I told her what I was planning to study at university. 'And what would you do with it for a job? You might be able to sort me out. I'll probably be in a mental hospital by the time you finish; you can come and visit me. Tell them that you're a psychologist and they'll let you in, night or day. That would be a wee perk of the job; you could visit your old mother.'

When she got home from work and talked about how one of the rollers was causing the thread to come through with too many knots, I would sit there trying to show interest. 'How many knots is too many?' I would enquire, as I watched television. But she always thought I was just trying to be funny at her expense. 'That's right, you little snob, you look down at me out there working away, to support you at that bloody snob *school of yours.' So I'd normally slip out just before five and go for a walk. That particular day was warm for the golden flux of mid-autumn, so it was the park with the loud cak cak cak of crows above empty sharp nests balancing in the long thin branches of the already bare chestnut trees, stripped naked by the wind through the iron railings and the boys with short fat sticks out collecting cheesers. The thin branches standing out against the grey sky, like blue veins running up the back of an old greying hand holding up some thorned prize. The crows were circling overhead in the park. I could never work out what set them off. It would all be nice and quiet and then they'd be off squawking and screeching and getting excited about God knows what. Once they were out of their sharp, dark, tangled nests they made themselves busy. One of them would go into a litter bin, the rest would wait for him to come out. I watched one large bedraggled crow drag some greasy paper right out of a bin and across the grass. The rest were in a noisy line behind it, jostling and complaining and every so often catching up with the first bird, and snatching lumps of paper stained with fat away from it. Cak, cak, cak, then silence as they wrestled and tugged the paper out of each other's beaks. Then more loud cries.*

I prodded the damp earth with a long stick. The leaves were turning brown, with darker speckles in the middle, like dead butterflies, the dead wings of the leaves crackling as I prodded them with a stick. Some pencil-thin old man came towards me with a small dog with short, bony, cantilevered legs. The crows parted for him to walk through, but they didn't fly off for him. They were far too busy. The man's cheeks were hollow and unshaven, covered in a white downy hair. His shirt was done up to the top, but he had no tie. His jacket was the top half of a suit. It wasn't the same colour as his trousers. His trousers didn't fit. They were pulled in at the waist with an old light brown leather belt with matadors on it. The clothes were from an older brother perhaps, recently deceased, leaving a full wardrobe of clothes which he wouldn't have wanted to go to waste. Or perhaps, the trousers had been bought for that man himself, the man he had once been. It was impossible to tell.

But it was the jacket of his best suit, the suit for weddings and funerals, all its revels and public sadness done. It was the jacket for taking the dog out now. He was past the rest. His family and friends were long gone. He gave me that look. I was sure he recognised me but didn't say hello. He looked at my blazer, with the gold and crimson crown, the wee snob in the park with the badge from the school with a 'Royal' in it, and just snorted, as if he couldn't be bothered wasting a greeting on the likes of me. The snort cleared his windpipes, and it acted as some sort of acknowledgement.

I could hear him coming before I saw him. Sucking in the breath, the air whistling as it left that bony white chest. A lifetime up in the mill, before it became a thread factory. Sucking in the flax dust, trying to whistle as he worked. He had a lifetime in that dry, dusty place, and he wanted me to be there on that bright, dry afternoon, to understand what life is really all about. It was a pity that the mill was really just a big store room for thread now, and that Belfast linen had gone the way of Sheffield steel, and no doubt Paris buns, for all I cared: made somewhere else for half the price so that the likes of me could be left alone. They didn't really make anything up there anymore, not in the way they once had done, not in the way they had made linen out of flax. Irish linen, the best in the world, was made up there from something that grew in our own native fields. But they didn't really make anything any longer. They just changed the thread around a bit, they put it on to reels and packed it and sent it off somewhere else. Nobody knew where exactly, that was the responsibility of the packing department, and the girls from the packing department were a bit odd, they didn't have a smoke and a wee chat with the rest of the girls at breaks. They kept themselves to themselves. They were very quiet.

I could feel his resentments, glancing at the wee posh boy who didn't have a life in the mill ahead of him; I could feel the old man looking straight at me. He pulled the dog along by its lead, its leaden chest rocked from side to side as it walked. They stopped just by me. Even the dog glowered my way, as if I was responsible for its discomfort and the fact that the old man wouldn't let it go in peace.

I watched the two of them walk off, pulling against each other. They had their routine, I had mine. I'd go off in a few minutes and sit on a swing, and wait until about six, the wee snob enjoying the autumn sun, without a care in the frigging *world, back to a night of 'amo, amas, amat' (word perfect, word perfect every time, it had to be) and other dead linguistic codes with Greek symbols and then Dostoevsky and Checkov and Turgenev and long, convoluted formulae written in a neat blue hand across page after page (to make it a grade A once again, to narrowly skirt the abyss of failure, which was anything but this A).*

I knew what prejudices felt like, both as a source and as a target, and growing up when I did, it wasn't just a simple Protestant-Catholic dimension. There were prejudices of aspiration and hope and knowing your place or rebelling against what was on offer. There were prejudices all around me. And these experiences make me realise that any analyses that psychologists provide have to be, at the very least, as powerful and as detailed as our own experiences. But my own experiences also make me ask essential questions about the psychological theories and their own intellectual and personal origins. What had Allport written? '. . . most of the business of life can go with less effort if we stick together with our own kind.' But perhaps he had too egocentric a view of the social world, perhaps his host community felt much more cohesive and familiar to him, much more comfortable than perhaps any I had known. Was his personal background an important contributory factor to the development of his own views? And some serious questions may follow from this. Is that contrast between what is familiar and known and the unfamiliar and strange a necessary prerequisite of prejudice? But what happens if you are born and grow up in a community that doesn't seem so familiar even when you are fully immersed in it? Does this then inoculate against prejudice against the stranger because there is no essential contrast in the first place? Or do you still end up with prejudice because you have less social support in your host community? In fact, could you end up with even more prejudice in this case (assuming that fear and uncertainty may be some of the key driving forces behind prejudice)?

I was intrigued about my own implicit scores on the Ethnic IAT. Was I protected in some way against any strong implicit bias because I did not seem to possess the reflex pull to the familiar? Like many people, I have often wondered whether I'm a real racist or not; the fact that I have had many intimate friends during the course of my life from a huge range of ethnic backgrounds does not necessarily reassure me: all of this social intercourse could well have been prompted by some desire to prove to myself that I was not, in any way, subject to the old familiar biases and prejudices that dominated my childhood (that is the problem with allowing the unconscious back into psychological theorising, you have to potentially allow for Freudian mechanisms to operate, perhaps not all but some, like reaction formation). The test was over quickly. Like many tests, I could not really tell how it went. Explicitly in terms of the Likert and Thermometer Difference scores I was right in the middle, so was I going to turn out to be one of those people who say one thing but deep down inside feel something completely different? Did I, indeed, have a racist heart? One of my team read the result out to me. I shielded my eyes, by letting my head slump forward into them, like Gordon Brown in that radio station during the British General Election of 2010, when Jeremy Vine played back the tape of his comment about the 'bigoted' pensioner in Rochdale, picked up in his car when he thought that his microphone was switched off.

'Your score was 0.14; you are neutral, you have no automatic preferences one way or the other.'

The team all laughed; I wasn't sure what they were expecting. They had just discovered that their boss was not a racist; all three of them looked at me with a great deal of obvious joy written all over their pure white faces.

- Many people may feel familiar and comfortable with those that they grew up with, some do not.
- This degree of felt separation may, or may not, inoculate you against other forms of prejudice or bias.
- I am not a racist, or so it seems. I am very relieved.
- It's probably as odd finding out that you're not an implicit racist as finding out that you are.
- What does any of this actually mean? (And what are the implications, if any?)

15

Why aren't we saving the planet? Another example of unconscious bias in action

It is probably good to remind ourselves that all that we have actually done so far is to devise a computerised test that seems to show that White participants are quicker at pressing keys on a keyboard when certain images and words are put together than when certain other images and words are put together. A number of psychologists want to claim that this means that in the minds of our participants the concepts of 'White' and 'Good' are more associated than 'non-White' and 'Good', and that 'non-White' and 'Bad' are more associated than 'non-White' and 'Good'. But what are the possible implications of this?

The IAT, after all, is not without its critics. Fiedler and colleagues (2006) raise a number of important issues. They argue that it can be problematic using evaluative associations like this to infer underlying attitudes. 'More generally, equating attitudes and evaluative associations is by definition problematic because the attitude construct is then one-dimensional (referring to approach versus avoidance tendencies), whereas the laws of association can be multi-dimensional' (ibid.: 83). They want to argue that the evaluative associations revealed by the IAT, are:

> more about the lexicon or the symbol system, or knowledge of cultural consensus, than about the attitudinal structure of individual persons. Because of these and other complicating factors, the universal assumption that attitude strength can be inferred

unambiguously from the closeness of associations would appear to be hard to defend. (ibid.: 84)

Fiedler and colleagues also raise the issue of whether, given that the IAT involves 'an active sorting process', participants may have the opportunity to use different (uncontrolled) strategies when engaged in completing the IAT. They suggest that one such strategy could be that participants classify stimuli according to self-reference as in 'like me' or 'unlike me'.

From the standpoint of German participants, German stimuli are 'like me' and Turkish stimuli are 'unlike me', just as positive stimuli are 'like me' and negative stimuli are 'unlike me'. Such a self reference strategy is in principle independent of valence and attitudes. (ibid.: 87)

Fiedler and colleagues identify other strategies that could operate within the confines of the IAT including certain other types of mental reframing, where such mental reframing could be affected by the kinds of stimuli used in the IAT. Thus the inclusion of very positive iconic Black figures in the IAT, which impacts on D scores, as we have seen earlier, can lead to a certain type of mental reframing. Fiedler says about such effects:

Rather than assuming that such a treatment changes attitudes or prejudice within a few minutes, one might simply interpret the reversals or voluntary influences on the IAT as strategic effects, quite distinct from long-term memory associations between attitude objects and valence. (ibid.: 88)

In other words, not every psychologist is convinced that the IAT does provide a straightforward and unambiguous measure of an unconscious attitude.

But others have argued that the IAT does provide us with a very useful tool to predict subsequent behaviour, including behaviour that might be seen as highly discriminatory. For example Dovidio, Kawakami and Gaertner (2002)

analysed the implicit and explicit attitudes of their participants and then studied how these participants interacted
with a Black confederate. The experimenters analysed the
friendliness of the participants towards a Black confederate
in terms of both their verbal and non-verbal behaviour. They
found that the explicit measures of attitude were related
to verbal friendliness but were not related to non-verbal
friendliness, whereas the implicit scores correlated with
non-verbal friendliness but not verbal friendliness. The
Black confederates themselves were also asked to rate how
friendly they thought the interaction was, and it turned out
that their judgements were more affected by what had gone
on non-verbally in the interaction than verbally. In other
words, explicit attitudes do seem to predict more deliberative behaviours such as the expression of friendliness
verbally, whereas implicit attitudes seem to predict more
spontaneous and unconscious behaviours like the expression of friendliness non-verbally (see Towles-Schwen and
Fazio 2003). Of course, given that non-verbal behaviours
play a big role in regulating the smooth flow of conversation
(Beattie 1983, Beattie, Cutler and Pearson 1982), this might
predict why some interactions between Blacks and Whites
sometimes feel a little uncomfortable.

Using a similar paradigm, McConnell and Leibold
(2001) found that larger IAT effects (meaning a more pro-
White bias) predicted a longer speaking time, more smiling,
more spontaneous social comments, and fewer speech errors
and hesitations, often taken as a measure of social anxiety,
when interacting with a White rather than a Black experimenter (although interestingly in this study there was a
significant relationship between the IAT score and the
explicit measures of prejudice).

The sociologist Lincoln Quillian (2006: 319) writing in
the *Annual Review of Sociology* says:

> This evidence suggests that for behaviors where
> conscious regulation is difficult, such as body language
> or decisions made under time pressure, implicit biases
> are likely to influence behavior even among subjects with
> neutral or positive explicit attitudes towards the target.

The police officer's dilemma to shoot quickly or not to shoot a threatening subject, for example, is a case in which the necessity of a quick decision may prevent conscious inhibition of stereotype activation, as one experiment using a video game-shooting exercise with Black and White figures suggests. (Corell, Park, Judd and Wittenbrink 2002)

According to many authors implicit attitudes do influence behaviour, and indeed will only be inhibited when people have the opportunity and motive to do so. This is the basis of the MODE model (Fazio 1990). In Quillian's words (2006: 319):

The motive usually arises from nonprejudicial explicit beliefs or social desirability pressures. The opportunity is greatest for behaviors that can be deliberately controlled, most clearly verbal statements. For behaviors that are non-verbal or made quickly, however, the opportunity to control implicit biases is more limited, so implicit biases appear among even non-prejudiced subjects.

This seems to be a critical issue; Fazio (1990) and others have tried to work out under what conditions the various measures of underlying attitude predict actual behaviour. This has also been the subject of my research on implicit attitudes to sustainability, which does suggest that D scores might actually be of some consequence for behaviour (in this particular case, consumer choice). The motivation behind my sustainability research is simple enough – why aren't we doing more to save the planet? It would seem, after all, that a slow but accelerating change in our climate is occurring (Walker and King 2008) and there is no longer any real disagreement within the scientific community on the matter (see Beattie 2010). It is also now generally accepted that, as human beings, our patterns of consumption have been a major factor in all this, causing irreparable damage to our environment and climate (see, for example, the Stern Review 2006). The recommendations of the World Bank's *Annual World Development Report* (2010: xiii) are pretty

clear: 'We must act now, because what we do today deter-
mines both the climate of tomorrow and the choices that
shape our future.'

But where is this action supposed to come from – is it to
come primarily from governments who can develop and
enact greener policies? Or is it to come primarily from individuals who will somehow 'voluntarily' modify their own
individual behaviour? Despite this clarion call to action,
significant behavioural change may be far from straightforward (Beattie 2011b; Beattie, Sale and McGuire 2011). As
Walker and King (2008: 238) have noted,

> It's easy to believe that global warming is somebody
> else's problem – other people will suffer and other people
> will come up with the solution . . . it's as individuals that
> we live our lives and make our choices . . . now we will
> have to adapt our choices to the new realities of the
> twenty-first century.

Choice, and what governs it, is the absolutely critical
issue here. 'Individuals, as citizens and consumers, will
determine the planet's future. Although an increasing
number of people know about climate change and believe
action is needed, too few make it a priority, and too many
fail to act when they have the opportunity' (*World
Development Report* 2010: xxi). So the question becomes why
do so many people not make it a priority, even when they
could, for example by modifying their everyday patterns of
consumption or, alternatively, by limiting their overall
patterns of consumption? Why do they fail to act in these
kinds of regards? (See Beattie 2010.)

By changing our everyday patterns of consumption we
could, it seems, make a very real difference. If we focus
exclusively on the UK for the moment then according to
Forum for the Future (2007: 8):

> Retail has a vital role to play in delivering sustainable
> development. It is responsible for approximately 2.5%
> of the UK's carbon dioxide emissions and has a
> disproportionate influence over society and the economy

through its marketing, regular customer transactions and complex, globalised supply chains.

In short, if we could achieve a revolution in green consumption in the UK and elsewhere, we would be one step closer to mitigating climate change. Hence, a number of schemes have been introduced to guide consumer choice, including the labelling of products with carbon footprint information.

An assumption underlying such activity is that consumers will act in an appropriately sustainable manner, provided they are given the information and the opportunity to make these sustainable choices in the first place (Sustainable Consumption Roundtable 2006). Thus, carbon footprint information now appears on a whole range of commercial products including things like light bulbs, detergent, and orange juice (although whether this information is scanned in the relevant time frame for a typical shopping decision is another issue, see Beattie, McGuire and Sale 2010). Unfortunately, the inclusion of this information has not necessarily resulted in actual changes in the patterns of consumption towards the low carbon alternative (see University of Manchester's Sustainable Consumption Institute Report 'Consumers, business and climate change' 2009). Perhaps it is important to recall Gifford's (2008: 2) warning that,

individuals truly are the ultimate key to climate-change amelioration: policies, programmes, and regulations themselves do not change anything. For one thing, to be acceptable and efficacious to individuals, policies must be 'bought into' by individuals. In short, policy beckons or even commands, but persons accept or refuse its demands. Behavioural change does not occur until this happens.

If consumer choice is the key to mitigating climate change (as opposed to, say, more straightforward rationing of high carbon products), then we need to determine urgently whether we, as individuals, are ready to buy into low carbon consumption.

Market research (which measures self-report attitudes) seems to suggest that people are indeed ready to act in a more sustainable way. Thus, '78% say that they are prepared to change their behaviour to help limit climate change' (Downing and Ballantyne 2007), '84% say retailers should do more to reduce the impact of production and transportation of their products on climate change' (Ipsos MORI 2008), and '69% of consumers in China are willing to change their life-style to help reduce climate change' (see also Beattie 2010). If we take these statistics at face value it would appear that attitudes towards sustainability are already very positive. But, of course, there is one rather large fly in the ointment. The exclusive focus of research in this area has been on explicit attitudes which necessarily introduce a major issue of social desirability (and, of course, race does this with a vengeance). Everybody in our society knows that green is good and that people who are 'environmentally friendly' are almost certainly going to be perceived positively. Indeed, we now know that 'environmentally friendly' individuals are viewed as being 'considerate', 'thoughtful', 'caring', 'knowl-edgeable', 'selfless' and 'nice' (see Beattie 2010). The problem with this, of course, is that this social desirability, which is obviously very widespread throughout society, could be affecting the expression of explicit attitudes towards envi-ronmental behaviour. But few studies have attempted to measure implicit attitudes in the domain of sustainability (but see Beattie and Sale 2009; Vantomme, Geuens, De Houwer and De Pelsmacker 2005). In our first investigation into explicit and implicit attitudes towards carbon footprint, we created a carbon footprint version of the IAT that compared the categories of high and low carbon footprint products with the attributes 'Good' and 'Bad' (Beattie and Sale 2009). The carbon footprint IAT revealed that, in a sample of UK consumers in 2008, most participants showed a positive implicit attitude (but this was just one prelimi-nary sample). However, there was another significant feature of this particular dataset, namely that there was no significant correlation between the implicit and explicit scores. In other words, the implicit and explicit attitudes appeared to be 'dissociated' and a significant proportion of individuals were much more pro-low carbon on the explicit measure than they were on the implicit measure. The existence of such attitudinal divergence is not unusual in the light of previous attitude research. We already knew from a number of other domains that implicit attitudes may not relate that closely to reported explicit attitudes. But just imagine if this 'unconscious, automatic, unintended, impulsive and fast' system (the implicit one) came to very different, and much more negative, conclusions about carbon footprint information and the environment than our conscious and reflective system as revealed by the market research surveys. Where would that leave the whole philosophy of carbon labelling and the role of consumer choice in ecological stability (and maybe even the survival of the planet)?

The relationship between explicit and implicit attitudes, as we have seen, is a major issue for social psychology generally and for those wishing to promote behavioural change in many core areas. Greenwald *et al.* (2009) conducted a meta-analysis on the predictive validity of the IAT and concluded that, in general, when the IAT and explicit attitude measures are combined, they are together better predictors of behaviour than either measure alone. However, when attitudes are 'socially sensitive', and where social desirability concerns are inevitably present (as in attitudes to race, age, gender or the *environment*) then explicit measures are very poor predictors of behaviour, and in these situations the IAT would appear to be a much better predictor of behaviour than explicit measures. More recently, Greenwald, along with other researchers, has started to apply the IAT to consumer research, since it has become increasingly apparent that consumer behaviour does not necessarily involve conscious and rational decision making, but can also be influenced by all sorts of unconscious factors as well as mere habit. You can often see people in the supermarket picking up products without even properly looking at them, let alone making complex decisions based upon price or nutritional value or fat content. There might well be something at work here which is not based upon conscious, reflective, rational thought and slow decision making. There are 15 published studies which have used the IAT in the consumer domain as shown in Table 15.1, adapted from the Greenwald *et al.* (2009) study.

Table 15.1 The IAT as a potential predictor of consumer behaviour

Citation	Behavioural measure	Did the IAT successfully predict behaviour?
Brunel, Tietje and Greenwald (2004)	Study 1: Self-report of ownership and usage frequency of Mac and PC.	Both IAT and explicit predicted ownership and usage.
Friese, Hofmann and Wänke (2008)	Study 1: Behavioural choice task between apples and chocolate where working memory capacity is reduced.	When processing resources are 'ample' – explicit attitude measure is a better predictor of behaviour. When processing resources are 'taxed', 'behaviour appeared to be more strongly driven by impulsive processes as indicated by the increase in the implicit measure's predictive validity.'
Friese, Hofmann and Wänke (2008)	Study 2: Consumption of potato crisps after watching a film where emotions were either controlled (depleting 'self-regulatory strength') or not controlled.	'… when participants were depleted of their self-regulatory strength [by having to suppress their emotional response to a film], not only did the implicit measure gain considerable predictive power compared with the control condition but also the explicit measure was now unrelated to potato crisps consumption.'

(Continued overleaf)

Table 15.1 continued

Citation	Behavioural measure	Did the IAT successfully predict behaviour?
Friese, Hofmann and Wänke (2008)	Study 3: Beer consumption after watching a film where emotions were either controlled (depleting 'self-regulatory strength') or not controlled.	'When resources were scarce [because participants had to suppress their emotional response to a film] the implicit measure predicted behaviour well and showed incremental validity over and above both explicit self-report measures at the same time.'
Friese, Wänke and Plessner (2006)	Brand choice between generic or branded products in experimental conditions either under time pressure [5 seconds to make their choice], or not under time pressure [unlimited time].	'Participants whose explicit and implicit preferences regarding generic food products and well-known food brands were incongruent were more likely to choose the implicitly preferred brand over the explicitly preferred one when choices were made under time pressure. The opposite was the case when they had ample time to make their choice.'
Gibson (2008)	Brand choice between Coke or Pepsi in experimental conditions when cognitive load was manipulated (by asking participants to remember an 8 digit number, or not).	'. . . choice in this high load condition was related to implicit attitudes, while choice in the low load condition was not.

Hofmann and Friese (2008)	Candy consumption when participants had been drinking alcohol or not.	'Specifically, the predictive validity of implicit attitudes (as part of the impulsive system) was markedly increased for participants who had consumed alcohol as compared with sober participants.'
Hofmann, Rauch and Gawronski (2007)	Candy consumption after watching a film and being asked to either suppress emotions (depletion condition) or 'let emotions flow' (control condition).	'...automatic candy attitudes showed a positive correlation to candy consumption in the depletion condition but not in the control condition. That is, candy consumption significantly increased as a function of automatic positivity toward the candy in the depletion condition but not in the control condition.'
Karpinski and Hilton (2001)	Study 2: Behavioural choice between apples or candy bars.	'...explicit attitudes and the IAT are independent... explicit attitudes predicted behavior but the IAT did not.' (Note: there was no time pressure/drain on cognitive resources etc. operating here. In this study – participants 'were informed that they could choose only one of the objects [apple or candy bar] to eat or to take home with them.')
Karpinski and Steinman (2006)	Study 1: Brand choice between Coke or Pepsi.	Both IAT and explicit measures predicted choice of branded drink.

(Continued overleaf)

Table 15.1 continued

Citation	Behavioural measure	Did the IAT successfully predict behaviour?
Karpinski, Steinman and Hilton (2005)	Voting intention in the 2000 US Presidential election and also brand choice between Coke or Pepsi.	'… explicit attitude measures were better predictors of *deliberative* behaviors than IAT scores' (note: my italics).
Maison, Greenwald and Bruin (2001)	Study 1: Self-reported drinking of juices or soda, and self-reported dieting.	'… both studies resulted in significant correlation between the IAT and Ss' *self-reported* behavior.'
Maison, Greenwald and Bruin (2004)	Study 1: Self-reported consumption of yoghurt brands/eating at different fast food restaurants/consumption of Coke or Pepsi.	'A meta-analytic combination of the three studies showed that that the use of IAT measures increased the prediction of behavior relative to explicit attitude measures alone.'
Olson and Fazio (2004)	Study 3: Self-reported behaviour of apple and candy bar consumption.	IAT predicted behavior, particularly a more personalized IAT. '… the personalized IAT correlated more strongly with explicit measures of liking, past eating behavior, and behavioral intentions than did the traditional IAT.'

Scarabis, Florack and Gosejohann (2006)	Choice between chocolate and fruit.	The IAT a good predictor of actual choice, '... people rely more on automatic preferences that are independent from higher-order appraisals when they focus on their affective responses [what enjoyment they might get from the food] than when they think about the advantages and disadvantages of choice options.'
Swanson, Rudman and Greenwald (2001)	Study 2: Self-reported smoking behaviour or vegetarianism/non-vegetarianism.	The IAT and explicit attitude measures did predict vegetarianism/non-vegetarianism but not smoking.
Vantomme, Geuens, De Houwer and De Pelsmacker (2005)	Self-reported purchase intentions for real and fictitious brands of green and environmentally unfriendly cleaning products.	'The IAT, but not the explicit difference score, differentiated between respondents intending to buy the real ecological all-purpose cleaner and those intending to buy the real traditional all-purpose cleaner.'

These studies suggest a positive trend with respect to the predictive power of the IAT, particularly under certain types of conditions. When people are under any kind of time pressure, or when they are attempting to control their emotional state, or when they are under the influence of alcohol, the IAT seems to be a good predictor of behaviour. Explicit measures, on the other hand, are usually better when there is no mental load or time pressure, thereby allowing the person to make slower, deliberate and reflective behavioural decisions (see Fazio 1990). Supermarket shopping, however, is often not a slow, deliberate, reflective process, the shopper passes about 300 brands per minute (Rundh 2007) and each individual choice is often quick and automatic (Zeithaml, Bolton, Deighton *et al.* 2006). In such contexts, the IAT might well be a better predictor of consumer behaviour than a measure of explicit attitude.

Only one other study prior to Beattie and Sale (2009) had applied the IAT to issues to do with sustainability. Vantomme and colleagues (2005) examined explicit and implicit attitudes towards green cleaning products. They had expected to find that implicit attitudes would be less positive than the explicit attitudes (because of social desirability). In their first experiment they used fictitious cleaning products, introduced to participants in a 'learning phase' where participants were informed that one product was environmentally friendly whilst the other was harmful to the environment. They used fictitious products because of the dangers of brand image impacting upon the results. What they found, however, was that in contrast to their initial hypothesis, implicit attitudes towards the fictitious green cleaning products were far more positive than their explicit attitudes. In a second experiment, real brands were used and, this time, there was no difference in explicit and implicit attitudes towards the green cleaning products. So the results from this study are far from conclusive with respect to the underlying implicit attitudes that people might actually hold towards green products. Moreover, no study had attempted to compare the predictive value of measures of explicit and implicit attitudes to low carbon products for actual consumer choice.

Given the potential importance of this topic with respect to climate change, we argued that it is crucial to understand fully the nature of explicit and implicit attitudes towards green products. We need to understand this in order to assess consumers' willingness to change their patterns of consumption (given potentially the right kinds of triggers). Beattie and Sale (2011) explored this by measuring explicit and implicit attitudes towards high and low carbon footprint products and then used a consumer choice paradigm to see which measure (explicit or implicit) differentiated the choice of high/low carbon products. Given that most supermarket shopping is conducted under time pressure, we also explored the possible contribution of time pressure in consumer choice.

The results showed that nearly half (48.4%) of those who adamantly stated they were pro-low carbon in self-report measures actually held implicit attitudes that were discrepant with this (like the young dark-haired woman in Chapter 1). Clearly, a large proportion of people do exaggerate their green credentials. But what are the implications of these two different types of attitude for actual behavioural choice? We used 80 participants in this part of the research. After the participants completed the attitude tests, they had to choose a 'goody bag' containing either low (English apple, recycled pen, energy efficient light bulb) or high carbon footprint products (banana, biro, normal bulb). These objects were laid out behind participants but remained covered during the attitude testing. Participants were invited to make a choice under one of two conditions – time pressure (TP), where they had to make an immediate choice encouraged by the experimenter, or no time pressure (no TP), where they had as much time as required to make their choice. The bags covering the products were removed by an assistant (blind to the scores on the attitude scales) and participants were asked to point to the goody bag of their choice. Participants were randomly assigned to the condition (TP/no TP) on consecutive trials.

In terms of our current concerns, the critical result was that those who were pro-low carbon, as revealed by the IAT, were significantly more likely to choose the low carbon footprint goody bag. Explicit measures, on the other hand, were not a significant predictor of behavioural choice.

The implication of this finding is clear: we simply cannot rely on what people say to predict patterns of behaviour. If we are to genuinely produce a green revolution, then the concept of implicit attitudes must be kept firmly in focus and it may well be a matter of urgency to consider how to augment implicit attitudes to green products and, in addition, to ensure that these implicit attitudes translate to actual consumer behaviour, for example, by designing carbon footprint symbols that can impact on the implicit system. One important practical step is to think about the design of carbon labels. The detailed carbon footprint information currently on labels might work if consumer choice was a slow, reflective process directed by explicit attitudes (currently there is little visual attention to these carbon labels in the normal 5–10 second viewing frame, see Beattie *et al.* 2010). However, if consumer choice is much more automatic and unconscious then we may need a different labelling system which can impinge on more automatic processes. For example, we may need to use something like a traffic light approach, with red symbolising 'high carbon footprint' or 'danger' (hence producing relatively more right frontal cortical activation, see Elliot, Maier, Moller *et al.* 2007; Beattie 2010). Traffic signals might well influence consumer choice guided by these implicit processes in a way that the (very well meaning) current system does not.

The research also revealed that the condition under which the behavioural choice was made (i.e. under time pressure or under no time pressure) significantly predicted choice so that, when under time pressure, people were more likely to choose the high carbon footprint option (those choosing the high carbon option under time pressure had the least pro-low carbon footprint implicit attitude in the entire sample, suggesting that under time pressure implicit attitudes influenced behaviour). This finding has implications for supermarket shopping which, unfortunately (from this point of view), is an activity often conducted under a great deal of time pressure (see also Southerton 2003). Our research would suggest that the likelihood of consumers actually choosing the 'greener option' would be significantly reduced under these conditions if their implicit attitudes are not sufficiently pro-low carbon in the first place. Of course, we used just one type of behavioural choice in this study, and a choice with no economic consequences whatsoever for the consumer. Future research must consider the generality of this effect in a much more representative (and real) consumer domain. But what this research does tell us is that implicit attitudes might well predict behaviour in some specific contexts. The implication for implicit attitudes to ethnicity could be very important indeed.

- In the area of attitudes to the environment there is no significant correlation between people's self-reported attitudes and their implicit attitude.
- Their implicit attitude seems to be a better predictor of the 'green' choices they actually make.
- Implicit attitudes seem to predict behaviour best when people are under cognitive, emotional or time pressure.
- This may have serious implications for identifying those conditions under which we might see the behavioural consequences of implicit racial attitudes.
- Generalising from this research one might recommend that an individual should never rush into expressing an opinion about the suitability of someone from a different ethnic group for a post, if their D score has a certain polarity to it.*(Continued overleaf)*

16

How ethnicity and implicit attitudes may affect shortlisting for university posts

So, could implicit attitudes be a significant factor in the under-representation of Black and Minority Ethnic (BME) staff in universities? The assumption is that somehow the implicit attitudes which we have now measured are impacting on actual selection decisions. But how plausible is this and how big could the problem actually be?

Many have argued that racial inequality in recruitment between Minority Ethnic groups and the majority White population continues to represent a major persistent source of social and economic injustice (Bassanini and Saint-Martin 2008). I have already discussed this in the opening chapter. However, despite its obvious theoretical import, research attention has focused disproportionately on the prevalence of discrimination per se, rather than on the core psychological processes underpinning potential sources of bias in recruitment and hiring decisions. Research attention urgently needs to shift away from an exploration of the magnitude of 'ethnic penalties' (see Heath and Li 2007), and investigate instead the psychological conditions that give rise to discrimination and ultimately towards an understanding of what (if any) policy initiatives can be implemented during personnel recruitment to reduce potential bias in the decision-making processes that underpin selection.

A number of researchers have suggested previously that implicit biases might well operate in selection interviews. Sharon Purkiss and her colleagues (Purkiss, Perrewé, Gillespie *et al.* 2006) from California State University looked at possible implicit sources of bias about Hispanics on

interview judgements and decisions. They based their particular investigation on the work of Dovidio and Gaertner
(2000) who showed that when Black and White candidates
were being considered for the same post, the Black candidates were not selected as often as the White candidates
even when their qualifications were identical, but this only
occurred if they just fitted the criterion for the post. When
their qualifications were not sufficient or when their qualifications were absolutely sparkling then there was no racial
or ethnic bias apparent. In other words, when people are
being considered for any post then clearly there are a number
of factors that need to be taken into consideration, and when
you design studies to test for ethnic bias it is important to
bear this in mind.

Purkiss and her colleagues (2006: 155) were mindful of
this and also mindful of the fact that, in their words:

> A combination of ethnic minority cues (i.e. as opposed to
> a single cue) may be more likely to trigger an
> unconscious automatic negative reaction because of the
> salience of the cues and the ease in which one is more
> confident about placing someone in a class or category.

For this reason in their particular study they varied both the
name of the candidate (Hispanic versus non-Hispanic) and
the accent of the candidate, because they argued that when
both cues were present they were more likely to cue negative
automatic associations. The way they carried out the study
was they auditioned to find an actor for the role of the applicant who was able to speak equally well with a standard
American English accent and with a Hispanic accent. They
found an established actor who had experience of working
in the theatre and in commercials in both Spanish and
English. The actor they selected was a White male. The
participants in the study were given a job description and a
CV of someone applying for the post of Human Resource
Manager. The 'applicant' was called either 'Michael
Fredrickson' or 'Miguel Fernandez' and given a 3.7 Grade
Point Average in Human Resource Management from a
large state university. 'Miguel Fernandez' either spoke in a

Hispanic accent or a standard American English accent on the video, 'Michael Fredrickson' also either spoke in a Hispanic or American English accent. Participants then had a set of judgements to make. Purkiss and her colleagues did not use the Implicit Association Test to measure implicit bias against Hispanics but an adaptation of the Modern Racism Scale (see McConahay 1986). The Modern Racism Scale does not delve down into implicit or unconscious associations but nevertheless uses a rating scale which tries to 'inconspicuously measure prejudice'. It provides the participants with a set of 12 statements and they have to indicate whether they agree or disagree with the statements. The statements include items like 'Over the past few years, the government and news media have shown more respect to Hispanics than they deserve' and 'It is easy to understand the frustration of Hispanics in America'. Participants were also asked to rate the applicant on 26 bipolar pairs of adjectives using a seven-point scale and then to indicate their decision as to whether they would hire the applicant or not. They were also asked if they could understand the candidate's accent.

Purkiss and her colleagues found, as predicted, that the most unfavourable judgements about the applicants were triggered by a combination of the ethnic name and the ethnic accent. In other words, the most extreme negative judgements were made to 'Miguel Fernandez' speaking in a Hispanic accent. However, the researchers were surprised to find that the most *favourable* judgements of all did not occur when 'Michael Fredrickson' was speaking in a standard American-English accent but when 'Miguel Fernandez' spoke with a standard American-English accent.

To make sense of this the researchers looked outside the domain of implicit prejudice to 'Expectancy Violation Theory' (Jussim, Coleman and Lerch 1987) where it is suggested that we have lower expectations from minority groups but when these expectations are violated in a positive way then evaluations may change dramatically. In other words, when 'Miguel Fernandez' was sitting in the applicant's seat on the video, the participants had quite low expectations until Miguel started to speak and then suddenly they changed their minds. There was one other surprising finding from this study, namely that the measure of ethnic bias that was used seemed not just to predict negative evaluations of the 'Hispanic' applicant, rather it predicted negative evaluation of all applicants. In other words, those people who were most biased against Hispanics tended to evaluate negatively most other candidates as well. In the words of the researchers: 'Perhaps interviewer ethnic biases trigger a sceptical and guarded view of others, which is translated into more negative perceptions of applicants in general' (Purkiss *et al.* 2006: 163). Of course, this study did not use any measure of implicit attitude. The Modern Racism Scale is a self-report measure which claims to measure prejudice 'inconspicuously' but the items are fairly transparent, so it does not really answer the question about possible implicit and possibly *unconscious* biases.

One study which did consider the impact of automatic associations on employment decisions was conducted by Dan-Olof Rooth from Kalmar University in Sweden (Rooth 2010). Rooth used an IAT to measure possible implicit biases towards Muslim names compared to Swedish names. He also used a measure of explicit attitudes towards Arab-Muslims and Swedes which consisted of a number of different subtests, including a 'hiring preference rating' in which the employers had to choose one out of a set of alternatives (e.g. 'When hiring staff I strongly prefer Swedish men to Arab-Muslim men', ranging from a strong preference for Arab-Muslims to a strong preference for Swedish men). Another sub-test was a performance stereotype test in which participants had to rate items such as 'Swedish men perform much better at work than Arab-Muslim men.'

Rooth analysed the relationship between the measures of implicit and explicit attitude and the probability of a callback for interview for applicants with either an Arab-Muslim name or a Swedish name. The results were stark and clear:

This study was one of the first to examine the relation among automatically activated associations, explicit attitudes and stereotypes, and discriminatory behavior in a real hiring situation. We find strong and consistent negative correlations between the IAT score and the probability that the firm/recruiter invited the applicant with an Arab-Muslim sounding name for an interview. The results . . . show that the probability to invite job applicants with names such as Mohammed or Ali decreases by five percentage points when the recruiter has at least a moderate negative implicit association toward Arab-Muslim men in Sweden. On the other hand, no such stable, and statistically significant, correlations are found for the explicit measures and the probability to invite job applicants with Arab-Muslim sounding names. (ibid.: 529)

These are indeed stark conclusions: 'what our results then indicate is that there are recruiters who implicitly discriminate, but who would not explicitly do so. The results present evidence of that recruiting behavior is being affected by implicit prejudice rather than by explicit discrimination.' (Rooth 2010: 529.)

Son Hing, Chung-Yan, Hamilton and Zanna (2008) took separate measures of explicit and implicit attitude (again using the IAT) to create four different profiles with individuals high or low on the two dimensions (explicit/ implicit). They labelled each of these four groups: truly low prejudiced (double low), aversive racists (low explicit, high implicit), principled conservatives (high explicit, low implicit) and modern racists (double high). They wished to consider both factors to predict behaviour when it came to hiring or not (apparent) White or Asian job applicants who either clearly met or just met job specifications for posts in data analysis of human resources. One of the critical findings was that the aversive racists (low explicit, high implicit) were less likely to hire the Asian candidate compared with the identically qualified White candidate when their qualifications were just above threshold (rather than way above threshold). Truly low prejudiced individuals, however, gave the Asians and the Whites equivalent recommendations. What was also interesting was that the aversive racists were more likely to remember the negative parts of the qualifications of those from a different ethnic group. Their conclusion was that:

> aversive racists are able to maintain a self-image as egalitarian humanists. This might be possible because they do not discriminate in situations where such behavior would be obvious (e.g. when they have all relevant information on hand or when assessing a highly qualified candidate for a position). In addition, once aversive racists engage in discriminatory behavior, it appears that they protect their self-image with post hoc rationales. (Son Hing *et al.* 2008: 982)

But, of course, these studies all investigate quite specific ethnic groups: Muslim, Asian or Black candidates. Would these sorts of results generalise to something as inherently heterogeneous as a category like 'non-White'? And further, although research now seems to have shown discriminatory selection practices across a spectrum of occupations (Pager, Western and Bonikowski 2009) and even potentially identified one core mechanism in the form of implicit bias, one area which has not been explored in any great detail is the selection of staff for Higher Education Institutes (Leathwood, Maylor and Moreau 2009), and the operation of possible biases here.

But what we do know is that despite considerable efforts to deal with the underrepresentation of ethnic minorities among the higher academic and administrative grades of British universities, the statistics reveal that so far success has been, at best, limited (see the UK's Equality Challenge Unit, Equality in higher education: statistical report 2011). It is perhaps a little surprising, given the meritocratic principles on which universities are founded, as well as the liberal values that one might expect educated individuals to espouse, that the proportion of BME academic staff in UK universities is lower than that of the British working population for individuals qualified to perform an academic job (Equality Challenge Unit 2011). Moreover, recent data suggests that compared to equally qualified Whites, BME academic staff are more likely to be employed on short, fixed-term contracts (33.5% for BME staff vs. 28.1% for Whites; ibid.), and become increasingly underrepresented the more senior the academic grade. For example, 11.1% of all White (UK) academics are professors compared to 8.9% of BME (UK) academics (ibid.). Again this appears to be an international problem with a similar picture emerging from the US, where only 5.4% of all university full-time academic staff come from a BME background (US Department of Education 2007). According to the *Journal of Blacks in Higher Education*:

> If we project into the future on a straight-line basis the progress of Blacks into faculty ranks over the past 26 years, we find that Blacks in faculty ranks will not reach parity with the Black percentage of the overall American workforce for another 140 years. (Cited by Leathwood *et al.* 2009)

So how might implicit attitudes have been impacting on recruitment (and promotion) at the University of Manchester in particular? The statistics in many ways are quite stark (see Table 16.1), suggesting that women and BME staff are significantly underrepresented at the higher grades in the case of both the academic staff and the professional support services.

The university had been trying to address these issues, certainly since the creation of the new university in 2004 through Operational Performance Review (OPR) actions, including the close monitoring of data on age, gender, ethnicity and disability with respect to new staff profiles and promotions. Then there were 'Women in Leadership' and 'Race in Leadership' reports and recommendations and various positive actions emerging out of these: career development activities, mentoring, development sessions for academics, career development advice. But after three years of activity, there was still minimal change at a senior level. The problem in Patrick Johnson's words was that 'Senior Managers were absolutely convinced that the best people got the job and the right people got promoted' (personal

Table 16.1 So how diverse *really* is the University of Manchester in 2011?

	Female%	BME%
Academic staff		
Lecturer	44	13
Senior Lecturer/Reader	29	10
Professor	19	8
Professional support services	%	%
Grade 1–4	62	13
Grade 5–6	53	7
Grade 7	46	4
Grade 8–9	3	3

communication). And this, of course, is where I came in. So far we had found some D scores that seemed to be at odds with what people had written on their self-report questionnaires – but were they of any significance? We jumped straight in, to try to simulate that process of coming to the university as an employee.

We began by selecting two genuine job adverts that appeared on the vacancy section of the University of Manchester's website. One job advertised an academic position ('Lectureship in Health Psychology'; Figure 16.1); the other was an administrative post ('Postgraduate Administrator'; Figure 16.2), part of the Professional Support Services.

We then created four CVs for the lectureship post and four for the administrative post (each CV consisted of two or three pages of information; two in the case of some of the CVs for the administrative post). Each CV was designed to contain some positive and some negative information. Our reasoning was that most CVs have this basic feature (few are 100% excellent). For example, all of the academic applicants had studied at high-ranking British universities for their first degree (*positive information*), but at less prestigious

Lecturer in Health Psychology
Department of Psychology
University of Manchester – Faculty of Medical and Human Sciences
From £32,620 – £45,155 pa   Job Ref: 7715   Closing date: 31st January 2010

The Department of Psychology is seeking to appoint a Lecturer in Health Psychology with specific expertise in understanding the impact of negative cognitions on health behaviour and well-being. The post holder will develop their individual research programme in collaboration with existing academic staff and will take an active role in contributing to both postgraduate and undergraduate teaching. Specifically, the post holder will lecture to postgraduate students on our new M.Sc. programme in Clinical and Health Psychology as well as contributing in all three years on our undergraduate programme. In addition, the successful candidate will supervise small scale Tutorial Projects and third year projects in both their area of expertise and within the broader domain of health psychology. They will also supervise Masters' level students as well as Ph.D. students.

Qualifications
The successful applicant is likely to have a developing record of research and publications commensurate with the appropriate stage in their career, but clearly show international potential. Applicants should also have a good first degree in psychology and a Ph.D (or be nearing completion of a Ph.D.) in the area of health psychology. Interviews are scheduled for early February, 2011. For an informal discussion about this post, please contact Professor Howard Mansfield, Head of School, on 0161 275 2590 email: H.Mansfield@manchester.ac.uk.

Figure 16.1 **Advert for the academic post.**

Experienced Administrator Needed for Postgraduate Taught Course University of Manchester
School of Psychological Sciences
Reference: HUM/10559 £20,938 – £23,566 p.a. Closing Date: 15th November 2010

A post has arisen in the School of Psychological Sciences for a Postgraduate Administrator. You will be responsible for creating and maintaining academic and student records using Campus Solutions, linking academic advisement with programme plans, monitoring class enrolments, class scheduling, student course unit choices and recording degree classification. You will also be involved in organising formal feedback meetings with student representatives, and will work with the Examinations Officer coordinating the assessment process across a range of Postgraduate Taught Programmes. The role also involves compiling examination grids, monitoring students' progress and liaising with External Examiners. Other duties include organising introductory sessions at the start of the academic year and creating programme and dissertation handbooks for students and staff to use throughout the year, as well as liaising with academics and other administrators to ensure that information is accurate and concise.

Qualifications required:
You should have a good standard level of education, normally six GCSEs including passes in English and Maths grade C or above and 2 or more A-Levels, or equivalent qualification (e.g., City and Guilds or GNVQs). Preferably you will also have previous administrative experience in higher education and excellent IT, interpersonal and communication skills. For an informal discussion please contact Jenny Higgins, on 0161 275 2799 or email: J.Higgins@manchester.ac.uk

Figure 16.2 **Advert for the administrative post.**

institutions for their second degree (*negative information*), had some publications in high-impact journals (positive), but other papers in much less prestigious journals (*negative*). In relation to the administrative post, all candidates had a mixture of relevant (*positive*) and less relevant work experience (*negative*) with some unexplained gaps in their work history (*negative*), and pastimes that focused on learning new transferable skills, e.g. attending IT classes (*positive*), as well as hobbies that were less likely to appeal to a responsible employer, e.g. socialising in the pub with friends (*negative*). There were also some spelling mistakes in some of the CVs.

Of course, this positive/negative split was very subjective but was an attempt to crystallise a Manchester ethos on such matters; non-prestigious in the UK context meant not being a Russell Group university.

In the CV below, the A levels are very good, as is the 2:1 from University College London. However, the Masters degree was not completed and Edge Hill is a much less prestigious institution than UCL (Figure 16.3). In terms of the journal articles, two are prestigious (*British Medical Journal* and *Personality and Individual Differences*), the other two much less so (Figure 16.4). In terms of teaching, again there are some positive bits and some more negative bits: 55 per

Education and Qualifications

1998–2000 – *Eaton Road College, Bury:* A-Levels: Psychology (A), German (A), History (A)

2000–2003 – *University College London:* B.Sc. (Hons) Psychology (2:1).

2005–2006 – *University of Salford:* M.Sc. in Psychology and Neuroscience (didn't complete)

2006–2010 – *Edge Hill University:* (Ph.D. Psychology)
Thesis Title *"Exploring the Effects of Stress on the Duration and Severity of Illness"*

Figure 16.3 **Qualifications detailed on one of the CVs for the academic post.**

Academic Publications

Obagundu, Latoya. (2010). Effects of Cortisol and Stress on Antibiotic Resistant Infection. *Health Psychology Newsletter,* 2, 27–36.

Obagundu, Latoya. (2009). An Investigation into the Effects of Anxiety and Stress on the Duration of Influenza in Elderly Patients. *The Psychologist,* 7, 110–112.

Thomas, Michael, Turner, Mark and Obagundu, Latoya. (2008) Can Stressful Life Events Really Cause Cancer? A Meta Analytic Review of the Literature. *British Medical Journal,* 12, 112–123.

Soughton, Jonathan, Dempsey, Thomas and Obagundu, Latoya. (2007) The Effects of Stress on Secondary Cancers: A Two Stage Model? *Personality and Individual Differences,* 21, 234–246.

Figure 16.4 **Publications represented on one of the CVs for the academic post.**

cent of students saying that they were 'satisfied' with a course is not that good in these demanding times dominated by National Student Satisfaction scores (Figure 16.5).

The four CVs systematically varied the qualifications, publications and experience of the apparent applicant. Each CV was then assigned a White or a non-White identity of matching gender (Figures 16.6 and 16.7). All pictures were carefully selected to reflect applicants who

Relevant Experience

I gained valuable experience in teaching at *University College London* (2004–2005). I spent the year as a Teaching Assistant and gave a series of seminars in Health Psychology to first year undergraduates. Duties included preparing and giving a series of seminars, and assessing students' knowledge of Health Psychology through an essay-based assignment. As part of their final year exams, students sat an examination entitled "Social Cognition and the Psychology of Health" that I was partly responsible for moderating.

More recently, I have spent 3 months gaining teaching experience at *Edge Hill University* (between finishing my PhD in March 2010 and May 2010), where my role was to integrate a Health Psychology module into the existing syllabus. After creating the module, students were asked to rate how much they had enjoyed the course. Over 55% of psychology students said they were at least satisfied with the new Health Psychology course, with about 5% stating that they were 'very' satisfied with the course that I had created.

Figure 16.5 **Relevant experience detailed on one of the CVs for the academic post.**

Name	Photograph	Name	Photograph
Jennifer Peterson		Latoya Obagundu	
Victoria Glegg		Nazia Atwi	
Sarah Taylor		Ishia Nazariah	
Jayne Turner		Xia Lynn	

Figure 16.6 Matched female White and non-White names and images for the academic post.

were smiling and who were matched in terms of age and judged attractiveness.

Figure 16.8 shows the start of one CV for a White candidate and is followed by the identical CV for a non-White candidate (Figure 16.9).

We wanted to ensure that the CVs we had created were broadly equivalent in terms of the quality of each applicant. We tested this by asking 10 participants (five White and five non-White), who did not take part in any of our studies, to individually rate the suitability (using a 7-point Likert

Name	Photograph	Name	Photograph
Steven Phillips		Kim Wu	
John Thompson		Rezza Housseini	
Mark Pennington		Saleem Rajput	
Timothy Lewis		Reggie Nnamani	

Figure 16.7 **Matched male White and non-White names and images for the administrative post.**

Scale) of each of the eight CVs for the target job, on the basis of qualifications, work experience and, where appropriate, publication history. Critically the CVs that we asked our 10 participants to rate did not carry any information about the ethnicity of the applicant. In other words, there were no names or photographs attached to these particular CVs. The mean suitability ratings of CVs for the lectureship post was 4.74 (range 4.38 to 5.00) and 3.85 for the administrative job (range 3.67 to 4.05). These results showed that overall, when the CVs were neutral in terms of ethnicity, there was very

Jennifer Peterson

<u>Qualifications</u>

1996–1998: *Bolton Sixth Form College* – 3 A-Levels: Biology (A), English Language (B), Psychology (A)

1999–2002: *University of Liverpool* – B.Sc. (Hons) Psychology (First Class)

2002–2004: *University of Bradford* – M.Res. (Pass) (Part-Time)

2004–2010: *Liverpool John Moores University* PhD in Psychology (Part-Time) *The Role of Social Support in the Treatment of Eating Disorders*

Figure 16.8 White version of first page of one CV for the academic post.

Ishia Nazariah

<u>Qualifications</u>

1996–1998: *Bolton Sixth Form College* – 3 A-Levels: Biology (A), English Language (B), Psychology (A)

1999–2002: *University of Liverpool* – B.Sc. (Hons) Psychology (First Class)

2002–2004: *University of Bradford* – M.Res. (Pass) (Part-Time)

2004–2010: *Liverpool John Moores University* PhD in Psychology (Part-Time) *The Role of Social Support in the Treatment of Eating Disorders*

Figure 16.9 Non-White (matched) version of first page of one CV for the academic post.

little variation in how our participants rated the quality of each applicant. If, on the other hand, White and non-White participants rate the quality of the CVs differently when the candidates are assigned an ethnic identity, then we can be relatively confident that any difference is due to some sort of ethnic bias.

Participants in our study (mainly university students) were shown the advert for the lectureship post, followed by four CVs, and also the advert for the administrative post, followed by the relevant second set of CVs. Participants always saw two White and two non-White applicants after each advert (the order in which the job adverts appeared and order of candidates were randomised throughout). After viewing each candidate for a given post, participants rated the suitability of the candidate on a 7-point scale. In this first study, all of the applicants for the academic post were female and all the applicants for the administrative post were male.

Participants were then given a further minute to reflect on their initial suitability judgement. We wanted to monitor their eye movements during this critical period because people tended to read the CVs linearly and sequentially (but, of course, at different speeds). This 'critical minute' formed the basis of our eye-tracking analysis as during this time period participants appear to *scan* rather than read the CVs and now their unconscious eye movements are being directed at certain points in the CV in preparation for some sort of decision. After seeing all four applicants for a given post, participants were then asked to shortlist two candidates. This procedure was then repeated for the remaining job advert. Afterwards, we measured both explicit and implicit attitudes to White and non-White candidates using the Likert Scale, the Feeling Thermometer and our new Ethnic IAT.

By way of illustration, Figures 16.10 and 16.11 show how two participants, both White, scanned the first page of a CV of one White and one non-White candidate, with the dots indicating individual fixation points (the data is simplified here using event sampling; every fifth 40-millisecond fixation point is sampled). Look at the level of fixation on the university from which Ishia, the non-White candidate, obtained her PhD (not a Russell Group university) and the fixation on the photograph and particularly on the headscarf. The participant does scan Ishia's very good A Level results but during the critical period he does not look back once at the First Class degree from Liverpool. Rather, the

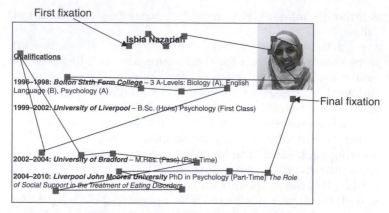

Figure 16.10 Pattern of gaze fixation of one White participant looking at the first page of a non-White candidate's CV for the academic post.

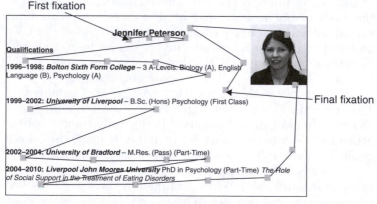

Figure 16.11 Pattern of gaze fixation of one White participant looking at the first page of a White candidate's CV for the academic post.

participant jumps across this line of information. Compare this with a different White participant in Figure 16.11, this time looking at a White job applicant, Jennifer. This time the participant does glance at the First Class degree result in the critical period and interestingly at the end of the period they again glance at the face, and then at the name, the A Level results and the degree result in that order. These two figures suggest that there may well be an effect of participant ethnicity on how participants scan the CV of applicants from different ethnic backgrounds.

Figures 16.12 and 16.13 show two non-White participants scanning White and non-White CVs. The main features of these two figures is that the information about the First Class degree from Liverpool (clearly representing good information) is scanned in both cases.

In total, *240,000 data points* were individually coded and analysed (as follows):

- Each fixation point lasts for 40 ms (25 fixations per second).
- Participants saw each CV for 1 minute = 1,500 fixations
- Each participant saw 8 CVs = 12,000 fixations.
- 20 participants were used = 240,000 frames analysed in total.

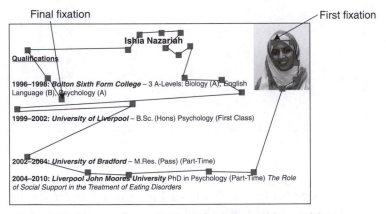

Figure 16.12 **Pattern of gaze fixation of one non-White participant looking at the first page of a non-White candidate's CV for the academic post.**

First fixation   Final fixation

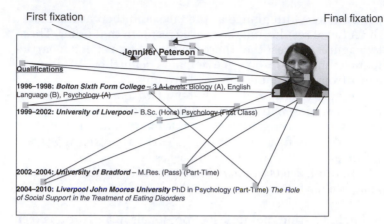

Figure 16.13 **Pattern of gaze fixation of one non-White participant looking at the first page of a White candidate's CV for the academic post.**

Table 16.2 **The shortlisting of candidates for an academic post by White participants**

White participants	2 non-Whites	1 White and 1 non-White	2 Whites
1			X
2			X
3			X
4			X
5			X
6			X
7			X
8		X	
9			X
10		X	

The first question we asked was which candidates (all female remember) were shortlisted for the academic job by *White* participants? See Table 16.2.

Table 16.3 shows which candidates were shortlisted for the academic job by *non-White* participants.

Table 16.3 The shortlisting of candidates for an academic post
by non-White participants

Non-White participants	2 non-Whites	1 White and 1 non-White	2 Whites
1		X	
2	X		
3		X	
4		X	
5		X	
6		X	
7	X		
8	X		
9		X	
10		X	

It would seem to be the case that White participants
were more likely to shortlist White applicants than non-
White applicants (with identical CVs) for the academic post.
This was a very small sample, but transforming the frequen-
cies to a log scale reveals a significant statistical effect. We
then asked which candidates (all male) were shortlisted for
the administrative job by *White* participants. See Table 16.4.

Table 16.4 The shortlisting of candidates for an administrative post
by White participants

White participants	2 non-Whites	1 White and 1 non-White	2 Whites
1		X	
2	X		
3		X	
4		X	
5			X
6		X	
7		X	
8		X	
9		X	
10		X	

And then we focused on which candidates were short-listed for the administrative post by non-White participants. See Table 16.5.

Here we found that ethnicity of participants had no significant effect on the proportion of White and non-White applicants shortlisted for the administrative post.

Next we analysed the results of both the explicit and implicit attitudinal measures to see if there was any connection between these measures and the ethnicity of the candidates who were shortlisted (see Tables 16.6 to 16.8). The measures of explicit attitude do not show any real pattern

Table 16.5 The shortlisting of candidates for an administrative post by non-White participants

Non-White participants	2 non-Whites	1 White and 1 non-White	2 Whites
1		X	
2			X
3		X	
4		X	
5		X	
6		X	
7		X	
8		X	
9		X	
10	X		

Table 16.6 The mean Likert scores of participants shortlisting candidates from different ethnic backgrounds

	2 non-Whites shortlisted	1 White and 1 non-White shortlisted	2 Whites shortlisted
Academic post	3.00	2.40	3.00
Administrative post	3.00	2.89	3.00

Table 16.7 **The mean Thermometer Difference scores of participants shortlisting candidates from different ethnic backgrounds**

	2 non-Whites shortlisted	1 White and 1 non-White shortlisted	2 Whites shortlisted
Academic post	−0.33	−0.33	0.25
Administrative post	0	−0.12	0

Table 16.8 **The mean D scores of participants shortlisting candidates from different ethnic backgrounds**

	2 non-Whites shortlisted	1 White and 1 non-White shortlisted	2 Whites shortlisted
Academic post	0.50	0.63	0.93
Administrative post	0.13	0.62	2.82

and tend to fall within the neutral band of the scale (3 is neutral for the Likert Scale; 0 is neutral for the Thermometer Difference Scale). Participants shortlisting two White or two non-White candidates for either post had exactly the same Likert score (3.00), exactly in the middle of the scale.

What is interesting about the D scores is that there does seem to be a pattern in that the D scores of those shortlisting two White candidates are the highest (and above the critical threshold of 0.8, which indicates a strong preference for Whites compared to non-Whites). Those participants who shortlisted two non-White candidates had the lowest mean D scores (although still pro-White in the case of the academic job but essentially neutral in the case of the administrative post).

In this exploratory study there did seem to be a pattern, but the pattern, such as it was, only occurred with the measures of implicit attitude. The explicit attitudes that people reported were not that relevant to their actual judgement when shortlisting for university posts.

But did anything happen with their unconscious eye movements in that critical minute when they had already scanned the data on the CVs but before they had to make their actual shortlisting judgement? We analysed the individual gaze fixations by considering the proportion of time spent looking at the following categories:

- positive information, such as good qualifications and publications;
- negative information, such as poorer qualifications and publications;
- face, i.e. photograph of candidate;
- name, i.e. name of candidate.

Plus, there were residual categories of:

- 'movement', namely eye movements outside of target area;
- 'tracker loss', namely eye movements that could not be captured.

So where did our White participants look when they scanned the CVs of candidates from different ethnic backgrounds? The tables below show the proportion of total time spent looking by White participants (Table 16.9) and non-White participants (Table 16.10) at various types of information (excluding tracker loss).

Table 16.9 **The proportion of total time spent looking by White participants at positive and negative information of White and non-White candidates (excluding tracker loss)**

		Positive%	*Negative%*
Academic post (Female)	White candidate	39.7	32.2
	Non-White candidate	30.9	40.1
Administrative post (Male)	White candidate	49.6	27.0
	Non-White candidate	37.0	38.0

Table 16.10 **The proportion of total time spent looking by non-White participants at positive and negative information of White and non-White candidates (excluding tracker loss)**

		Positive%	*Negative%*
Academic post (Female)	White candidate	34.5	41.7
	Non-White candidate	34.9	34.2
Administrative post (Male)	White candidate	36.4	39.3
	Non-White candidate	44.0	32.1

There are a number of things which should be apparent from these tables. Firstly, White participants spent more time looking at positive information on the CVs of White candidates and negative information on the CVs of non-White candidates for the academic post. They also spent a lot more time looking at the positive information of White candidates for the administrative post, but in the case of the non-White candidates for the administrative post they looked at positive and negative information equally often.

In the case of non-White participants shortlisting for an academic post, they spent slightly more time looking at the negative information than at the positive information of White candidates, but they looked at the positive and negative information of the non-White candidates equally. When non-White participants were shortlisting for the administrative post they looked more at the positive information of the non-White candidates than at the negative information, but in the case of White candidates they looked more evenly at positive and negative information. In other words, there seemed to be an interaction between the ethnicity of the participant and the ethnicity of the candidate, as shown in Figures 16.14 to 16.17.

This interaction between the ethnicity of the participant and the ethnicity of the candidate is perhaps shown

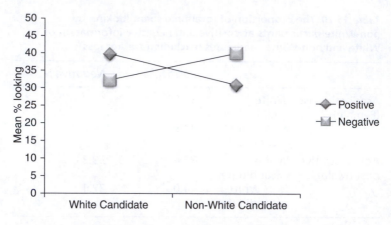

Figure 16.14 White participants viewing candidates for the academic post.

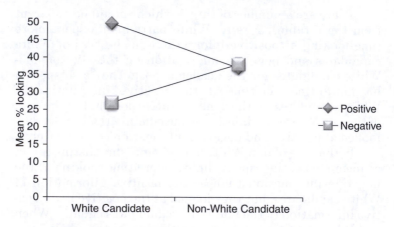

Figure 16.15 White participants viewing candidates for the administrative post.

most clearly in Figure 16.18, which averages across both posts (academic and administrative): the trend seems to be that non-White participants look at the positive information on the CVs of White and non-White candidates approximately equally, the White participants do not. In other words, there would appear to be a selective bias in

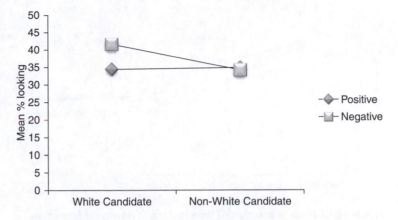

Figure 16.16 **Non-White participants viewing candidates for the academic post.**

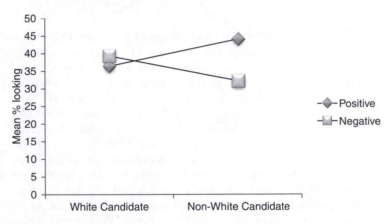

Figure 16.17 **Non-White participants viewing candidates for the administrative post.**

perception operating here. Our assumption throughout is that these eye movements are unconscious but highly selective. The implicit attitude seems to be directing these unconscious eye movements to build up a representation to form the basis for rational decision making. In other words, the unconscious is to some extent directing the rational mind.

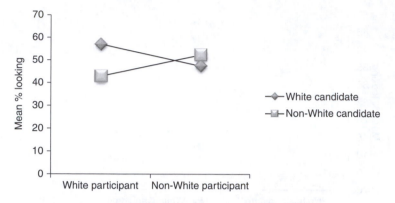

Figure 16.18 **Mean proportion of time looking at positive information of White and non-White candidates by White and non-White participants.**

The final analyses here considered whether there was any relationship between measures of implicit attitudes (D scores) and where participants looked at the CVs of candidates from different ethnic backgrounds. High D score participants were defined as those above the median, and low D score participants were defined as those below the median. The analyses revealed that those participants with high D scores (mean = 1.32) spent more time looking at the positive information of White candidates (58.91%) than those participants with lower D scores (mean = 0.30) and this difference was marginally significant. Those participants with high D scores similarly spent less time looking at the positive information on the CVs of non-White candidates compared with participants with lower D scores. In other words, measures of implicit attitude do seem to predict selective focus on parts of CVs even in the relatively small sample used here (see Table 16.11).

You can imagine how this selective focus could feed into 'rational' judgements about the relative appropriateness and inappropriateness of candidates for various posts. Our implicit attitude would seem to be directing our unconscious eye movements to provide exactly the information it

Table 16.11 **Proportion of time participants high or low in D score spent looking at positive and negative information of White and non-White candidates**

D Score of participants (mean)	Positive info. White candidates	Negative info. White candidates	Positive info. non-White candidates	Negative info. non-White candidates
High (1.32)	58.91	41.09	47.25	52.76
Low (0.30)	52.19	47.81	50.86	49.15

wants for a 'rational' decision. This is both extraordinary and very worrying.

I considered the data so far quite exploratory with a small sample of 20 participants, but the results looked potentially very interesting, and far too interesting not to follow up in a more systematic way. The problem with eye-tracking, however, is that, in our experience (and certainly with the equipment that we had available) it is exceptionally time consuming to do well with all of the individual dots having to be coded by human observers. For this reason we decided to increase the size of the sample but drop the eye-tracking component. But importantly we decided to counter-balance the design of the study so that both men and women were considered for both the academic and the non-academic posts. So now we used 96 participants (48 White and 48 non-White) who were presented with the CVs of four applicants (two White and two non-White) for an academic post ('Lectureship in Health Psychology'), and the CVs of a different set of four applicants (two White and two non-White) for an administrative position ('Postgraduate Administrator') at The University of Manchester. These figures should also give us a better estimate of how D scores vary depending upon the participants' own ethnicity, particularly in the case of non-White participants.

All of our 96 participants were British born, the majority again were university students. In fact, while the White group comprised exclusively White British participants, the non-White (BME) group was made up of a variety of British born, non-White, ethnic minority groups (namely, Asian [43.8%], Mixed Race Asian [20.8%], Chinese [14.6%], Black African [12.5%], and African Caribbean [8.3%]). These categorisations were based on the responses of our participants to the question: 'What ethnicity do you consider yourself to be?' We asked them this question right at the end of the experiment, in order not to sensitise them to the fact that the study was about attitudes to race.

Both the order in which the jobs were presented (academic versus administrative) and the order in which the applicants appeared (White versus non-White) were randomised throughout. Additionally, the names (Anglo-Saxon versus Black or Minority Ethnic) and faces (White versus non-White) were fully randomised. In order to reduce the possible biasing effects of gender, candidates either saw exclusively male or exclusively female applicants for each job. In other words, for the academic job half of our 48 White participants saw the CVs of four women (two White and two non-White), and were presented with the CVs of four men (two White and two non-White) for the administrative job. The other half of our White participants were presented with the CVs of four men (two White and two non-White) for the academic job, and four women (two White and two non-White) for the administrative job. Likewise, half of our non-White participants were presented with the CVs of four female applicants for the academic job, and four males for the administrative post, while the order was reversed for the remaining half of our non-White participants. We decided not to show any participants the CVs of male and female applicants for a target job, because they may have associated one job as stereotypically gender-specific. For example, research conducted by the UK's Equality Challenge Unit (2011) shows that across British Universities, 56% of academic staff were male, compared to 44% of female. Similarly, members of academic staff in professorial roles were significantly more likely to be male (80.9%) than female (19.1%). In contrast, professional and support staff were made up of a greater proportion of women (54.1%) than men (45.9%) (Equality Challenge Unit's Equality in higher education: statistical report 2011).

The order in which each job was presented (academic versus administrative) was counterbalanced, so that half of our participants were asked to select applicants for the academic job first and were subsequently instructed to choose applicants for the administrative post, while the remaining participants were presented with each job in the reverse order (i.e. administrative job *followed by* the academic post).

Participants were asked to make a judgement about the suitability of each applicant. Applicant suitability was measured using the following 7-point Likert Scale:

7   extremely suitable
6   very suitable
5   quite suitable
4   neither suitable nor unsuitable
3   quite unsuitable
2   very unsuitable
1   extremely unsuitable.

Finally, after viewing all four applicants for a post, participants were asked to select the *two* candidates that they wanted to put forward for interview. They were then shown the second job description and the process was repeated. There were a large number of analyses, described in detail in Appendix 2.

In all, this larger study yielded a rich and complicated data set that highlighted clear and distinctive biases based around ethnicity in the shortlisting for both academic and administrative posts in universities. These biases affect who is shortlisted for various posts, and the measure of implicit attitude towards people from different ethnic groups that derives from the IAT does seem to predict the nature and extent of the bias. The biases were found particularly in our White participants, but many of our non-White participants seemed to have a pro-White bias. The biases were most pronounced for the more prestigious academic post. Of course, none of these processes that we studied were real shortlisting decisions but the majority of our experimental participants came from a large metropolitan university in the UK and I really do suspect that they, as much as I, would not have been pleased by these results. The main results are summarised below. The details of the study are to be found in Appendix 2, which does require slow and careful reading by anybody interested in racial or ethnic prejudice today.

- Previous research has shown that when Black and White candidates were being considered for the same post the Black candidates were not shortlisted as often as the White candidates even when their qualifications were identical.
- Implicit attitudes have been shown in the past to predict bias in the shortlisting of Arab-Muslim men.
- Our new study reveals that a measure of implicit attitude does discriminate between participants who shortlisted two White candidates compared to two non-White candidates when the CVs of the candidates were identical.
- Self-report measures of attitude towards different ethnic groups do not predict behavioural preferences for shortlisting White candidates.
- The ethnicity of participants affected where they looked at the CVs of White and non-White candidates in the minute before they had to make their shortlisting decision.
- White participants spent more time looking at good information on the CVs of White candidates, and bad information on the CVs of non-White candidates, for an academic post.
- White participants spent longer looking at the good information than at the bad information of White candidates applying for an administrative post.
- White participants looked at good and bad information equally of the non-White candidates applying for the administrative post.
- Non-White participants spent slightly more time looking at the bad information than at the good information of White candidates applying for an academic post.
- Non-White participants looked at the good and bad information equally of non-White candidates applying for an academic post.
- Non-White participants looked at the good information rather than the bad information on the CVs of non-White candidates applying for an administrative post.

- There is a significant statistical interaction between the ethnicity of the participant and the ethnicity of the candidate when it comes to scrutinising CVs.
- People may think that they are making rational decisions in shortlisting for university posts but exactly what they fixate on when they are looking at a CV is affected by their ethnicity and that of the candidate.
- Those participants with high D scores (strong pro-White bias) spent more time looking at the good information on the CVs of White candidates compared with participants with lower D scores (less strong pro-White bias).
- Our implicit (and unconscious) attitude to people from different ethnic backgrounds seems to direct our unconscious eye movements when we consider their CVs.
- Our 'rational' decisions about the suitability of candidates are based on this biased pattern of fixation.
- This is both extraordinary and very worrying.

- In the second study reported in this chapter, and described in detail in Appendix 2, there was an overall moderate pro-White bias in this sample (with a mean D score of 0.68).
- The mean D score for the White participants was 0.93, which indicates a strong pro-White bias.
- The mean D score for the non-Whites was 0.43, which indicates a slight pro-White bias (in contrast to a neutral preference from the smaller sample of non-Whites in the first empirical investigation reported in Chapter 13).
- White participants tended to shortlist White candidates for the academic post rather than non-White candidates with identical CVs.
- White participants were ten times more likely to shortlist two White candidates for the lectureship post than two non-White candidates with the same CV.
- The shortlisting of candidates for the academic post often did not correspond that closely to the judged suitability of the candidates.
- The IAT score of those White participants who shortlisted two White candidates for the lectureship post was 1.17, which indicates a strong pro-White bias.
- The implicit attitude of White participants significantly predicted the ethnicity of those candidates who were shortlisted for the academic post.
- White participants who shortlisted a White and a non-White applicant for the academic post appeared to

select candidates based on merit (i.e. they nominated the two candidates that they had previously rated as most suitable for a subsequent interview).

- Non-White participants tended to shortlist one White and one non-White candidate for the academic post.
- The majority of non-Whites appeared to select candidates for the academic post on merit (i.e. they put forward the two candidates that they had previously rated as most suitable).
- The implicit attitude of non-White participants did not significantly predict the ethnicity of those candidates who they shortlisted for the academic post.
- White participants tended to shortlist one White and one non-White candidate for the administrative post.
- The IAT score of those White participants who shortlisted two White candidates for the administrative post was 1.82, which indicates a strong pro-White bias.
- The implicit attitude of White participants significantly predicted the ethnicity of those candidates who were shortlisted for the administrative post.
- Non-White participants tended to shortlist one White and one non-White candidate for the administrative post.
- The IAT score of those non-White participants who shortlisted one White and one non-White candidate for the administrative post was 0.53, which indicates a medium pro-White bias, and was significantly higher than that of non-White participants who shortlisted two non-White candidates.
- It seems that we all do have a racist heart, at times, but some have it more strongly and more regularly than others.
- If non-White people really do have an underlying pro-White bias, as both Greenwald's data and the data presented in this chapter suggests, then it would seem that their implicit biases around race/ethnicity are weaker and closer to neutral than for White participants, allowing non-Whites to consider White and non-White applicants more fairly.

17

So what can we do about any of this?

Every book is written in a particular time and in a particular place, and time and place are necessarily woven into the very fabric of every manuscript, and this book is no exception. This book addresses an important and sensitive topic at an important and sensitive time for us all in terms of questions about race and fairness and discrimination, explicit or implicit, at the institutional level or personal level. I started on the final chapter of this book in the week that President Barack Obama, the first Black President of the US ('Oh! How things have moved on', they were saying), made his inaugural visit to the UK, and made his fine speeches in the Palace of Westminster. He dined with the Queen at Buckingham Palace. Michelle Obama, originally from the south side of Chicago but more recently a product of Princeton University and Harvard Law School, had taken a group of school children from a north London secondary School, the Elizabeth Garrett Anderson School, where 90 per cent of the pupils are BME, to Oxford University for an 'immersion experience', to show them this hallowed scholarly ground, and to urge them to make this great distinguished institution their aspiration. It was an uplifting sort of week, in many ways, for those interested in questions of colour, race and equality.

And yet that very week, coincidentally or not, was buzzing with claims and accusations of the racism that sits just below the surface. In the Letters page of the *Guardian*, Sharon Grant from the Bernie Grant Trust wrote:

How impressive to see that on the visit to the UK of the first black president of the US, Britain's finest were entertained in such style by Her Majesty (Report, 25 May). Such a shame, however, that apparently we had no Black Britons fine enough to be invited?' (the *Guardian*, 26th May 2011: 41)

I did not get the opportunity to scan that sea of White faces again to see how accurate this accusation was. Were there really no Black Britons present, not even a single one? I had caught part of Michelle Obama's visit to Oxford on a television in a hotel bar, and I heard one White middle-aged man comment to his friend:

Why are so many of the kids that she has with her either Black or Muslim? Aren't there enough White girls to take with her to Oxford? Why couldn't she have brought kids from a working-class White school? How is that going to impact on the aspirations of young White, working-class girls from the UK? They'll think they haven't got a chance around here. You have to be Black or Muslim to have any chance of getting into Oxford, unless you're born with a silver spoon in your mouth.

And that very same day I caught the fuss about the soap product 'Dove' who, in great tabloid speak, had 'landed them-selves in hot water after sparking a race row'. The advert for Dove showed three attractive female models, one Black, one Latino and one White (and blonde), each just wearing a white towel and nothing else. There was a caption above the Black woman's head saying 'before' and above the blonde woman's head saying 'after'. This campaign for a body wash was to promote how this particular product can make you feel. But the internet was buzzing with people complaining that the advert seemed to be implying that the Black woman was the 'before' look and the White woman was the 'after' look. This, they said, was the implicit message in the advert. 'Dove body wash turns black women into Latino women, into white women,' one blogger had written; 'at least, that's what one could possibly infer by the left-to-right before and after progression in this advert.' Another blogger had written: 'Bye-bye black skin, hello white skin! (Scrub hard!) Can this ad be for real?' A Dove spokesman had commented that 'All three women are intended to demonstrate the "after" product benefit'. It would seem that putting the 'before' and 'after' labels above the heads of the Black and the White models was purely coincidental, although many begged to differ.

There was clearly no getting away from claims of racism, explicit or implicit, in adverts or guest lists, and in this week of all weeks, it made one's heart sink. And yet when Saturday came I found my spirits lifting, not because there was positive news about any of this but rather the opposite, a whole page of the *Guardian* devoted to the topic that has guided this book from the start. The headline read '14,000 British professors – but only 50 are black'. The text continued:

> Leading black academics are calling for an urgent culture change at UK universities as figures show there are just 50 black professors out of more than 14,000, and the number has barely changed in eight years, according to data from the Higher Education Statistics Agency. Only the University of Birmingham has more than two black British professors, and only six out of 133 have more than two black professors from the UK or abroad.

There was a great deal of hand wringing in the article about what was going on and what could be done to rectify this. There was a picture of Harry Goulbourne, Professor of Sociology at London's South Bank University, who was quoted as saying that 'Universities are still riddled with "passive racism"'. The *Guardian* reported that,

> as a black man aspiring to be a professor he [Professor Goulbourne] had to publish twice as many academic papers as his White peers. He said he had switched out of the field of politics, because it was not one that promoted minorities. He called for a 'cultural shift' inside the most prestigious universities.

Heidi Mirza, an emeritus professor at the Institute of Education, University of London, said that UK universities were 'nepotistic and cliquey. It is all about who you know.' Nicola Dandridge, the chief executive of Universities UK, the organisation for Vice Chancellors of British universities, was quoted in the article as saying: 'We recognise that there is a serious issue about lack of black representation among senior staff in universities, though this is not a problem affecting universities alone, but one affecting societies as a whole.'

In this book we have seen evidence of what might be behind some of this. It is not necessarily what you might call 'active, deliberate nepotism' or 'intentional, targeted cliquishness', it is more a kind of 'passive' racism, as good a term as any, that derives from implicit processes. The book clearly reveals bias connected to the ethnicity of applicants in shortlisting for posts in universities. Can I imagine a situation where there are a number of candidates for a chair position and because one of them is Black he or she has to present with twice as many papers (*of the same quality*) simply because of his or her racial background? Not really, because experience tells me that in these kinds of decision-making situations (where there is going to be debate and challenge) most of the decisions tend to be slow, careful and deliberative and therefore tend not to be governed by the kinds of implicit processes that we have seen at work in the previous chapters. But can I imagine a subtle shift in attention or focus to the less strong papers on the CV of the BME candidate (after all it's not about quantity; it's all about quality) to find evidence to back up the original emotional prejudgement driven by implicit processes? Unfortunately, I can.

This book has tried to expose the role of implicit biases in everyday life and tried to show how they might have an impact in a variety of situations, including employment-based decision making in one particular context, the modern, meritocratic British university. The book shows that there are distinct ethnic biases which do operate in decision making here and that these ethnic biases are connected to measures of implicit attitude. These implicit attitudes are quick, automatic and not subject to conscious reflection, but they do seem to impact on shortlisting decisions, and ethnicity also impacts on patterns of unconscious eye movements where people build up the 'rational' evidence for making a decision one way or another. We are all rational creatures, after all, especially in great meritocratic universities, and it will be disconcerting for some to see how some of these rational processes can be at the mercy of something much more basic and vulgar at times. Of course, the experiments were all surrogates, no decisions were actually made that affected people's real lives, but most of the experimental participants were connected to the university in some way, as either staff or students, so principles of fairness and rational decision-making should have been embedded within each and every one of them.

But can we do anything about any of this? Some have been reasonably upbeat about this in the past. In his acceptance speech for the Nobel Peace Prize in 1964, Martin Luther King Jr. famously said: 'I refuse to accept the view that mankind is so tragically bound to the starless midnight of racism and war that the bright daybreak of peace and brotherhood can never become a reality.' As the psychologist Laurie Rudman and her colleagues from Rutgers, the State University of New Jersey (2001) commented:

> his remarks were characterized by optimism and resolve. Having weathered the storms of desegregation and the violent backlash against it, he accepted his honor on behalf of the Civil Rights Movement, even while acknowledging that the movement had not yet fulfilled its promise to African Americans. Nearly 40 years later, that promise remains to be fulfilled . . . if researchers were to rely solely on self-report measures of attitude towards Blacks, they would be hard-pressed to conclude anything other than that prejudice has become, if not outdated, at least unfashionable. In reality, however, prejudice continues to dog America's footsteps, even as we make progress toward an egalitarian ideal . . . In summary, despite dramatic reductions in self-reported prejudice, other indicators suggest that racism persists, even on the part of avowed egalitarians. (Rudman, Ashmore and Gary 2001: 856)

So what is to be done about all of this persistent and insidious and implicit racism?

Binna Kandola, in his book *The Value of Difference* (2009: 171) is still fairly positive that a solution can be found:

> Prejudice is one of the most complex problems we have in our society. But complex problems often have simple solutions. We can't see the solutions to our problems, so we assume the solutions are of the same order of complexity as the problem – with which we are all too familiar.

I want to believe this because I do want to see a solution but when you read Kandola's recommendations for combating implicit biases, you can't help but feel that they are perhaps a little bit over-optimistic. One of the principal weapons in his armoury is called an 'implementation intention', a bit of contingent self-talk, which specifies:

> where, when and how we will behave in a particular way. It's not exactly programming, and it's certainly not brain-washing. But it is a way of directing our attention to particular contexts in which we are likely to act from unconscious habit rather than conscious intention. We train ourselves to recognise certain situations in which we want to act differently.
> (ibid.: 175)

According to Kandola, the benefit of these implementation intentions is that they allow:

> people to respond automatically – in the way that they want to respond – in particular situations that they expect to encounter in the future. The plan creates a kind of memory of the future. The pattern laid down by the plan creates a strong association between environmental cues and intended behaviour . . . When the anticipated situation arises, the memory traces formed by the plan are readily accessed and the desired behaviour is activated. (ibid.: 175)

In other words, what he is trying to do here is to break the 'natural' connection between a situation and the automatic behaviour that arises because of implicit processes by using a degree of pre-planning to insert something in between the two. Kandola tried to use such implementation intentions to remove unconscious race bias. One of the groups in his study was the implementation intention group and it was given an implementation intention as well as a goal. The goal that they were given was:

> 'Don't be prejudiced' and the implementation plan was 'If I see a dark face then I'll ignore skin colour'. According to Kandola 'those participants given an implementation plan performed significantly different to those in the control group. Their IAT scores were reduced to near zero – meaning an absence of prejudice. (ibid.: 177)

This is in many senses an extraordinary result, although it becomes quite difficult to evaluate in retrospect because unfortunately it seems never to have been published (it was merely an oral presentation at a conference). My problem with this claim is that it just seems a little too easy and a little too straightforward. It's as if a little bit of self-talk, directed at one level and one level only, can change everything for the better. The whole point about implicit biases is that they operate without conscious awareness. When do you start the self-talk? How do you know when the implicit processes are about to commence? 'If I see a dark face then I will ignore skin colour' (before the selection panel? Before perusing the CV? On getting up in the morning?). And what about making these implementation intentions a little more specific? Might that not work better? For example,

> If I see a dark face then I will consciously override my natural tendency to look at the worst bits of the CV; instead I will consciously and deliberately direct my eye gaze to the best bits so that I can arrive at a more balanced and fairer view of the candidate.

This latter implementation intention might be well worth trying. Or what about:

> If I am shortlisting for a position and I notice that I have only shortlisted candidates from a particular racial or ethnic group, when the applicants themselves come from a range of racial or ethnic groups, then I will look at the CVs once again to make sure that some sort of implicit processes were not at work in my decision making.

It is clearly not that I am against the concept of implementation intentions, or against actively trying to do something to interfere with the 'implicit bias in attitude' – 'explicit bias in judgement' connection; rather, I am concerned that if we conceive of this too narrowly or too simplistically, and it does not work, then we may end up more pessimistic and depressed than when we started.

So perhaps, implementation intentions can work in particular situations, although exactly how effective they are at preventing implicit bias does need to be carefully evaluated. But, of course, there may be other simpler ways of preventing implicit biases from operating in certain contexts. For example, we may be able to interfere with the connection between automatically activated associations and behaviour in interviews by never asking for a 'first impression' or a 'preliminary thought' or a 'gut response' at any point during the selection interview. We may well want to leave 'gut feelings' altogether out of the selection process since such responses are more likely to derive from implicit processes that may be biased in particular ways. If you want a reminder of why this is important just think of the work on sustainability, presented in Chapter 15. The research here found that under time pressure, the implicit processes (more pro-high carbon than the explicit measures would have us believe) had a much more direct impact on the actual behaviour, the choice of a goody bag that was not so good for the environment in terms of carbon footprint, than when the individuals concerned were not under time pressure. So, if implicit biases are present (as the research in this book suggests that they are) avoid eliciting any kinds of social judgement ('first impression'/'preliminary thought'/'gut response') which necessarily have to be made under time pressure. Indeed, the whole issue of the social organisation of selection panels and interviews might well need to be re-thought in the light of the research described in this book. The more time pressure, the more rushed they are, the more complex the decision making is in terms of what is expected of the panel, the more tasks the interview panel are being given simultaneously, the more 'intensely' they are chaired with shorter latencies of response between turns and more overlapping talk by the panel members (see Beattie 1983, for example, for an attempt to characterise the so-called 'temporal' characteristics of a number of forms of verbal interaction), the less time there will be for individual reflection and decision making and the more likely the outcomes will be biased in particular ways.

In other words, if we accept that implicit biases do exist then our number one and immediate priority has to be to prevent them manifesting themselves in ways that can prevent fairness from operating. Daniel Kahneman (2011: 417) comes to the same sort of conclusion in his excellent book *Thinking, Fast and Slow*:

> 'What can be done about biases? How can we improve judgments and decisions, both our own and those of the institutions that we serve and that serve us? The short answer is that little can be achieved without a considerable investment of effort. As I know from experience, System 1 is not readily educable . . . The way to block errors that originate in System 1 is simple in principle: recognize the signs that you are in a cognitive minefield, slow down, and ask for reinforcement from System 2.

Of course, in many senses, the big question that the research described in this book ultimately leads to is 'What can we do to change implicit attitudes?' Is System 1 not educable at all? Indeed, are these implicit biases the true 'starless midnight of racism', in Martin Luther King's words, so dark and never ending and infinite that they allow no light for any journey of equality and diversity to even begin? The good news is that there is now a growing body of evidence from within experimental psychology about how to modify automatically activated associations. Dasgupta and Greenwald (2001) examined whether exposure to admired and disliked racial 'exemplars' can produce a change in automatic preference for White and Black Americans. They used the IAT as the diagnostic measure of implicit bias. In one study they showed pictures of 40 well-known Black and White individuals who were either –

- admired and Black, e.g. Denzel Washington;
- admired and White, e.g. Tom Hanks;
- disliked and Black, e.g. Mike Tyson;
- disliked and White, e.g. Jeffrey Dahmer.

The task was presented as a general knowledge test for assessing participants' familiarity with these famous or infamous Americans so that each picture was accompanied by a person's name together with a correct and an incorrect description of them. So, for example, Martin Luther King's picture was accompanied by a correct description that read 'Leader of the Black Civil Rights movement in the 1960s' and the incorrect description read 'Former Vice President of the United States'. The task for the participants was to identify the correct description. What Dasgupta and Greenwald found was that exposure to the positive Black exemplars had a significant effect on the automatic racial associations, such that the 'D' score, which derives from the IAT, was significantly reduced after exposure to the admired Black exemplars. They also found that this reduction in D score was maintained one day after the original experiment (they did not test D scores after this time). Further, they found that although this manipulation had a significant effect on implicit attitudes, it did not have a significant effect on explicit self-reported attitudes. Dasgupta and Greenwald's conclusion are that the studies they carried out here 'provide a strategy that attempts to change the social context and, through it, to reduce automatic prejudice and preference' (Dasgupta and Greenwald 2001: 800). They go on to specify some of the practical ways in which society could play a role in this, thus:

> The mass media have been frequently criticized for disproportionately emphasizing stereotypic images of minorities and women (Greenberg and Brand 1994; Harris 1999). Interestingly, even when disliked members of dominant groups are portrayed in the popular media (e.g. news stories about White criminals like Jeffrey Dahmer), their race is typically not made salient. Rather, they are presented as deviant individuals, not members of a particular group. By contrast, news stories about Black criminals often highlight the individual's race. In our study, by forcing people to classify admired and disliked individuals by race, we emphasized the exemplars' group membership as well as their valence. These data imply that if media representations were to become more balanced, reminding people of both admired members of out-groups and less-than-stellar members of in-groups with emphasis on their group membership, the combined effect may be able to shift implicit prejudice and stereotypes. (Dasgupta and Greenwald 2001: 808)

So what these psychologists are saying is not that every time a White criminal does something terrible we must note his race ('As that White serial killer Jeffrey Dahmer said . . .'), rather there should be a degree of balance in mentions of race attached to crime (so we might like to mention Dahmer's race, at least, some of the time). And, in addition, we might like to mention race more when BME individuals do something good.

Other psychologists have suggested even more focused experimental techniques to reduce automatic prejudice. Olson and Fazio (2004). have suggested using implicit evaluative conditioning to reduce automatically activated individual prejudice. Implicit Evaluative Conditioning is a non-conscious learning process where, for example, experimental participants believe they are taking part in an experiment about 'attention and surveillance', in which they would see a stream of 'randomly assembled images' on a computer screen. In reality, on the computer screen various images are paired in particular ways such that images of Black or White individuals appear on the screen in association with either positive or negative words or images. This is essentially a form of classical conditioning (pairing the unconditioned stimulus, the US, in this case positive words or images, with the conditioned stimulus, the CS, which in this case were images of White or Black individuals). The basic idea is that the US produces a certain response in participants and through repeated association the CS starts to produce a similar effect on its own (rather like Pavlov's bell causing salivation through its association with food), and this all happens below the level of conscious awareness. Olson and Fazio claim that this type of associative learning does reduce automatically activated racial attitudes and that they stay low for at least two days following the experiment (again they stopped testing after two days). The societal implication of this is that we have to be careful about how we present information about Black and White individuals to the public at large because what this experiment seems to suggest is that mere association can either increase or decrease implicit bias. So the argument would go that by bringing a set of BME school children to Oxford University, Michelle Obama is a conduit for conditioning us to think more positively about BME children on the basis of the mere association (Oxford = scholastic aspiration and excellence = BME school children). Whereas, in the Dove advert, whether it is done intentionally or not, the Black model is being associated unconsciously in our minds with the concept of something that needs to be cleansed to become purer and whiter and cleaner. When the great and the good are shown in the Palace of Westminster or in Buckingham Palace, the predominance of White faces again is an association that is being laid down in all our minds (the great and the good = White) and we are being conditioned to think one way or another. Some psychologists say that there are grounds to be optimistic here, that although parts of the brain may fire more automatically when we view people from ethnic backgrounds different to our own that this is not fixed for all time and everything can be changed. But you can see how close to the start of the journey we really are when you remind yourself that the effects of these psychological experiments are tested over a period of one or two days. We clearly have a long way to go into this starless midnight of implicit racism.

This book has been both academic (I hope) and extremely personal at times; as I have tried to lay bare some of my own processes of psychological development, including my own acquisition of racial, ethnic and religious biases, growing up in the Troubles in Northern Ireland, where prejudice seemed to be everywhere, even inside the family itself. I make no apologies for the personal aspects of the book: I believe that psychology makes most sense when it connects to ordinary human lives, including my own, if that's what I've got to work with. The book has been a journey, and what this journey has persuaded me is that we all do have some sort of implicit attitudes that can emerge in many situations and that much of what goes on in life is guided by these implicit and unconscious processes. Psychology suggests that these processes might not be fixed for all time but we need to start thinking immediately and with much more urgency about how to speed up the processes of change. We need to uncover how best to identify and modify these implicit attitudes, and to work out how to interfere with the operation of these natural insidious processes. If we don't, then we are clearly letting not just ourselves down, but all of those generations that follow on. And let me tell you that this would be unforgiveable for a whole host of reasons, but I'm sure that I don't have to labour the point and be too explicit.

But you will get this point, I am sure, even without any more conscious effort on my part, in your growing natural emotional discomfort, because that is, after all, how implicit processes normally work. And these processes do usually find a way of getting out and impacting on behaviour, as we have repeatedly seen, to get us to do what we have to do, with their help, with their gentle and insidious nudges, below consciousness, below reason, but not beyond hope.

- Remember that other important implicit biases, as well as race/ethnicity, almost certainly exist.
- In the future, we may well want to consider the role of implicit biases regarding weight, social class, accent, religion (in certain parts of the world), and even physical attractiveness in selection for jobs.
- It is not easy being from the gutter, but I suspect that it's easier than other things.
- It is amazing how we act 'rationally' in applicant selection through our gaze fixation patterns.
- Don't fool yourself about your sound judgement regarding other people based on the evidence before you.
- We need to change.
- We need to change now.
- Don't let the irrational mind win.

Appendix 1

Before leaving this Part on measures of implicit attitudes, I just want to mention some other data that we collected, which represents more than just a methodological footnote to the chapter. When we were deciding what kinds of stimuli to use in our new 'Ethnic' IAT, we considered whether the faces should be of younger or older adults. So many of the stimuli used in Project Implicit seemed to represent just young people and I was wondering if this was the case because most of the people who take part in psychology experiments are themselves young and most commonly undergraduates (and not just undergraduates, but psychology undergraduates; see, for example, Sears 1986 for some systematic analyses of the inherent biases that affect who is recruited for psychological research). Using young faces might therefore be more 'salient' for the sample of participants, or so the reasoning might have gone. But we did wonder what would happen if you used old rather than young faces in the IAT.

We tried this in a sample of just 51 participants but again the results were highly informative. The mean pro-White bias (D score from the IAT) with the older faces was substantially higher (with a mean of 1.25 versus 0.69) and slightly more variable in terms of standard deviation than with the young faces (see Table A1.1 and Figures A1.1 to A1.3). One interpretation of these results is that the pro-White bias is even more pronounced when participants view older adults, or to turn it the other way round, there is a pro-White bias irrespective of the age of the people displayed but

Table A1.1 **Descriptive statistics for the Young IAT, Old IAT and Mixed IAT**

IAT version	Minimum	Maximum	Mean	Standard deviation
Young	−3.41	5.11	0.69	1.99
Old	−2.68	7.15	1.25	2.09
Mixed	−2.12	5.40	0.74	0.90

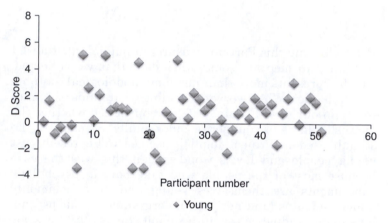

Figure A1.1 **Distribution of D scores for the 'Young IAT'.**

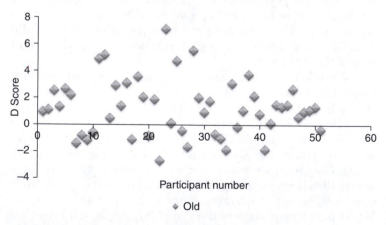

Figure A1.2 **Distribution of D scores for the 'Old IAT'.**

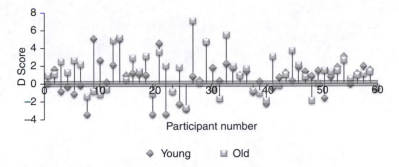

Figure A1.3 **D Score distribution for the Young IAT and the Old IAT compared.**

this is ameliorated to some extent with younger people. For this reason, we used pictures of people from a range of ages in the IAT we used in Chapter 12 and the results from this 'Mixed IAT' (with a larger sample of 130 participants included for comparison in Table A1.1). But it is worth remembering that the results so far could have been even more extreme if we had changed the age of the people we chose to depict in the IAT.

Appendix 2

Implicit biases operating in the academy: the detailed results

Analysis 1: Were our White participants affected by implicit bias in shortlisting candidates for an academic post?

The first important thing to note is that the analysis of the D scores for the 96 participants analysed here revealed that there was an overall moderate pro-White bias in the sample (with a mean D score of 0.68). The mean D score for the White participants was 0.93, which indicates a strong pro-White bias, and the mean D score for the non-Whites was 0.43 which indicates a slight pro-White bias (in contrast to a neutral preference from the smaller sample of non-Whites in the first empirical investigation reported in Chapter 13).

Table A2.1 demonstrates that almost 80 per cent (77.1%) of applicants who were recommended for interview by White participants were of Caucasian descent, while less than a quarter (22.9%) of candidates short-listed for interview came from a Black and Minority Ethnic (BME) background.

That is, despite the CVs being matched identically in terms of human capital, non-White applicants appear to be around *three and a half times* less likely than Whites to be

Table A2.1 **Number of White versus non-White applicants put forward for interview for the academic post by White participants**

White	Non-White
74 out of a possible 96	22 out of a possible 96
77.1%	22.9%

shortlisted for interview, when White participants were
making the recommendations (see also Figure A2.1).

The next analysis examines the number of White participants who shortlisted two White candidates, two non-
Whites, or one White and one non-White for the academic
post (see Table A2.2).

Table A2.2 demonstrates that over 60 per cent of White
participants shortlisted exclusively White candidates for
the academic post, while only 6.3 per cent recommended
exclusively non-White candidates (with identical CVs). Only
one third of White candidates selected a White and a

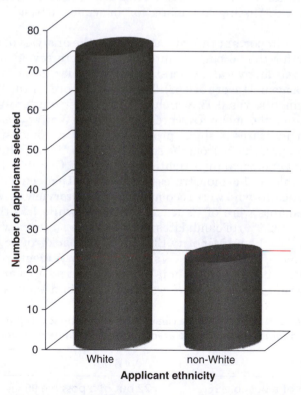

Figure A2.1 **Number of White and non-White applicants shortlisted
by White participants (academic post).**

Table A2.2 Number of White participants shortlisting candidates from different ethnic backgrounds for the academic post

Both candidates White	One candidate White and one non-White	Both candidates non-White
29 out of 48	16 out of 48	3 out of 48
60.4%	33.3%	6.3%

non-White applicant. This information is shown graphically in Figure A2.2.

Given that the applicants' CVs varied only by name and face, it seems that the only plausible explanation for the apparent bias towards White candidates is an underlying ethnic bias.

Another way of trying to understand what might be going on here is to consider whether those White participants who selected exclusively White applicants put forward those candidates that they considered to be the *most* suitable for the position on the basis of the rating scale. That is, did the White participants put forward the two applicants that they had judged to be the best for the job based on the 7-point rating scale of suitability, which they had filled in previously? Or, alternatively, were the White participants scoring White and non-White applicants equally on the scale of suitability, but putting forward more White applicants irrespective of the initial ratings, presumably based on something else?

In order to examine this, we compared the suitability ratings given to White and non-White applicants by the 29 White participants who put forward only White candidates. This was done by summing the suitability ratings given to the two White applicants and comparing them to the summed suitability judgements for the two non-White candidates (i.e. those who were not selected). The median rating of suitability was identical in the two groups (5.00 for each candidate) and the difference was not statistically significant. In other words, White participants were more likely to select White than non-White candidates, even though they considered all applicants to be essentially comparable in terms of their suitability for the post. Their shortlisting judgement did not

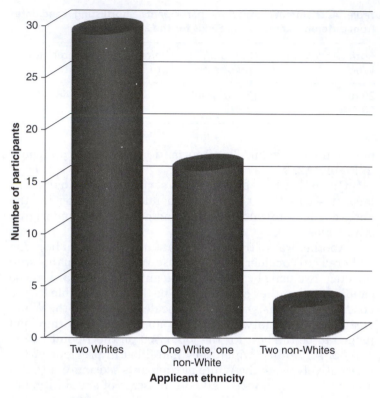

Figure A2.2 **Number of White participants as a function of who they shortlisted for the academic post.**

correspond with their (perhaps more careful and deliberative) previous judgement of suitability.

A second statistical test was run, this time focusing on whether the 16 participants who put forward one White and one non-White candidate selected those applicants that they considered to be most suitable for the job on the basis of their rating scale judgement. This time the median suitability of those shortlisted candidates was 5.5, while the median suitability judgement for those applicants who were not invited for interview was 4.5 and this difference was significant. In other words, this set of 16 participants were selecting candidates based on some kind of merit, in that they put forward the two candidates to whom they had previously awarded the highest suitability ratings.

IAT Data

The mean D score observed across participants, irrespective of ethnicity, was 0.68. As anticipated, the mean D score for White participants (mean D = 0.93) was statistically higher (i.e. more pro-White) than for non-White participants (mean D = 0.43), although non-Whites still exhibited a moderate preference for Whites.

The next stage of the analysis aimed to determine whether the D scores of the participants was related to the ethnicity of the candidates put forward for interview (see Table A2.3).

The D score of the participant does appear to be related to the ethnicity of the applicants who were shortlisted, at least in the case of the White participants in our sample. That is, those White participants who put forward two White candidates had an average D score of 1.17 (indicating a strong preference for Whites). Those who recommended one White and one non-White applicant had a mean D score of 0.71 (indicating a moderate preference for Whites), while those who recommended two non-Whites had a mean D score of –0.22 (equivalent to a slight preference for non-Whites, but almost neutral). Although these scores may not 'map directly' onto the usual verbal descriptions of the D score

Table A2.3 Mean D scores of White participants as a function of who they recommended for interview (academic post)

Shortlisted two White applicants	Shortlisted one White and one non-White applicant	Shortlisted two non-White applicants
Mean D score		
1.17 (strongly pro-White)	0.71 (moderately pro-White)	–0.22 (slightly pro-non-White)

(e.g. it might be expected that those who recommended two Whites would have a score of 0.8 or above, as was observed, but those who put forward one White and one non-White should have a neutral score rather than a medium score), they do seem to show a clearly defined pattern.

Statistical analyses revealed that those participants who put forward two Whites had significantly higher D scores than those White participants who put forward a White and a non-White applicant or two non-White applicants (and both tests were highly significant; in other words the results were very, very unlikely to have arisen by chance). A further statistical analysis revealed that the D scores of those participants who recommended one White and one non-White applicant for the job had significantly higher D scores than those who put forward exclusively non-White applicants.

Analysis 2: Were our non-White participants affected by implicit bias in shortlisting candidates for an academic post?

Table A2.4 demonstrates that 61.5 per cent of candidates who were recommended for interview by non-White participants were non-White, while 38.5 per cent of candidates short-listed for interview were White. This shows that non-White participants also had a bias for certain applicants as a function of ethnicity, but the bias was less marked than for our White participants (see Table A2.1). Perhaps this could be due to the fact that non-White participants in the experiment did not represent a single homogeneous group in the way that the Whites did. After all, all of the White applicants in the study were Caucasian whereas the non-White applicants include

Table A2.4 Number of White versus non-White applicants put forward for interview for the academic post by non-White participants

White	Non-Whites
37 out of a possible 96	59 out of a possible 96
38.5%	61.5%

candidates from Black African (Latoya Obagundu), Asian (Kym Wu) and Arab-Muslim (Rezza Housseini) backgrounds.

These results are represented graphically in Figure A2.3.

The next stage of the analysis was to look at the pattern of shortlisting for the academic job by the non-White participants (i.e. did they shortlist two White candidates, two non-Whites, or one White and one non-White?) (Table A2.5).

Table A2.5 demonstrates that, in contrast to our White participants, who typically recommended exclusively White candidates for the academic post (60.4%), non-Whites overwhelming selected one White and one non-White candidate (68.8%). Indeed, this is more than double the

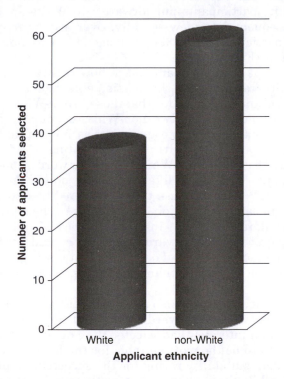

Figure A2.3 **Number of White and non-White applicants shortlisted by non-White participants (academic post).**

Table A2.5 Number of non-White participants shortlisting candidates from different ethnic backgrounds for the academic post

Both candidates White	One candidate White and one non-White	Both candidates non-White
2 out of 48	33 out of 48	13 out of 48
4.2%	68.8%	27.1%

proportion of White participants who selected a White and a non-White applicant (which was 33.3%; see Table A2.2) for the academic position. However, while 6.3 per cent of White participants did recommend two non-Whites for the post (see Table A2.2), Table A2.5 reveals that only 4.2 per cent of non-White participants put forward two White applicants for subsequent interview. Finally, over a quarter of non-White participants (27.1%) recommended two non-White applicants (Figure A2.4).

Again it was important to see how this related to the suitability ratings that the participants had also made. Statistical analyses revealed that those 13 non-White participants who put forward two non-White candidates for the post did rate the non-White applicants as more suitable than the White candidates (with a median rating of 4.5 for the White and 6.0 for the non-Whites). In other words, non-White participants were more likely to select non-White candidates than Whites, because they considered them to be the 'best' applicants for the job on the basis of their previous, considered, rating. This is in sharp contrast with the White participants who put forward two White candidates for the post, even though they had not rated Whites as significantly more suitable for the job than non-Whites on that particular scale.

Statistical analyses also revealed that the 33 non-White participants who put forward both a White and a non-White applicant for interview had selected the candidates that they considered to be the most suitable for the lectureship post. The median suitability rating for the successful applicants was 5.5, while the median rating for the unsuccessful applicants was 4.5.

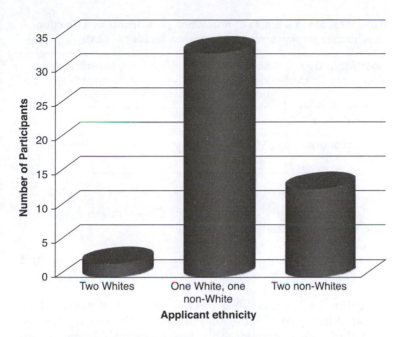

Figure A2.4 **Number of non-White participants as a function of who they shortlisted for the academic post.**

IAT Data

The next stage of the analysis aimed to determine whether the D score of the non-White participants was related to the ethnicity of the candidates put forward for interview (see Table A2.6).

Again, as with the White participants, it looks like the mean IAT scores of non-White participants could have a direct effect on the ethnicity of who they recommend for interview. That is, those non-White participants who put forward two White candidates had an average D score of 1.01 (indicating a strong preference towards Whites) whereas those who recommended one White and one non-White candidate, had a mean D score of 0.52 (indicating a moderate preference for Whites), while those who recommended two non-Whites had a mean D score of 0.10 (equivalent to no

Table A2.6 Mean D scores of non-White participants as a function of who they recommended for interview (academic post)

Shortlisted two White candidates	Shortlisted one White and one non-White candidate	Shortlisted two non-White candidates
Mean D score		
1.01 (strongly pro-White)	0.52 (moderately pro-White)	0.10 (neutral)

preference towards either group). These differences were not, however, statistically reliable.

Analysis 3: Were our White participants affected by implicit bias in shortlisting candidates for an administrative post?

In Table A2.7 a pro-White bias is again demonstrated by whom White participants shortlisted for the administrative post, but this is considerably less pronounced than when White participants shortlisted applicants for the academic post, where they overwhelmingly put forward White candidates (77.1%; see Table A2.1).

This information is represented graphically in Figure A2.5.

The next analysis considers the ethnicity of the applicants shortlisted for the administrative post by our White participants.

Table A2.8 demonstrates that when it comes to the administrative position, the majority of White participants

Table A2.7 Number of White versus non-White candidates put forward for interview by White participants for the administrative post

White	Non-Whites
53 out of a possible 96 55.2%	43 out of a possible 96 44.8%

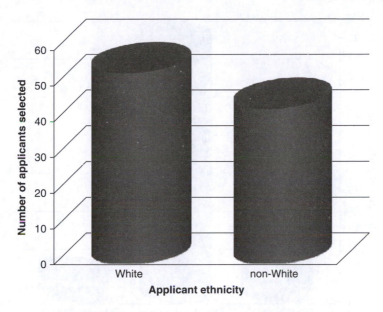

Figure A2.5 **Number of White and non-White applicants shortlisted by White participants (administrative post).**

(72.9%) shortlisted one White and one non-White applicant compared to just 33.3 per cent of White participants who recommended both a White and a non-White for the academic post (see Table A2.2). This information is represented graphically in Figure A2.6.

Again, it is important to see how this shortlisting decision relates to the prior judgement of the suitability of the candidates. Statistical analyses revealed that the

Table A2.8 **Number of White participants shortlisting candidates from different ethnic backgrounds for the administrative post**

Both candidates White	One candidate White and one non-White	Both candidates non-White
9 out of 48	35 out of 48	4 out of 48
18.8%	72.9%	8.3%

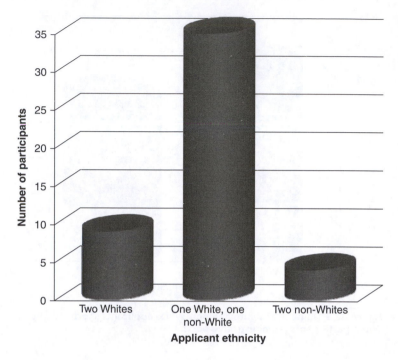

Figure A2.6 **Number of White participants as a function of who they shortlisted for the administrative post.**

35 participants who put forward one White and one non-White candidate were significantly more likely to shortlist those applicants who they considered to be most suitable for the job. The median suitability for selected candidates was 4.5, while the median suitability judgement for those applicants who were not to be invited for interview was 4.0.

Next to be investigated were the suitability ratings of White and non-White applicants given by the nine White participants who put forward *two* White applicants. Again, this was calculated by summing the suitability ratings given to the two White applicants and comparing them to the summed suitability judgements for the two non-White applicants (i.e. those who were not selected). The median rating of suitability was 5.5 for the White applicants and 4.5 for the non-Whites. The difference was not statistically robust. Given that prospective applicants differ only in terms of name and face, this again suggests that some sort of racial bias is a major factor in why these nine White participants recommended two White applicants, even though they had not rated them as significantly more suitable than the two non-Whites for the post. Of course, one problem with this conclusion is that here the sample size is very small.

IAT Data

Once more, the D scores (Table A2.9) appear to relate to shortlisting decisions, with participants who shortlisted two White candidates having a stronger pro-White bias (1.82) than any of the other groups, and with those shortlisting one White and one non-White candidate falling somewhere between the other two groups.

Again, statistical analyses revealed that White participants who shortlisted two White candidates for the administrative post did have significantly higher D scores than those White participants who recommended one White and one non-White candidate. In addition, those White participants who shortlisted one White and one non-White candidate did have significantly higher D scores (more pro-White) than those who shortlisted two non-White candidates. Finally, it was observed that White participants who shortlisted two White candidates had significantly higher D scores than those who shortlisted two non-Whites.

Table A2.9 Mean D scores of White participants as a function of who they recommend for interview (administrative post)

Shortlisted two White candidates	Shortlisted one White and one non-White candidate	Shortlisted two non-White candidates
Mean D score		
1.82 (strongly pro-White)	0.83 (strongly pro-White)	−0.18 (neutral)

Analysis 4: Were our non-White participants affected by implicit bias in shortlisting candidates for an administrative post?

Table A2.10 demonstrates that the proportion of White versus non-White candidates shortlisted for the administrative job by the non-White participants was almost equal, although there was a very slight preference for non-White applicants.

This information is represented graphically in Figure A2.7.

The next analysis considers the ethnicity of the candidates shortlisted for the administrative post by our non-White participants (Table A2.11).

Table A2.11 demonstrates that 83.3 per cent of non-White participants shortlisted one White and one non-White applicant for the administrative job. There was also only a 4.1 per cent bias towards non-White candidates (10.4%–6.3%) in terms of the proportion of non-White participants who selected two non-White versus two White candidates. This is shown in Figure A2.8.

Statistical analyses also revealed that the 40 non-White participants who shortlisted a White and a non-White applicant had selected the candidates that they considered to be (significantly) more suitable for the administrative post (the median suitability rating for the successful applicants was 5.5 while the median rating for the unsuccessful applicants was 4.5).

IAT Data

Here, statistical comparisons are much less meaningful because most of our participants shortlisted one White and

Table A2.10 **Number of White versus non-White applicants put forward for interview by non-White participants for the administrative post**

White	Non-Whites
46 out of a possible 96	50 out of a possible 96
47.9	52.1

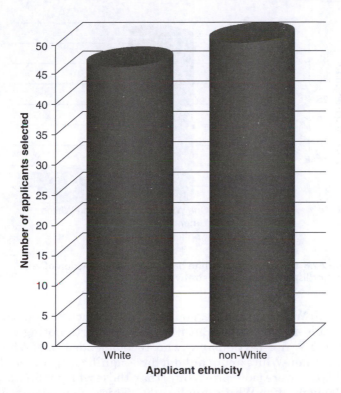

Figure A2.7 Number of White and non-White applicants shortlisted by non-White participants (administrative post).

Table A2.11 Number of non-White participants shortlisting candidates from different ethnic backgrounds for the administrative post

Both candidates White	One candidate White and one non-White	Both candidates non-White
3 out of 48 6.3%	40 out of 48 83.3%	5 out of 48 10.4%

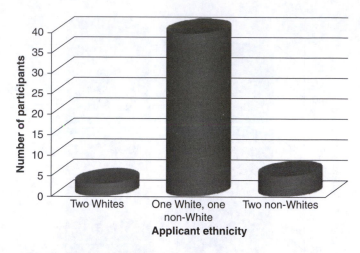

Figure A2.8 Number of non-White participants as a function of who they shortlisted for the administrative post.

one non-White candidate, so there is not much to compare with this middle group. But it is perhaps worth noting that our non-White participants who recommended one White and one non-White applicant did have significantly higher D scores (i.e. were more pro-White) than those who put forward exclusively non-White applicants. This apparent trend clearly did not apply to the three non-White participants who shortlisted two Whites for the post, whose scores were essentially neutral (Table A2.12).

Table A2.12 Mean D scores of non-White participants as a function of who they recommend for interview (administrative post)

Shortlisted two White candidates	Shortlisted one White and one non-White candidate	Shortlisted two non-White candidates
Mean D score		
0.05 (neutral)	0.53 (moderately pro-White)	−0.13 (neutral)

References

Ajzen, I. (1991) The theory of planned behaviour. *Organizational Behavior and Human Decision Processes* 50: 179–211.

Allport, G. W. (1935) Attitudes. In C. Murchison (ed.), *Handbook of Social Psychology*. Worcester, MA: Clark University Press, pp. 798–884.

—— (1954/1979) *The Nature of Prejudice*. Cambridge, MA: Addison Wesley.

—— (1967) Gordon Allport. In E. Boring and G. Lindzey (eds), *A History of Psychology in Autobiography*. New York: Appleton-Century-Crofts, Vol. 6, pp. 3–25.

—— (1968) An Autobiography. In G. Allport (ed.), *The Person in Psychology: Selected Essays*. Boston, MA: Beacon, pp. 376–409.

Arber, E. (2007) *The Dunbar Anthology. 1401–1508 AD*. Whitefish, MO: Kessinger.

Banaji, M. R. (2001) Implicit attitudes can be measured. In H. L. Roediger, III, J. S. Nairne, I. Neath and A. Surprenant (eds), *The Nature of Remembering: Essays in Honor of Robert G. Crowder*. Washington, DC: American Psychological Association, pp. 117–150.

Banton, M. (1998) *Racial Theories*. Cambridge: Cambridge University Press.

Bargh, J. A., Chen, A. and Burrows, L. (1996) Automaticity of social behaviour: Direct effects of trait construct and stereotype activation on action. *Journal of Personality and Social Psychology* 71: 230–244.

Bassanini, A. and Saint-Martin, A. (2008) The price of prejudice: Labour market discrimination on the grounds of gender and ethnicity. In *OECD Employment Outlook*, Chapter 3.

Bateson, G., Jackson, D. D. and Weakland, J. (1956) Toward a theory of schizophrenia. *Behavoral Science* 1: 251–264.

Beattie, G. (1980) The skilled art of conversational interaction: Verbal and nonverbal signals in its regulation and management.

In W. T. Singleton, P. Spurgeon and R. B. Stammers (eds), *The Analysis of Social Skills*. New York: Plenum.

—— (1983) *Talk: An Analysis of Speech and Non-Verbal Behaviour*. Milton Keynes: Open University Press.

—— (1986) *Survivors of Steel City: A Portrait of Sheffield*. London: Chatto & Windus.

—— (1992) *We Are the People: Journeys through the Heart of Protestant Ulster*. London: William Heinemann.

—— (1998) *The Corner Boys*. London: Victor Gollancz.

—— (2003) *Visible Thought: The New Psychology of Body Language*, London: Routledge.

—— (2004) *Protestant Boy*. London: Granta.

—— (2010) *Why Aren't We Saving the Planet? A Psychologist's Perspective*. London and New York: Routledge.

—— (2011a) *Get the Edge: How Simple Changes can Transform your Life*. London: Headline.

—— (2011b) Making an action film. *Nature Climate Change* 1: 372–374.

Beattie, G. and Doherty, K. (1995) 'I saw what really happened.' The discursive construction of victims and perpetrators in first-hand accounts of paramilitary violence in Northern Ireland. *Journal of Language and Social Psychology* 14: 408–433.

Beattie, G. and Shovelton, H. (1999a) Do iconic hand gestures really contribute anything to the semantic information conveyed by speech? An experimental investigation. *Semiotica* 123: 1–30.

—— (1999b) Mapping the range of information contained in the iconic hand gestures that accompany spontaneous speech. *Journal of Language and Social Psychology* 18: 438–462.

—— (2000) Iconic hand gestures and the predictability of words in context in spontaneous speech. *British Journal of Psychology* 91: 473–492.

—— (2001) An experimental investigation of the role of different types of iconic gesture in communication: A semantic feature approach. *Gesture* 1/2: 129–149.

—— (2002a) An experimental investigation of some properties of individual iconic gestures that affect their communicative power. *British Journal of Psychology* 93: 179–192.

—— (2002b) What properties of talk are associated with the generation of spontaneous iconic hand gestures? *British Journal of Social Psychology* 41: 403–417.

—— (2005) Why the spontaneous images created by the hands during talk can help make TV advertisements more effective. *British Journal of Psychology* 96: 21–37.

—— (2006) When size really matters: How a single semantic feature is represented in the speech and gesture modalities. *Gesture* 6: 63–84.

Beattie, G. and Sale, L. (2009) Explicit and implicit attitudes to low and high carbon footprint products. *International Journal of Environmental, Cultural, Economic and Social Sustainability* 5: 191–206.

—— (2011) Shopping to save the planet? Implicit rather than explicit attitudes predict low carbon footprint consumer choice. *International Journal of Environmental, Cultural, Economic and Social Sustainability* 7: 211–232.

—— (2011) An exploration of the other side of semantic communication: How the spontaneous movements of the human hand add crucial meaning to narrative. *Semiotica* 184: 33–51.

Beattie, G., Cutler, A. and Pearson, M. (1982) Why is Mrs Thatcher interrupted so often? *Nature* 300: 744–747.

Beattie, G., McGuire, L. and Sale, L. (2010) Do we actually look at the carbon footprint of a product in the initial few seconds? An experimental analysis of unconscious eye movements. *International Journal of Environmental, Cultural, Economic and Social Sustainability* 6: 47–66.

Beattie, G., Sale, L. and McGuire, L. (2011) 'An Inconvenient Truth?' Can extracts of a film really affect our psychological mood and our motivation to act against climate change? *Semiotica* 187: 105–125.

Bertrand, M. and Mullainathan, S. (2004) Are Emily and Gregg more employable than Lakisha and Jamal? A field experiment on labor market discrimination. *The American Economic Review* 94: 991–1013.

Billig, M. (2011) Writing social psychology: Fictional things and unpopulated texts. *British Journal of Social Psychology* 50, 4–20.

Bluemke, M. and Friese, M. (2005) Do features of stimuli influence IAT effects? *Journal of Experimental Social Psychology* 42: 163–176.

Booth, A., Leigh, A. and Vaganova, E. (2009). Does racial and ethnic discrimination vary across minority groups? Unpublished paper.

Brunel, F. F., Tietje, B. C. and Greenwald, A. G. (2004) Is the Implicit Association Test a valid and valuable measure of implicit consumer social cognition? *Journal of Consumer Psychology* 14: 385–404.

Bruner, J. (1957) On perceptual readiness. *Psychological Review* 64: 123–152.

Carlsson, M. and Rooth, D. (2007) Evidence of ethnic discrimination in the Swedish labor market using experimental data. *Labour Economics* 14: 716–729.

Chaiken, S. and Trope, Y. (eds) (1999) *Dual Process Theories in Social Psychology*. New York: Guilford.

Cienki, A. and Müller, C. (eds) (2008) *Metaphor and Gesture*. Amsterdam: John Benjamins.

Clarke, H. M. (1911) Conscious attitudes. *American Journal of Psychology* 32: 214–249.

Cohen, D., Beattie. G. and Shovelton, H. (2010) Nonverbal indicators of deception: How iconic gestures reveal thoughts that cannot be suppressed. *Semiotica* 182: 133–174.

Correll, J., Park., B., Judd., C.M. and Wittenbrink, B. (2002) The police officer's dilemma: Using ethnicity to disambiguate potentially threatening individuals. *Journal of Personality and Social Psychology*, 83: 1314–1329.

Craib, I. (1986) Review of M. Mulkay, *The Word and the World* (London: Allen & Unwin, 1985). *Sociology* 20: 483–484.

Danesi, M. (1999) *Of Cigarettes, High Heels, and Other Interesting Things. An Introduction to Semiotics.* New York: St Martin's Press.

Dasgupta, N. and Greenwald, A. G. (2001) On the malleability of automatic attitudes: Combating automatic prejudice with images of admired and disliked individuals. *Journal of Personality and Social Psychology* 81: 800–814.

Devine, P. G. (1989) Stereotypes and prejudice: Their automatic and controlled components. *Journal of Personality and Social Psychology* 56: 5–18.

—— (2005) Prejudice with and without compunction: Allport's inner conflict revisited. In J. F. Dovidio, P. Glick and L. A. Rudman (eds), *On the Nature of Prejudice: Fifty years after Allport*. Oxford: Blackwell, pp. 327–342.

Dollard, J. and Miller, N. E. (1950) *Personality and Psychotherapy*. New York: McGraw-Hill.

Doob, L. (1947) The behavior of attitudes. *Psychological Review* 54: 135–156.

Dostoevsky, F. (1864/1972) *Notes from the Underground.* Harmondsworth, UK: Penguin.

Dovidio, J. F. and Gaertner, S. L. (2000) *Reducing Intergroup Bias: The Common Ingroup Identity Model.* Philadelphia, PA: Psychology Press.

—— (2004) Aversive racism. In M. P. Zanna (ed.), *Advances in Experimental Social Psychology.* San Diego, CA: Academic Press, Vol. 36, pp. 1–51.

Dovidio, J. F., Kawakami, K. and Gaertner S. (2002) Implicit and explicit prejudice in interracial interaction. *Journal of Personality and Social Psychology* 82: 62–68.

Dovidio, J. F., Glick, P. and Rudman, A. (2005) *On the Nature of Prejudice, Fifty Years after Allport.* Oxford: Blackwell.

Downing, P. and Ballantyne, J. (2007) *Tipping Point or Turning Point? Social Marketing and Climate Change* (Online). Ipsos MORI. http://www.ipsos-mori.com/_assets/pdfs/turning%20point %20or%20tipping%20point.pdf (accessed: 5 January 2009).

Drydakis, N. and Vlassis, M. (2010) Ethnic discrimination in the Greek labour market: Occupational access, insurance coverage and wage offers. *The Manchester School* 78: 201–218.

Edwards, D., Ashmore, M. and Potter, J. (1995) Death and furniture: The rhetoric, politics and theology of bottom line arguments against relativism. *History of the Human Sciences* 8: 25–49.

Elliot, A. J., Maier, M. A., Moller. C., Friedman, R. and Meinhardt, J. (2007). Color and psychological functioning: The effect of red on performance attainment. *Journal of Experimental Psychology* 136: 154–68.

Elms, A. C. (1993) Allport's Personality and Allport's Personality. In K. H. Craik, R. Hogan and R. N. Wolf (eds), *Fifty Years of Personality Psychology (Perspectives on Individual Differences)*. New York: Plenum Press.

Faber, M. (1970) Allport's visit with Freud. *The Psychoanalytic Review* 57: 60–64.

Fanon, F. (2006) *The Fanon Reader*. London: Pluto Press.

Fazio, R. H. (1990) Multiple processes by which attitudes guide behavior: The MODE model as an integrative framework. In M. P. Zanna (ed.), *Advances in Experimental Social Psychology* 23: 75–109.

Festinger, L. A. (1957) *A Theory of Cognitive Dissonance*. Stanford, CA: Stanford University Press.

Fiedler, K. and Bluemke, M. (2005) Faking the IAT: Aided and unaided response control on the implicit association test. *Basic and Applied Social Psychology* 27: 307–316.

Fiedler, K., Messner, C. and Bluemke, M. (2006) Unresolved problems with the 'I', the 'A' and the 'T': A logical and psychometric critique of the Implicit Association Test (IAT). *European Review of Social Psychology* 17: 74–147.

Fiske, S. (2005) Social cognition and the normality of prejudice. In J. F. Dovidio, P. Glick and L. A. Rudman (eds), *On the Nature of Prejudice: Fifty Years after Allport*. Oxford: Blackwell Publishers, pp. 36–53.

Fiske, S. T. and Ruscher, J. B. (1993) Negative interdependence and prejudice: Whence the affect? In D. M. Mackie and D. L. Hamilton (eds), *Affect, Cognition, and Stereotyping: Interactive Processes in Group Perception*. San Diego: Academic, pp. 239–268.

Franklin, J. H. (1965) The two worlds of race: A historical view. *Daedalus* 94: 899–920.

Friese, M., Wänke, M. and Plessner, H. (2006) Implicit consumer preferences and their influence on product choice. *Psychology and Marketing* 23: 727–740.

Friese, M., Hofmann, W. and Wänke, M. (2008) When impulses takes over: Moderated predictive validity of explicit and implicit attitude measures in predicting food choice and consumption behaviour. *British Journal of Social Psychology* 47: 397–419.

Gaertner, S. L. and McLaughlin, J. P. (1983) Racial stereotypes: Associations and ascriptions of positive and negative characteristics. *Social Psychology Quarterly* 46: 23–30.

Gibson, B. (2008) Can evaluative conditioning change attitudes toward mature brands? New evidence from the implicit association test. *Journal of Consumer Research* 35: 178–188.

Gifford, R. (2008) Psychology's essential role in alleviating the impacts of climate change. *Canadian Psychology* 49: 273–280.

Gladwell, M. (2005) *Blink: The Power of Thinking without Thinking.* New York: Little, Brown.

Goldberg, D. T. (1993) *Racist Culture. Philosophy and the Politics of Meaning.* Oxford: Blackwell.

Goldin-Meadow, S. (1997) When gestures and words speak differently. *Current Directions in Psychological Science* 6: 138–143.

Govan, C. L. and Williams, K. D. (2004) Changing the affective valence of the stimulus items influences the IAT by re-defining the category labels. *Journal of Experimental Social Psychology* 40: 357–365.

Greenberg, B. S. and Brand, J. E (1994) Minorities and the mass media: 1970s to 1980s. In J. Bryant and D. Zillman (eds), *Media Effects: Advances in Theory and Research.* Hillsdale, NJ: Erlbaum, pp. 273–314.

Greenwald, A. G. (1990) What cognitive representations underlie attitudes? *Bulletin of the Psychonomic Society* 28: 254–260.

Greenwald, A. G. and Banaji, M. R. (1995) Implicit social cognition: Attitudes, self-esteem, and stereotypes. *Psychological Review* 102: 4–27.

Greenwald, A. G. and Nosek, B. A. (2008) Attitudinal dissociation: What does it mean? In R. E. Petty, R. H. Fazio and P. Brinol (eds), *Attitudes: Insights from the New Implicit Measures.* Hillsdale, NJ: Erlbaum, pp. 65–82.

Greenwald, A. G., Klinger, M. R. and Liu, T. J. (1989) Unconscious processing of dichoptically masked words. *Memory and Cognition* 17: 35–47.

Greenwald, A. G., Schuh, E. G. and Engell. K. (1990) Ethnic Bias in Scientific Citations, Unpublished manuscript, University of Washington, Department of Psychology.

Greenwald, A., McGhee, D. and Schwartz, J. (1998) Measuring individual differences in implicit cognition: The Implicit Association Test. *Journal of Personality and Social Psychology* 74: 1464–1480.

Greenwald, A. G., Poehlman, T. A., Uhlmann, E. and Banaji, M. R. (2009) Understanding and using the implicit association test: III. Meta-analysis of predictive validity. *Journal of Personality and Social Psychology* 97: 17–41.

Gregg, A. P. (2008) Oracle of the unconscious or deceiver of the unwitting? *The Psychologist* 21: 762–766.

Harris, R. J. (1999) *A Cognitive Psychology of Mass Communication* (3rd edn). Mahwah, NJ: Erlbaum.

Hart, A. J., Whalen, P. J., Shin, L. M., McInerney, S. C., Fischer, H. and Rauch, S. L. (2000) Differential response in the human amygdala to racial outgroup vs. ingroup face stimuli. *Brain Imaging* 11: 2351–2355.

Hazlitt, W. (1826) *On the Pleasure of Hating*. London: Penguin.

Heath, A. and Li, Y. (2007) *Measuring the Size of the Employer Contribution to the Ethnic Minority Employment Gap*. Consultation Paper for the National Employment Panel. London.

Hoare, Prince (1820) *Memoirs of Granville Sharp Esq*. London: Henry Colburn.

Hofmann, W. and Friese, M. (2008) Impulses got the better of me: Alcohol moderates the influence of implicit attitudes toward food cues on eating behaviour. *Journal of Abnormal Psychology* 117: 420–427.

Hofmann, W., Gawronski, B., Gschwendner, T., Le, H. and Schmitt, M. (2005) A meta-analysis on the correlation between the Implicit Association Test and explicit self-report measures. *Personality and Social Psychology Bulletin* 31: 1369–1385.

Hofmann, W., Rauch, W. and Gawronski, B. (2007) And deplete us not into temptation: Automatic attitudes, dietary restraint, and self-regulatory resources as determinants of eating behaviour. *Journal of Experimental Social Psychology* 43: 497–504.

Holland, R., Hendriks, M. and Aarts, H. (2005) Smells like clean spirit. Nonconscious effects of scent on cognition and behaviour. *Psychological Science* 16: 689–693.

Hooff, J. van (1972) A comparative approach to the phylogeny of laughter and smiling. In R. A. Hinde (ed.), *Non-Verbal Communication*. Cambridge: Cambridge University Press, pp. 209–241.

Ipsos MORI (2008) *Carbon Labelling – Just a Load of Hot Air?* (Online). Ipsos MORI. http://www.ipsosmori.com/researchspecialisms/publicaffairs/reputationcentre/carbon.ashx (not available).

Jacoby, L. L., Kelley, C. M., Brown, J. and Jasechko, J. (1989) Becoming famous overnight: Limits on the ability to avoid unconscious influences of the past. *Journal of Personality and Social Psychology* 56: 326–338.

Jefferson, G. (1985) An exercise in the transcription and analysis of laughter. In T. Van Dijk (ed.), *Handbook of Discourse Analysis* (Vol. 3). London: Academic Press.

Jones, E. and Sigall, H. (1971) The bogus pipeline: A new paradigm for measuring affect and attitude. *Psychology Bulletin* 76: 349–364.

Jordan, R. and Beattie, G. (1998) Understanding male interpersonal violence: A discourse analytic approach to accounts of violence on the door. *Semiotica* 2003: 101–141.

Jowell, R. and Prescott-Clarke, P. 1970. Racial discrimination and white-collar workers in Britain. *Race and Class* 11: 397–417.

Jussim, L., Coleman, L. M. and Lerch, L. (1987) The nature of stereo – of self-fulfilling prophesies in interracial interaction. *Journal of Experimental Psychology* 10: 109–120.

Kahneman, D. (2011) *Thinking, Fast and Slow*. London: Penguin.

Kandola, B. (2009) *The Value of Difference. Eliminating Bias in the Organisation*. Oxford: Pearn Kandola.

Karpinski, A., and Hilton, J. L. (2001) Attitudes and the Implicit Association Test. *Journal of Personality and Social Psychology* 81: 774–788.

Karpinski, A. and Steinman, R. B. (2006) The single category Implicit Association Test as a measure of implicit social cognition. *Journal of Personality and Social Psychology* 91: 16–32.

Karpinski, A., Steinman, R. B. and Hilton, J. L. (2005) Attitude importance as a moderator of the relationship between implicit and explicit attitude measures. *Personality and Social Psychology Bulletin* 31: 949–962.

Katz, I. and Hass, R. G. (1988) Racial ambivalence and American value conflict: Correlational and priming studies of dual cognitive structures. *Journal of Personality and Social Psychology* 55: 893–905.

Keith, A. (1931a, 1973 Reprint) *The Place of Prejudice in Modern Civilisation*. Saratoga: Quest.

—— (1931b) *New Discoveries Relating to the Antiquity of Man*. London: Williams and Norgate.

Kita, S. (2000) How representational gestures help speaking. In D. McNeill (ed.), *Language and Gesture*. Cambridge: Cambridge University Press, pp. 162–185.

Kluckhohn, C. M. (1949) *Mirror for Man*. New York: McGraw-Hill

Kogan, I. (2011) New immigrants – old disadvantage patterns? Recent immigrants into Germany. *International Migration* 49: 91–117.

Landy, D. and Sigall, H. (1974) Beauty is talent: Task evaluation as a function of the performer's physical attractiveness. *Journal of Personality and Social Psychology* 29: 299–304.

Leathwood, C., Maylor, U. and Moreau, M. (2009) *The Experience of Black and Minority Ethnic Staff Working in Higher Education*. London: Equality Challenge Unit.

Lefranc, A. (2010) Unequal opportunities and ethnic origin: The labor market outcomes of second-generation immigrants in France. *American Behavioral Scientist* 53: 1851–1882.

McConahay, J. B. (1986) Modern racism, ambivalence, and the modern racism scale. In J. F. Dovidio and S. L. Gaertner (eds), *Prejudice, Discrimination, and Racism.* New York: Academic Press, pp. 91–126.

McConnell, A. R. and Leibold, J. M. (2001) Relations among the Implicit Association Test, discriminatory behaviour, and explicit measures of racial attitudes. *Journal of Experimental Social Psychology* 37, 435–442.

McNeill, D. (1992) *Hand and Mind. What Gestures Reveal About Thought.* Chicago, IL: University of Chicago Press.

McNeill, D. (2000) Growth points in thinking-for-speaking. In D. McNeill (ed.). *Language and Gesture.* Cambridge: Cambridge University Press.

McNeill, D. (2005). *Gesture and Thought.* Chicago, IL: University of Chicago Press.

Maison, D., Greenwald, A. G. and Bruin, R. (2001) The Implicit Association Test as a measure of consumer attitudes. *Polish Psychological Bulletin* 2: 61–79.

Maison, D., Greenwald, A. G. and Bruin, R. H. (2004) Predictive validity of the Implicit Association Test in studies of brands, consumer attitudes and behavior. *Journal of Consumer Psychology* 14: 405–415.

Muller, G. E. and Pilzecker, A. (1900) Experimentelle Beitrage zur Lehre vom Gedachtnis. *Zeitschrift fur Psychologie, Ergänzungsband* 1: 1–128.

Munasinghe, M., Dasgupta, P., Southerton, D., Bows, A. and McMeekin, A. (2009) *Consumers, Business and Climate.* Manchester: The Sustainable Consumption Institute.

Myers, D. G. (1987) *Social Psychology* (2nd edn). New York: McGraw-Hill.

Nelson, K. (2007) *Young Minds in Social Worlds: Experience, Meaning, and Memory.* Cambridge, MA: Harvard University Press.

Nietzsche, F. (1871/1962) *Twilight of the Idols.* Harmondsworth, UK: Penguin.

Nordin, M. and Rooth, D. (2009) The ethnic employment and income gap in Sweden: Is skill or labor market discrimination the explanation? *Scandinavian Journal of Economics* 111: 487–510.

Nosek, B. A. (2005) Moderators of the relationship between implicit and explicit evaluation. *Journal of Experimental Psychology: General* 134: 565–584.

Nosek, B. A. and Hansen, J. J. (2008) The associations in our heads belong to us: Searching for attitudes and knowledge in implicit evaluation. *Cognition and Emotion* 22: 553–594.

Nosek, B. A., Banaji, M. R. and Greenwald, A. G. (2002) Harvesting implicit group attitudes and beliefs from the demonstration website. *Group Dynamics* 6: 101–115.

Olson, M. A. and Fazio, R. H. (2004) Reducing the influence of extra-personal associations on the Implicit Association Test: Personalizing the IAT. *Journal of Personality and Social Psychology* 86: 653–667.

Osgood, C. E. (1957) A behavioristic analysis of perception and language as cognitive phenomena. In *Contemporary Approaches to Cognition*, Cambridge, MA: Harvard University Press, pp. 75–118.

Pager, D., Western, B. and Bonikowski, B. (2009) Discrimination in a low-wage labor market: A field experiment. *American Sociological Review* 74: 777–799.

Pendakur, K. and Pendakur, R. (1998) The colour of money: Earnings differentials among ethnic groups in Canada. *Canadian Journal of Economics* 31: 518–548.

Petrie, W. M. F. (1895) *Race and Civilization. Report of the Smithsonian Institution for 1895*, p. 597.

Phelps, E. A., O'Connor, K. J., Cunningham, W. A., Funayama, E. S., Gatenby, C. J., Gore, J. C. and Banaji, M. R. (2000) Performance on indirect measures of race evaluation predicts amygdala activation. *Journal of Cognitive Neuroscience* 12: 729–738.

Porier, G. W. and Lott, A. J. (1967) Galvanic skin responses and prejudice. *Journal of Personality and Social Psychology* 5: 253–259.

Potter, J. and Wetherell, M. (1987) *Discourse and Social Psychology*. London: Sage.

Purkiss, S. S. L., Perrewé, P. L., Gillespie, T. L., Myers, B. T. and Ferris, G. R. (2006) Implicit sources of bias in employment interview judgements and decisions. *Journal of Organizational Behaviour and Human Decision Processes* 101: 152–167.

Quillian, L. (2006) New approaches to understanding racial prejudice and discrimination. *Annual Sociology Review* 32: 299–328.

Rankin, R. E. and Campbell, D. T. (1955) Galvanic skin response to negro and white experimenters. *Journal of Abnormal and Social Psychology* 51: 30–33.

Richards, G. (1997) *Race, Racism and Psychology*. London: Routledge.

Rojahn, K. and Pettigrew, T. F. (1992) Memory for schema-relevant information: A meta-analytic resolution. *British Journal of Social Psychology* 31: 81–109.

Rooth, D. O. (2010) Automatic associations and discriminations in hiring: Real world evidence. *Labour Economics* 17: 523–534.

Rothbart, M. and John, O. P. (1985) Social categorization and behavioural episodes: A cognitive analysis of the effects of inter-group contact. *Journal of Social Issues* 41: 81–104.

Rudman, L. (2004) Sources of implicit attitudes. *Psychological Science* 13: 79–82.

Rudman, L. A. and Goodwin, S. A. (2003) Gender differences in automatic in-group bias: why do women like women more than men like men? *Journal of Personality and Social Psychology* 87(4): 494–509.

Rudman, L. A., Ashmore, R. D. and Gary, M. L. (2001) 'Unlearning' automatic biases: The malleability of implicit prejudice and stereotypes. *Journal of Personality and Social Psychology* 81(5): 856–868.

Rundh, B. (2007) The multi-faceted dimension of packaging: marketing logistic or marketing tool? *British Food Journal* 107: 670–684.

Sacks, H., Schegloff, E. A. and Jefferson, G. A. (1974) A simplest systematics for the organization of turn-taking in conversation. *Language* 50: 697–735.

Scarabis, M., Florack, A. and Gosejohann, S. (2006) When consumers follow their feelings: the impact of affective or cognitive focus on the basis of consumers' choice. *Psychology and Marketing* 23: 1005–1036.

Schaller, M. and Conway, L. G. (2001) From cognition to culture: The origins of stereotypes that really matter. In G. Moscowitz (ed.), *Cognitive Social Psychology: On the Tenure and Future of Social Cognition*. Mahwah, NJ: Lawrence Erlbaum Associates, pp. 163–176.

Sears, D. O. (1986) College sophomores in the laboratory: Influences of a narrow data base on social psychology's view of human nature. *Journal of Personality and Social Psychology* 51: 515–530.

Sheatsley, P. B. (1965) White attitudes towards the Negro. *Daedalus* 95: 217–238.

Sherif, M. and Sherif, C. W. (1953) *Groups in Harmony and Tension: An Introduction to Studies in Intergroup Relations*. New York: Harper and Row.

Sigall, H. and Page, R. (1971) Current stereotypes: A little fading, a little faking. *Journal of Personality and Social Psychology* 18: 247–255.

Sollors, W. (1986) *Beyond Ethnicity: Consent and Descent in American Culture*. Oxford: Oxford University Press.

Son Hing, L. S., Li, W. and Zanna, M. P. (2002) Inducing hypocrisy to reduce prejudicial responses among aversive racists. *Journal of Experimental Social Psychology* 38: 71–78.

Son Hing, L. S., Chung-Yan, G. A., Hamilton, L. K. and Zanna, M. P. (2008) A two-dimensional model that employs explicit and implicit attitudes to characterize prejudice. *Journal of Personality and Social Psychology* 94: 971–987.

Southerton, D. (2003) Squeezing time: Allocating practices, co-ordinating networks and scheduling society. *Time & Society* 12: 5–25.

Stangor, C. and McMillan, D. (1992) Memory for expectancy-congruent and expectancy-incongruent information: A review of the social and social-developmental literatures. *Psychological Bulletin* 111: 42–61.

Stanovich, K. E. and West, R. F. (2000) Individual differences in reasoning: Implications for the rationality debate. *Behavioral and Brain Sciences* 23: 645–665.

Stern, N. H. (2006) *The Economics of Climate Change: The Stern Review*. Cambridge: Cambridge University Press.

Stevenson, G. and Keehn, B. (2006) *I Will if You Will*. Towards Sustainable Consumption. Manchester: Sustainable Consumption Roundtable.

Strachey, C. (ed.) (1925) *The Letters of the Earl of Chesterfield to his Son*. New York: G.P. Putnam's Sons.

Swanson, J. E., Rudman, L. A. and Greenwald, A. G. (2001) Using the Implicit Association Test to investigate attitude–behavior consistency for stigmatized behaviour. *Cognition and Emotion* 15: 207–230.

Talaska, C., Fiske, S. T. and Chaiken, S. (2008) Legitimating racial discrimination: A meta-analysis of the racial attitude-behavior literature shows that emotions, not beliefs, best predict discrimination. *Social Justice Research: Social Power in Action* 21: 263–296.

Thomas, W. I. (1912) Race psychology: Standpoint and questionnaire, with particular reference to the immigrant and the Negro. *The American Journal of Sociology* 17: 725–775.

Tobias, M., Bhattacharya, A. and White, P. (2008) Cross classification of the New Zealand population by ethnicity and deprivation: Trends from 1996 to 2006. *Australian and New Zealand Journal of Public Health* 32: 431–436.

Towles-Schwen, T. and Fazio, R. S. (2003) Choosing social situations: The relation between automatically activated racial attitudes and anticipated comfort interacting with African Americans. *Psychological Science* 29: 170–182.

Uhlmann, E., Dasgupta, N., Elgueta, A., Greenwald, A. G. and Swanson, J. (2002) Subgroup prejudice based on skin color among Hispanics in the United States and Latin America. *Social Cognition* 20: 198–225.

Vantomme, D., Geuens, M., De Houwer, J. and De Pelsmacker, P. (2005) Implicit attitudes toward green consumer behaviour. *Psychologica Belgica* 45: 217–239.

Vygotsky, L. S. (1986) *Thought and Language*. Edited and translated by E. Hanfmann and G. Vakar. Revised and edited by A. Kozulin. Cambridge, MA: MIT Press.

Walker, G. and King, D. (2008) *The Hot Topic: How to Tackle Global Warming and Still Keep the Lights On*. London: Bloomsbury.

Webster, R. J., Saucier, D. A. and Harris, R. J. (2010) Before the measurement of prejudice: Early psychological and sociological papers on prejudice. *Journal of the History of the Behavioural Sciences* 46: 300–313.

Westie, I. R. and DeFleur, M. L. (1959) Autonomic responses and their relationship to race attitudes. *Journal of Abnormal and Social Psychology* 58: 340–347.

Wetherell, M. and Potter, J. (1992) *Mapping the Language of Racism. Discourse and the Legitimation of Exploitation*. London: Harvester Wheatsheaf.

Willhelm, S. M. (1970) *Who Needs the Negro?* Cambridge, MA: Schenkman.

Wilson, T., Lindsey, S. and Schooler, T. Y. (2000) A model of dual attitudes. *Psychological Review* 107: 101–126.

Wood, M., Hales, J., Purdon, S., Sejersen, T. and Hayllar, O. (2009) *A Test for Racial Discrimination in Recruitment Practice in British Cities*. London: Department for Work and Pensions (Research Report No. 607).

World Bank (2010) *WDR 2010: Development and Climate Change*. Washington, DC: The World Bank.

Young, K. (1933) *Source Book for Social Psychology*. New York: F.S. Crofts.

Zeithaml, V., Bolton, R. N., Deighton, J., Keiningham, T., Lemon, K. N. and Peterson, J. A. (2006) Forward-looking focus: Can firms have adaptive foresight? *Journal of Service Research* 9: 168–183.

Index